Internationalization and Localization Using Microsoft .NET

NICHOLAS SYMMONDS

Internationalization and Localization Using Microsoft .NET

Copyright ©2002 by Nicholas Symmonds

ISBN (pbk): 1-59059-002-3

Printed and bound in the United States of America 12345678910

Trademarked names may appear in this book. Rather than use a trademark symbol with every occurrence of a trademarked name, we use the names only in an editorial fashion and to the benefit of the trademark owner, with no intention of infringement of the trademark.

Technical Reviewer: Brian Jones

Editorial Directors: Dan Appleman, Peter Blackburn, Gary Cornell, Jason Gilmore, Karen Watterson

Managing and Production Editor: Grace Wong

Project Manager: Tracy Brown Collins

Copy Editor: Anne Friedman

Compositor: Impressions Book and Journal Services, Inc.

Indexer: Rebecca Plunkett

Cover Designer: Tom Debolski

Marketing Manager: Stephanie Rodriguez

Distributed to the book trade in the United States by Springer-Verlag New York, Inc., 175 Fifth Avenue, New York, NY, 10010

and outside the United States by Springer-Verlag GmbH & Co. KG, Tiergartenstr. 17, 69112 Heidelberg, Germany

In the United States, phone 1-800-SPRINGER, email orders@springer-ny.com, or visit http://www.springer-ny.com.

Outside the United States, fax +49 6221 345229, email orders@springer.de, or visit http://www.springer.de.

For information on translations, please contact Apress directly at 901 Grayson Street, Suite 204, Berkeley, CA 94710.

Phone 510-549-5938, fax: 510-549-5939, email info@apress.com, or visit http://www.apress.com.

The source code for this book is available to readers at http://www.apress.com in the Downloads section. You will need to answer questions pertaining to this book in order to successfully download the code.

This book is dedicated to my wife, Celeste. Her unwavering faith in me has brought me further in life than I ever dreamed I could go.

Contents at a Glance

Contents

About the Author

Nicholas Symmonds is a degreed electrical engineer who found an affinity for computers during that first college course so long ago. The 6502 processor was his first foray into machine code and still brings back fond memories. Nick has been programming since 1985 and still knows—and uses—most of the DOS batch file commands. He has worked in varying capacities in both the electronic engineering and software fields, often combining both areas of expertise. He currently works for the Security and Safety Solutions division of Ingersoll-Rand. He writes access control software in Visual Basic, C++, and now .NET. Nick lives with his wife and three children in the northeast hills of Connecticut. When not programming, Nick can often be found with his wife on their motorcycle traveling the wine trails of southern New England. He can be reached at nicksymmonds@attbi.com.

About the Tech Reviewer

Brian Jones fell in love with programming computers 36 years ago in a Tucson, AZ, high school IBM 1440 AutoCoder class. A degree in systems engineering led him to Silicon Valley where he developed software and systems solutions in assembly, C, C++, and bitslice microcode for CDC, Versatec, and Xerox Engineering Systems. In 1988 he gave up his 70 mile round trip commute and moved with his wife and two sons to a home on a hill near Burlington, VT, where he has been a telecommuting programmer for the past 13 years. He is currently working with Recognition Systems, Inc. providing access control security solutions in C++/MFC/, and.NET. Brian is the owner of Verdack Software, LLC., a provider of custom programming services. He can be reached at BrianJones@admont.com.

Preface

If you have picked up this book, you must want to learn about localization. Perhaps you have already done localization projects in another programming language such as Visual Basic 6 (VB 6) but now your company is moving to .NET. Well, this book is for you. Whether you are new to localization techniques or they are old hat to you, this book shows you not only how to localize from the start but also how to take what you know and apply it to .NET.

I am an old hand myself at localization techniques in both the PC arena and in the embedded world so let me start out by saying how impressed I am with the .NET environment. The more I use it, the more neat stuff I find that it can do. It is logically put together and I have found that I can do quite a few things I could never do with VB and C++.

As the title of this book implies, this book covers the new Visual Studio .NET from Microsoft. As I am sure you know by now, programming in .NET is a whole new paradigm. Perhaps you come from a Visual Basic or from a C++ background. Either way the rules have changed. It does not matter what programming language you have used now that you are now writing in .NET.

One of the changes brought about by VS .NET is the way resource files are handled. Visual Basic had resource file capability but it was limited at best and kind of awkward. C++ was better, but only slightly. The .NET version of Visual Studio was designed to allow localization to be done properly, and with relative ease. As you will see in later chapters, the resource file capability of .NET is very powerful indeed.

One of the things that most impresses me is the new multinational capability built right into .NET. Writing multinational programs with VB and C++ the right way has always involved quite a bit of work to get around the limitations of the languages. It seems, however, that all the work-arounds I came up with have been anticipated and eliminated in .NET. The level of integration of the Internationalization features inside .NET is very nice to see. Some of the features that I find most impressive are:

- The types of resource files. These files are used to hold text, pictures, fonts, and so on, that have to do with what the user sees in your program.

- Windows Forms are externalized to an XML resource file.

- Tools are available for the localizer to visually alter and localize forms without having access to source code.

- A fallback scheme for finding resources.

NOTE *I cover these tools and features of .NET Internationalization in Chapter 7.*

Between these covers I hope to show you what can be done to make your programs work well in any location. I also hope to tell you a bit about localization in general, why you need a book on the topic, and how this book is organized.

What Is Localization?

There are several terms relating to internationalizing software. Often these terms are used interchangeably but they do have slightly different meanings.

Multilingual

Multilingual means that your software has been translated into more than one language. Usually this refers to the strings and not much else. I have seen quite a few programs in the embedded world, as well as in the PC world, that only had their strings translated before being sold overseas. The numbers, and time, and so on were still represented as they are in the United States such as using a period for a decimal point and using AM/PM for time.

Internationalize

Internationalization is a more encompassing and more specific term for your software. This means that not only the code strings are multilingual but that the rest of the elements—time, numbers, formatting, and so on—have also been adapted to work properly in international markets.

Internationalizing software however, does not necessarily take into account dialects or cultural differences between countries that may even speak the same language. Translating a program to work in Spain may mean that it would work in other Spanish-speaking countries, but it does not take into account the cultural differences of those other countries. To make your program multinational you also need to localize.

Why Localize?

The marketplace is global. Companies realize that there may be a market for their products beyond their home base. The ease of sharing information electronically simplifies worldwide distribution. With electronic information being so fast and prevalent in most of the world it is not hard to find a market for your goods and services. If there is a need for your product over here you can bet there is a need for it somewhere else as well. Trade agreements are also making it easier to sell products across international lines.

I have worked in a scientific and technology–based industry most of my career. Quite a few of the software products I designed are intended as an adjunct to some other hardware. Increasingly this hardware needs user interface and management software. Some of this software is quite complex. Companies that sell hardware-based products overseas also need to send your software with it. Enter *localization.*

Mail services, rental cars, airlines, and so on are multinational. Look at FedEx. It sends packages everywhere in the world. The company needs a single software package with a user interface that can be used by anyone, anywhere. When you go the FedEx web site, the very first thing it asks you is to choose your country. This is localization at work.

Suppose you rent a car in Aachen, Germany and want to drive it to Paris, France. You can bet the rental software is the same in both places. You can also be sure that the software is in French in France and in German in Germany.

The United States prides itself on its cultural diversity. Let's say you wrote software that is to be used in a U.S. convenience store chain. Although you could write it only in English, you would probably increase your business by being multilingual. What if your convenience store chain wants to open stores in Miami, Florida? Southern Florida has a huge population of Cubans. Think of the market advantage of having your software run in Spanish, as well.

If you are building a new product, plan for localization features at the start of the process. Even if you don't use the localization features initially, when the need arises you will be ready with your internationally aware software. Fixing a program after it has been released is much harder and far more perilous than doing it right the first time.

Once completed, the actual localization usually requires no code changes. The effort of retrofitting a program for multilanguage capability is very costly in terms of the time it takes and the testing and bug fixing that inevitably goes on when code is changed.

Why a Book on Localization?

I have written this book to help guide you along the correct path to making your applications ready for the international marketplace. I have localized software after the fact and have also designed it in to new software. Designing in localization is so much easier. Both approaches are demonstrated in this book.

Perhaps many of you have had to write programs and have then been asked to translate them into another language. It is just some strings, you say. . . how hard can it be? You look in the MSDN for some help and start to discover that there is far more to localization than just translating a few strings.

Writing international software is far more than just translating some strings or learning how to work with resource files. You need to ask yourself questions such as:

- What do I know about the culture for which I am writing?

- What icons or graphics are acceptable. . . or not?

- How should I present time, numbers, and calendars?

- What is the intended platform?

- Should I make use of code pages or Unicode?

- Do I have online help? How can it be localized?

- Will the program be able to switch languages at runtime, or will the language be chosen during installation?

How This Book Is Organized

The first half of this book is intended to be a brief guide to what you need to do to properly localize your applications. A complete reference on localization in general would be beyond the scope of this book.

The first two chapters deal with design and pertinent issues that go into making a successful and extendible multinational program. It is not my intention to be a complete reference or to add weight to this book with tables and in-depth explanations that can easily be found elsewhere. But I do mention the resources I use to help me with projects as well as let you know where you can find more details.

The second half of this book deals with applying localization to your VS .NET code. This is where you get into the nitty-gritty of programming details.

NOTE *I do not consider you, the reader, to be a dummy or an idiot. I assume you are a professional programmer who needs to expand his or her company's market for its software.*

I spend some time explaining how to localize a program. I hope I convey that doing it correctly takes some thinking—in particular about design—up-front. When I get into the real code sections of this book, you can actually use the examples. You can then apply these the techniques to your next project in .NET.

Who Should Read This Book?

I assume that you are familiar with the basics of .NET, and such features as:

- Namespaces

- Structured error handling

- File I/O

- Basic XML

- Windows Forms and basic use of the IDE

- Console applications

Visual Basic and C++ Programmers

Notice that the title of the book does not say anything about being specific to VB or to C#. The beauty of the CLR (Common Language Runtime) makes the techniques shown in this book easily applicable to either language. The examples I show are in both Visual Basic and in C#. In fact, there are as many as 25 other .NET languages in the works. The use of resource files, namespaces, and tools used in one .NET language will apply to all of them. This is way cool!

I also use features of .NET that you may not have seen or are just getting to know. Not only will you write programs that are Windows Forms–based but you spend quite a bit of time in console mode. Those of you from the C and C++ world will be very familiar with console programs but to the VB crowd this is very

new. You also spend as much time outside of the IDE as in it. There are quite
a few tools for localization and .NET in general that require you to run them from
the command line.

Although my programs are not difficult, I suggest that if you have never
played with VB .NET or C# then perhaps you should also pick up one of the
Apress books that goes into the basics of Visual Studio .NET.

Let's get started!

Acknowledgments

Well, the book is finally done and this is where I get to say thank you to everyone who provided support and guidance throughout the last few months.

While the content and style is mine, I cannot say that this book is a solo effort. Not by any means. First of all this book would not have been possible without the editorial staff at Apress being willing to take a chance on a new author. For this I will always be grateful.

Like most of you I took English in high school and college, but the elements of style in regards to computer books was never taught to me. I have learned more in the last few months from my editor Tracy Brown Collins and copy editor Anne Friedman than I ever did in those courses so long ago. Thank you both for your patience and words of wisdom. If nothing else, I have learned a great deal from you both.

I develop software for a living and I am a big advocate for code reads and quality testing. I cannot imagine letting out a program without another set of eyes looking it over. For this project, my other set of eyes was Brian Jones. He is as enthusiastic about .NET as I am and his technical review was first class. Brian's thoughtful comments are woven throughout this book.

When I started this book my whole family was quite enthusiastic and proud. They are even more so now. I owe them much for their support and guidance. I hope to make up for those long nights and missed weekends writing.

I hope that you, the reader, get as much out of this book as I got writing it. It's been fun. Cheers.

CHAPTER 1

General Localization Concepts

SOFTWARE LOCALIZATION REQUIRES more than just good programming. Translating some strings into another language and then selling the product is nowhere near good enough. Your users expect to be able to use and understand your program as they would one written originally in their country. Achieving this requires that you, the programmer, develop an awareness of other cultures and their mores— what is commonplace in the United States may not make sense or may be offensive in other nations.

For example, if you have ever traveled to Europe you know that for the most part time is related as 24-hour military time (6:00 PM is 18:00 hours). Almost nowhere in Europe do people use AM/PM when speaking of time. In math in Europe, the period is used to separate thousands (10.000) and the comma is used to separate units from fractions (1,4). You need to adapt your code to the changes in these formats.

To further support my claim that localization is beyond mere translation, consider localizing a product from United States to the English market in England. Citizens of both countries speak the same language, right? (Just a bit more proper—that's all.) But although you may not need to translate any strings, quite a bit of work still needs to be done. In England, as in much of the world, dates are given Day/Month/Year. In the United States, dates are given in Month/Day/Year. Time in England is represented in military time, and currency has the decimal for thousands separators. You get the picture. Localization is about more than language. This chapter gives you some tips on the types of things to avoid when localizing software.

Multilanguage Support

Multilanguage support is the ability to change your program from one language to another. How do you achieve this? Never hard code any strings. This is the localization mantra and it bears repeating: no hard-coded strings. All strings should be external to the program and only referenced when needed. Why do this? When you have a constant, such as the number pi (3.1428) or the maximum people that can fit in a bus (60), you use these numbers as constants. What happens when you refer to pi or the maximum number of people in a bus throughout your program? If your bus expands capacity, you have to change the number you use (60) to a larger number at every instance in your program. This is a tedious process that opens the chance for error. It also makes the program less readable. If you *refer* to the constants, you only need to change the number once, and then recompile. The change would be reflected throughout the program. The same goes for strings. Although you may not ever exchange text that says "*No*" for anything else, you can at some point have it translated to "*Nein.*" Imagine having to make this change in a program that uses it 500 times? You would be bound to miss something.

Constants can be defined in a separate file that is referenced by other files in your program. In the same way, strings can be kept in a separate file. Visual Basic (VB) and C++ use resource files to help with this. Visual Studio .NET uses resource files as well, but as you will see, the .NET resource files have quite a bit more functionality to them.

Any good programming language has some kind of error-handling mechanism. VB has the On Error Goto error mechanism and C++ has structured error handling, as does the .NET Common Language Runtime (CLR).

Make sure that you take the error strings out and include them in your resource file. My point here is that all well-written programs have error strings to help the user define what goes wrong. Why should the user have a nice interface to work with, but when an error occurs why should the user see an incomprehensible error message?

NOTE *You are flagging errors aren't you? Let me see by a show of hands how many of you go back and put in error handling after your program is done. I don't mean to harp but error checking and error messages are just as important to your program as the actual code. It is all a matter of perception by the user. Bad or nonexistent error messages give your program and your company a bad rep. Include error handling in the design.*

Choosing Graphics

What should you do about icons that represent elements of a program that are not so common? Some examples are icons that represent a modem for communication, a lawn mover for a rental company, or perhaps a lock to represent security.

If your program is for patients of a specific hospital, you might include a small graphic of a restaurant menu on a toolbar where patients could choose their meals. The patients could choose between the red and the green Jell-O. This graphic, or icon, could take the place of a string that says, "Choose today's lunch." The icon in this case is probably universal enough not to require different versions for different countries.

There are quite a few standard sets of international pictograms. There is an ISO standard detailing international pictograms that are broken down by classifications such as transportation, safety, communications, and so on.

Here are some tips for choosing graphics for your program.

- **Choose graphics that do not offend.** For example, the Japanese find disembodied body parts such as eyes and mouths unappealing.

- **Avoid using text elements in your icons and pictures.** Text only serves to tie your icon to a particular location. This minimizes the need for different versions to account for varying languages.

- **Research how common items are represented.** A mailbox in the United States looks completely different than one in the U.K. The same goes for a phone booth. (Superman uses the U.S. version and Dr. Who uses the U.K.'s.)

- **Make sure your icons convey the intended task.** The more basic the icon, the more widespread its acceptance.

- **Make sure that the universal signs you see all the time are not copyrighted.** For example, the smiley face that is so ingrained in American society is free for use in the United States but copyrighted overseas.

The point is to choose your graphics with care. Do not gloss over this, or "give it the short shrift," as my mom would say, as using the appropriate icon can greatly reduce the amount of text you need to write and translate.

A Word About Color

Although it may not be obvious, different colors have different meanings in different cultures. Early Celtic peoples ascribed different colors to different elements, as do Native Americans. Early Christianity banned green as a pagan color. Colors are rich in hidden meaning and symbolism.

Suppose in the United States your bride wore red? It might be shocking at a wedding in Alabama. However in China it is expected. Language also can be a barrier to the perception of color. The Shona language in Zimbabwe and the Boas language in Liberia have no words that distinguish red from orange.

Therefore, these people do not perceive different colors because of the limitations of their languages.

Practically every race and culture uses color symbolically, assigning qualities and objects to certain colors. Color conveys moods that transfer quite easily to human feeling.

A truly rich program would take advantage of color to convey messages and intent that go beyond the written word. A sample of colors in some religions is shown in Table 1-1.

Table 1-1. Sacred Colors in Various Cultures

COLOR(S)	REGION	RELIGION
Blue, White, Gold	European	Judeo-Christian
Green, Lt Blue	Middle Eastern	Islam
Saffron Yellow	Asian	Buddhism

Table 1-2 lists some colors and their meaning on a regional basis.

Table 1-2. Colors and Their Regional Meanings

COLOR	WEST EUROPE & USA	CHINA	JAPAN	MIDDLE EAST
Red	Danger, anger, stop	Joy	Anger, danger	Evil
Yellow	Caution, cowardice	Honor, royalty	Grace, nobility	Happiness
Green	Sexual, nature, go	Youth, growth	Future, energy	Fertility, strength
White	Purity, cleanliness	Mourning	Death, mourning	Purity, mourning
Blue	Authority, purity	Strength, power	Villainy	
Black	Death, evil	Evil	Evil	Evil

There was a study done by the Pantone Color Institute. They polled many Americans to learn what people thought about different colors. The results are very telling and can be used to your advantage. Blue is the favorite color of both men and women. Green is second, but first among "influential" people and trendsetters. Purple came in third because many people consider it a bridge between the warm and cooler colors. Red came in close behind purple and is thought to be an exciting color. Interestingly black is considered the most mysterious and powerful color for wealthy women. Most middle-aged men and women still consider black the color of death and mourning.

Choose strong deep colors to emphasize stability. Use bright colors to grab people's attention. Try using some of the softer shades to invoke warmth and cheer.

Resource File Concepts

I explain resource files in relation to VS .NET later. Here I discuss resource files in general.

Resource files are external files that contain program resources. But you knew that! Okay, so what *are* these resources? Most programmers think of resource files as a place to store strings that need translation. Although strings are certainly the lion's share of what make up a resource file, they are by no means the only things. As I mentioned earlier, you also need to store icons and bitmaps in your resource file. I do this all the time in VB 6, and in VS .NET it is just as easy. You can even store .wav files as resource files.

Resource files can be external to an application or they can be linked. VB 6 forced you to link your resource file but .NET allows either method.

Most program languages have some sort of resource file editor in their IDEs. VB 6 allowed you to create a resource file using the resource editor or create one using a normal text editor.

VS .NET also has a resource file editor. It is automatically invoked in the case of an XML-based resource file. This kind of resource file has the extension .resx. I cover kinds of resource files in detail later. VS. NET also has classes that allow you to write resource files in any of the formats that VS .NET expects.

> **NOTE** *I will say this now about the built-in resource editor for .NET: I find it no more helpful than the built-in resource editor in VB 6. It has many of the same drawbacks, as I explain in Chapter 4.*

String Resources

What should be in a string resource file? Perhaps it would be better to talk about *how* strings should be put in a resource file. Here is where you can add clarity or confusion to your translated program.

Translating Simple Strings

I define *simple strings* as single words, or short phrases or sentences. Simple strings are usually fairly easy to translate, as they often are self-explanatory. Translating the words "Help" or "OK" or "Cancel" usually needs no explanation. For the majority of single-word strings, this is true. However, single-word strings need a context in order to be translated properly.

If you are a programmer who has worked for a while in a particular industry, you know that you tend to use some words that describe an item or action that is specific to your company. Suppose you had the string probe. How would this be translated? Perhaps you use the word *probe* as a verb, meaning to explore something. However, it is unlikely that you will use a single verb as a string, so perhaps you mean it as a noun. Is a *probe* some kind of an instrument?

Another example would be the word *set*. Do you mean a collection of items or something that has hardened, such as glue, or do you mean to put an item in a particular place? You get my drift. You sometimes need a context for your words, and that context is in the form of comments.

As a good programmer, you comment your code, right? Well, do the same for your string resource files. You could comment your strings as you write them. If you think a string can be interpreted differently, then write a comment describing what you mean. The .NET resource files you write have the capability to include comments.

You should also write a glossary in which you keep a list of industry-specific terms and their meanings. Always keep this file updated and send it along with your strings to be translated. This kind of preventive medicine gets rid of quite a bit of potential embarrassment later. It also helps keep your writing consistent. Get in the habit of using the glossary whenever you write software for your company. Not only is consistency within a program good, but consistency among your programs is also something to strive for.

Complex Strings

Complex strings are long sentences or entire paragraphs that need translation. Your program may have a set of Help tips for each window or tab the user can go to. These tips would not be in the Help system but rather in the string resource file. Some complex strings could also be error strings. It is nice to have informative error strings that not only tell you what is wrong but also give you a possible remedy. Such a string could be long indeed. Consider the following strings:

- "This screen is where you enter users. Click the users you want entered."

- "This screen is where you enter user data. Fill in all the fields."

- "This screen is where you delete a user. Click the user you want deleted."

You could conceivably have dozens of these. The temptation is great to break up the strings into substrings inside the resource file, as shown here:

```
SCREENENTER = This is where you
USERENTER = enter users. Click the users you want entered
DATAENTER = enter user data. Fill in all the fields
USERDELETE = delete a user. Click the user you want deleted.

. . .
```

Your code would look like this:

```
Message = LoadResString(SCREENENTER) + LoadResString(USERENTER)
```

Concatenating strings from a resource file is bad practice. Do *not* do this.

Yes, I know it is less work to enter in strings in the resource files this way but the strings will not be translated properly later. Different languages have different placements of verbs and nouns. If you concatenate strings that are meant to be whole sentences you end up with a very poor translation indeed. The reputation of your product will suffer with a badly translated user interface. It may even be an object of humor. If you feel that you need to break strings up, then keep them in a block within your resource file. Comment them at the beginning of the block. Use a comment such as "The following 82 strings are intended to be linked together in the following manner.. . ."

Avoid Slang

Most Americans are familiar with the beer commercial in which groups of people call each other and yell "WASSUUUP!" What does this mean? Another American commercial is a parody of this one where the actors say, "How are *you* doing?" The second phrase is easily translated. The first phrase is slang.

The point is we all use slang and tend toward the vernacular in our speech. It is only natural to use the same in our code. *Avoid this like the plague.* There is no need to sublocalize your original program with terms that identify you as being from the Bronx. Quite often we use one word in place of another in our daily talk. More than this, we often omit some words in our common spoken language because we expect the words to be understood. This is dangerous for the translator, as he or she may not know the vernacular. Try to use literary language.

For example, "Buffer size is maxed out," is a slang phrase. The resource file should contain the phrase "The maximum size of the buffer has been exceeded."

Abbreviations

Abbreviations are as precarious to include as slang. Most standard abbreviations are acceptable, such as Mr, Ms, and so on. Just make sure you leave enough space for a foreign translation.

However, making your own abbreviation by arbitrarily shortening a word or phrase to fit in a certain space is dangerous. Some abbreviations do not translate at all, and you may end up with a translation that is far longer than your abbreviated sentence. You have now defeated the whole purpose of abbreviating your sentence. If you must abbreviate, use abbreviations you find in the dictionary. Do not make up your own unless they are well commented. Even then don't do it.

One last thing about resource files in general concerns the length of your string. At times you will find it necessary to have a label of a maximum length. If this is the case, you must make sure that the string in the resource file is commented with that fact. Let the translator know what he or she is dealing with.

Resource Files Before .NET

My first brush with internationalization involved writing a DOS-based program in C that could be translated into Spanish. Back then the version of C that I was using had no native provision for managing external strings. I had originally written the program with embedded English strings and proceeded to do the same for the Spanish strings. I ended up with two different sets of source code for the same program. Later, when I had the time, I took all the strings out and put them in a simple text file and used compiler directives to generate separate executables depending on the language.

Things have come a long way since then. Over the years, while working with Visual Basic and C++ I made effective use of resource files. Although using the resource file capability of VB greatly simplified internationalization, there was a lack of elegance. To do what I truly wanted to do, I still had to use a little brute force by resorting to some WIN32 calls.

.NET to the Rescue

Along comes Visual Studio 7 in the form of .NET. I must admit that when I first started playing with VS .NET back in Beta, I was not really looking for any added localization capability. In the process of trying different things and delving into the documentation, I kept coming across ways to localize code. When I started digging into the resource file capability I was amazed. The folks at Microsoft had obviously spent quite a bit of time designing the CLR to be used anywhere.[1]

Quite a few of you have probably used VB 6 resource files in its basic form to externalize strings. Let's compare resource files in Visual Basic 6 to resource files in .NET.

---

[1] The documentation by the way is very good. It is several levels above what we are accustomed to from Microsoft.

VB 6 has the ability to have only one resource file. Although much was said about not having to change code to change languages, you did need to recompile your code to change resource files. You may not have introduced bugs into your code, but distribution involved a new executable for each language. .NET allows any number of resource files to be used in your program. Also these resource files are compiled as resources external to the program. (You can link them directly in to your assembly but more about that later.) There is no need to recompile your executable to get another language.

VB 6 had a resource editor built into the IDE. OK, so it wasn't built in but was an Add-in—essentially the same thing. The VB 6 resource editor was not a very useful tool mainly because the result was a compiled resource file. This tool had no provision to spit out a text file that you could send to your translator. Although it did allow multiple languages in the same resource file it did not allow multilanguage support within a single instance. .NET does have a native resource editor but it only deals with XML files. It also makes a .resources file directly instead of an intermediate .resx file. So far VB 6 and .NET seem like they have the same drawbacks. However, .NET is far more versatile. You create a multitalented resource file generator in Chapter 5. The most basic .NET resource file starts out as a text file. This can be formatted to your liking (within reason) and sent to a translator.

VB 6 does have a separate resource compiler that takes a text-based resource file and churns out a .res binary resource file. This is a good thing, and I encourage those of you who still need to use VB 6 to generate resource files this way. I explain a way to handle multiple resource files in VB 6 in Chapter 3. .NET has the ResGen.exe program that does essentially the same thing as the VB 6 RC.exe compiler.

The resource files in VB 6 are number-based. By this I mean that there is no provision to call any resource; string, icon, or otherwise in VB 6 without using a numerical argument. I consider this to be a major flaw in the way resource files are handled in VB 6.

Consider this piece of VB 6 code.

```
DIM s as string
s = LoadResString(1542)
```

Wouldn't this be better?

```
. . .
s = LoadResString(STR_FILENOTFOUND)
```

Write your code the first way and come back in three months and tell me what string you meant to load. Reading your code after writing it the second way allows anyone to see just what is supposed to happen.[2] Using named constants for strings takes a little effort but it is advisable and is something you should do. I have yet to read any MSDN documentation on calling up strings this way. My short VB 6 resource file program demonstrates this method.

Okay, now what about .NET? There are several ways to write a resource file in .NET, but as far as using named constants is concerned Microsoft hit the nail right on the head. Here is a single line from a hypothetical string resource file. (You can write a text-based resource file using any editor.) The setup for string resources is a key, value pair.

```
STR_FILENOTFOUND = Error: File Not Found
```

To retrieve this string from the resource file you use the following piece of code in VB .NET:

```
. . .
DIM ExtStr as ResourceManager = ResourceManager.
CreateFileBasedResourceManager ( "MyResourceFile", ".", Nothing )
    Console.WriteLine(ExtStr.GetString("STR_FILENOTFOUND"))
```

There are four overloaded constructors to the ResourceManager. This ResourceManager constructor takes three arguments; the name of the resource file, the location, and whether a record set is to be used. Once the ResourceManager is set up you can retrieve strings from the resource file using the GetString method. All you need is the key. This is simplicity itself. It also has some of the elegance I feel is missing from the VB 6 resource file management scheme. The resource manager is explained fully in Chapter 3.

Resources on the Loose

In this two-line example of getting a resource file string I used a feature of the resource file manager called "Loose resources." There are two ways to call up resources in .NET; the "managed" method and the "nonmanaged" method. The managed method entails a proper directory order and fallback scheme. The nonmanaged method is also referred to as using loose resources. This means that you can specify the resource file and directory where the assembly should look for the resource file. There is no fallback mechanism involved here.

So what other things can you do with VS .NET resource files in your program? Well you can have as many of them as you want. Resource files in VS .NET are

---

[2] Job security is a wonderful thing, but obfuscated code is not the way to achieve it. Well-written and documented code encourages management to appreciate you more. . . really.

intended to be single language (a different resource file for each language such as Spanish, French, and so on). This allows you to update your assembly with a new language without having to touch the existing resource files. Since you can have many resource files there is a naming scheme that Microsoft uses in VS .NET that is based on the ISO 2 letter abbreviations for regions and cultures.

Summary

This chapter has given you some insight into what localization is, in general terms, and I discussed some things to look out for when thinking about localizing your programs. Here are some points to remember:

- Always externalize your programs' text to resource files

- Choose graphics that have no associated text

- Choose graphics that do not offend

- Keep color symbolism in mind when presenting ideas in programs

- Try to keep your external strings complete and simple

- Do not concatenate strings from a resource file

- Avoid slang and abbreviations

Last I discussed the differences between .NET resource files and VB 6 resource files. The chapters that follow go into these subjects in greater depth.

CHAPTER 2

Aspects of Localization

THIS CHAPTER INTRODUCES some of the more common aspects of designing a multilingual program. You need to be aware of how dates, time, numbers, and calendars are affected by region. Of course, the one part of the program that may be as big as the program itself is the Help system. These elements are quite often left out of an internationalization project and if so could cause quite a bit of animosity to your program. The code for the programs in this chapter, as in the whole book, can be downloaded from the Apress web site at http://www.apress.com. The final section of this chapter introduces you to the Unicode standard, what it is, and how you may already be using it.

The most important part of any program is probably the design of the GUI itself, which I discuss next.

GUI Design for Mulitinational Programs

I would like to talk about basic GUI (Graphic User Interface) design strategy. There are tons of books available on how to design GUIs that contain rules for what you should and should not do. What I want to touch on here is GUI design specifically in relation to multilanguage programming.

I am sure most of you have experience coming up with screens, at the request of the marketing department, for those incredible programs you are developing.

Many demo screens, however, also tend to be the basis for the finished product. How many times have you shown a demo screen to your boss to explore a concept and then gone back and built the code around these same screens?

What is wrong with this approach? Most likely you have laid out the screens to be just the right size for the English words and phrases you use. The design needed for localization gets left out.

Keep in mind the lengths of the strings you use. It is common in GUI design to use short sentences or single words to label fields. Translated text can be considerably longer than the original English text. It is actually an inverse relation depending on how long the original text string is. Table 2-1 shows how much the string length will grow when translated.

Table 2-1. Buffer Size Growth Based on Original String Length

ENGLISH	OTHER
1 to 5	100%
6 to 20	70%
20 to 50	30%
> 50	15%

As you can see, the shorter the string length the more space in relation to the original string you need.

As you research some of the languages into which you will convert your program, you will find that some languages need entire phrases to literally translate one English word. The reverse is also true. You need to plan a little in the design of your GUI to allow for this kind of situation.

Here are some examples of single English words translated into German. While these words may not be typical of words you would use in a program, they give you an idea of the difference between languages.

Table 2-2. Some English Words and German Translations

ENGLISH	GERMAN	BUFFER GROWTH
Watch	Bewachung	80%
Obsolete	nicht mehr gebrauchlich	287%
Textiles	bekleidungsindustrie	250%

What about phone numbers and addresses? The ISO standard for the length of a phone number is 15 digits. Be sure to allow some extra room for things such as Private Branch Exchange (PBX) codes and country codes. Appendix A lists phone country codes.

Do not assume that the dash is the only number separator in a phone number. You need to allow spaces, dashes, commas, and periods.

An address in the United States includes some information that makes no sense elsewhere. Take for instance a state. This means nothing in Taiwan. It just adds a level of confusion. Be flexible with your address format and allow enough fields to locate an address anywhere.

In the United States a ZIP code is a 5+4 digit number with the extra 4 digits being optional. Be careful not to validate a ZIP code based just on this pattern.

Quite a few other countries use letters in their postal code and they may also be of differing lengths.

Here is the current address for Oxford University in England. Notice the U.K. equivalent of the ZIP code. If you do not allow for alpha characters your correspondence might never get there.

University of Oxford

University Offices

Wellington Square

Oxford. OX1 2JD. UK.

Message Boxes, Dialog Boxes, Maps, and Menus

Message boxes are used extensively in many programs and quite often the text they display is long. Message boxes also resize depending on the amount of text shown. A small message box in English could be quite large in German.

Dialog boxes may also grow, especially some of the common dialog boxes. If you can, try to make your dialog boxes large enough to prevent resizing controls. Plan for a text box that can wrap the text to another line. You are better off if you can avoid having to resize the dialog box.

Dialog boxes as well as forms are much easier to understand when they are not cluttered. Spread your fields out among logically constructed screens. You may find that a screen with many fields needs extra space to allow for text expansion when translated. If you do not leave extra space you may find that your translated text wraps and makes a messy screen. If you have space limitations in your text fields make a comment in your resource file noting this fact. Let the translator find the best word or phrase that fits.

Try to make sure that phrases are not split between labels or text fields. Quite often a sentence or phrase in English swaps words around when translated. If you have one part of a phrase separate from another part in the resource file, the translator will not be able to make the correct translated phrase out of the two separate pieces. For example, German sentences often have verbs at the ends of sentences, while English and French place them in the middle.

I once took over the task of localizing a program that used a series of dialog boxes of the same size. The author ran his program by placing these dialog boxes on top of each other in a modal fashion thus hiding the screen behind it. When I localized the program some of the new strings were much longer then the original English versions and the resize control allowed for this by resizing the dialog boxes. It ended up that he could no longer hide some dialog boxes behind others because they peeked through at the sides. His attempt to hide what he was doing failed once his program was translated into another language. This was poor design indeed.

The dialog boxes in question were actually different executables. The programmer was trying to simulate multithreading in VB. I disagreed with this approach, but I was not the one making the decisions.

A menu system is one where you can really get into trouble with localization. The topmost menu items in a menu list are always meant to be displayed on the screen. If you have quite a few menu items you probably have tried to make them all fit on just one line. If you have so many choices that you needed to "make them all fit" then you need to rethink your design. The menu will most probably grow quite a bit in size when localized and you will end up wrapping your menu. This is something you definitely need to take into account.

This century has seen boundary lines on maps redrawn countless times. We have seen new countries spring up and several countries combine into one. Even today many parts of the world are in flux and border disputes abound. If you need to display a map make sure you have the latest version for that region. You do not want your program to offend anyone who may take exception to the map you show.

Fonts and Keyboards

These days Windows has a large number of fonts natively available depending on the language version of Windows you have.

You may find that some of your characters are coming out with question marks and other characters that are not what you expect. If this is the case you most likely need a new font for your program.

If you find that you are translating to languages that are not supported by the built-in fonts you may need to include them with your program. Consider localizing the fonts you need in a resource file. You can then load the font you need at runtime without cluttering up the destination PC.

Keyboard layouts change according to locale. In some countries certain character do not appear on the keyboard at all. In such cases there are shortcut key combinations that are used to get the right character. If you need to set up shortcut keys, remember to use only keys that you are sure are on the keyboard at that locale. If you want to be independent of locale then use the function keys to do this.

To summarize; here are some pointers to keep in mind when designing user screens.

- Do not split phrases between label or text controls on your screen.

- Don't try to jam all your fields on one screen. Nothing is worse than a busy screen in English that when translated to another language has all kinds of word wrapping.

- Leave room for word expansion in your text fields.

- Truncate strings to the maximum length of a text field. This prevents unwanted word wrapping.

- Do not concatenate translated words or phrases to make sentences. Word order will invariably trip you up.

- Use proper English wherever possible. Slang translates poorly.

- Be careful of abbreviations or industry specific terms. Build up a glossary as you go along.

- Do not depend too much on the size of message boxes. They change in relation to the number of characters displayed.

- Make your dialog box large enough to handle translated text. Resizing a dialog box could lead to unexpected results.

- If you have quite a few first-level menu choices be prepared for them to wrap after being translated.

- Consider keeping nonstandard fonts in a resource file.

- Try to keep pictures of international maps to a minimum. Map divisions can be a hot point with quite a few people.

Formatting International Time

Remember when mom taught you to tell time on an analog clock? Pretty confusing when you consider that it can be 11 o'clock twice a day. Of course when you are 5 or 6-years-old you say "in the morning" or "in the afternoon." Only later did you learn the AM/PM part.

NOTE   *AM and PM stand for ante meridian/post meridian.*

That was okay for us in the United States. What about overseas? Most nations have standardized on military time. Most of us here in the United States only know it through John Wayne war movies where he asked people to synchronize watches at 0600 hours. Go to Europe and 9 PM is most always 21:00 when written. When you think of this in terms of programming, military time is definitely easier to work with (sort, add, subtract).

Try to make an algorithm to take the difference between 10 AM and 3:45 PM. It takes a little doing in analog time but military time is trivial.

Okay, I know what you are thinking. What happens at midnight? Well both 00:00:00 and 24:00:00 mean the same thing. However to remove ambiguity you should refer to midnight as 00:00:00. Digital clocks do not display 24:00:00.

In general the world standard for time is hh:mm:ss. Where hh is the number of complete hours that have passed since midnight (00-24), mm is the number of complete minutes that have passed since the start of the hour (00-59), and ss is the number of complete seconds since the start of the minute (00-60). If the hour value is 24, then the minute and second values must be zero.

Formatting Dates

Want a date? How about "3/4/05"? What date is this? Is it March 4, 2005 or March 4, 1905 or April 3, 2005 or April 3, 1905. Any of these interpretations is feasible depending on your location and your age.

Time is basic and you can pretty much tell what someone means when it is displayed. As you can see, dates are a different story.

You might see dates in the following formats. 8/7/99, 7/8/99, 99/7/8, 8.7.1999, 07-OCT-1999, 7-October-1999. And there are quite a few more. It can be quite confusing.

The international date standard notation is YYYY-MM-DD. This based on the Gregorian calendar where YYYY is the year. MM is the month between 01 and 12. DD is the day between 01 and 31.

The ISO has passed a language-independent international time and date standard called the International Standard ISO 8601. Aside from solving confusion over what date notation to use, the advantages of this standard are many.

- The standard is easily readable and writeable by software (no 'JAN', 'FEB', ... table necessary.)

- It is comparable and sortable with a trivial string comparison.

- Provides consistency with the common 24h time notation system.

- Strings containing a date followed by a time are easily comparable and sortable.

- The notation is short and has constant length, which makes both keyboard data entry and table layout easier.

- This date notation is already used in much of the world.

ISO date and time standards are very helpful to both the programmer and to the end user. Why the programmer? How many times have you had to add and subtract time or dates based on a 12-hour clock? Perhaps you have tried to find the day of the year and the number of days left in the year for a scheduling program you are writing. The algorithm for using a 12-hour clock and day and month names is very difficult. The ISO standard formats dates in the slowest moving time to the fastest. This makes date and time very easy to sort and calculations very easy to compute.

What about the end user? Quite a few countries, such as Japan, Korea, Hungary, Sweden, Finland, Denmark, and others, as well as people in the United States, are already used to at least the "month, day" order. This format is already used in much of the world. The end user also benefits from easier and more constant keyboard entry. Entering in May 24 (04-24) is the same as entering in September 24 (09-24).

Both time and dates are stored in different formats programmatically. Whatever the format, you should use some kind of formatting command to display the time based on a setting the user chooses or based on the regional settings of your computer. Both Visual Basic and Visual Studio .NET have such format commands.

Formatting Dates in Visual Basic 6

Visual Basic had some basic date formatting parameters that converted a date value to text based on the regional settings of your computer. An example of this is:

```
format ( now(), "General Date" )
```

This returns a string representation of the date and time according to your system settings. Other date formats that are displayed according to system settings are:

- "Long Date"

- "Medium Date"

- "Short Date"

- "Long Time"

Formatting Dates the .NET Way

The .NET way of doing this is somewhat different. .NET does not need a separate function to handle transformation of basic data types.

Now for a little review on .NET architecture. The most basic lesson of .NET is this: Everything inherits from the object class. . .*everything*. This means that all basic data types you are familiar with are actually objects. This includes integers, strings, longs, and dates.

As you study the basic data types in .NET you will find there are two kinds: value and reference types. The short explanation is that they can be treated the same ways. If you declare an integer and use it only for simple math operations it stays a value type. If you want a little more out of it such as determining what type it is then through the magic of "boxing" it becomes a reference type. It is now an object. I encourage you to review the documentation on boxing and play with boxing until you understand it. Knowing when a type is boxed and unboxed can make a difference in how you program a particular algorithm.

In VB a date is essentially a double. This stems from the fact that VB 6 is COM-based, and a date in the COM world is an OLE automation date, which is a double. All types in .NET inherit from the base object class. Because of this, the date type is also an object. All well-written objects (.NET has only well-written objects) have a certain amount of what I call "programmed instinct." They know what they are and what they are capable of doing. Most good objects can also transform their data to another form if appropriate.

This is all true for the date type (object). If you want to print out a date in one of several formats you would use the following piece of code.

C# Example:

```
DateTime MyDate = new DateTime(2001, 8, 2);
MyString = MyDate.ToString("F");
```

VB .NET Example:

```
Dim MyDate = new DateTime(2001, 8, 2)
MyString = MyDate.ToString("F")
```

The result of this code would be "8/2/2001" if the current culture was U.S. English.

The DateTime structure has seven overloaded constructors. You can initialize it with just about any kind of date or time you can think of. As you can see, the DateTime object can return a string according to the current culture settings. A partial listing of output formats with default patterns are:

- "d"   M/D/YYYY

- "D"   dddd, MMMM dd, yyyy

- "s"   yyyy-MM-dd HH:mm:ss

The last one conforms to the ISO standard 8601. There are quite a few others, and I encourage you to visit the VS .NET Help files to familiarize yourself with them.

Whatever you do in regard to displaying dates and times, make sure you are consistent throughout your program.

The Calendar

There are several calendars still in use around the world. The most popular is the Gregorian calendar. The Gregorian calendar was devised as a way to fix the problems with the Julian calendar. These problems had to do with the way Easter was calculated and the length of the tropical year. The Julian calendar lost one day every 128 years. Although the Julian calendar was dropped by most of the world in the 1500s, it is still used today by the Russian Orthodox Church and other orthodox churches.

The main calendars in use today are:

- Hebrew

- Chinese

- Japanese

- Julian

- Gregorian

- Islamic

- Balinese

- Baha'i

- Ethiopian

While the details of each calendar are out of the scope of this book I will say that most of the time the Gregorian calendar is the predominant one. Visual Studio .NET does allow date calculations in other calendars. If you find that you are making a date-centric application such as an HR program, it would behoove you to make use of these functions.

The System.Globalization namespace in VS .NET has the following calendar implementations.

- GregorianCalendar class

- HebrewCalendar class

- HijriCalndar class

- JapaneseCalendar class

- JulianCalendar class

- KoreanCalendar class

- TaiwanCalendar class

- ThaiBuddhistCalendar class

Each of these classes allows manipulation of dates within the particular calendar you are working with. This is not only way cool but allows easy implementation of different calendar types within your program. The good folks at Microsoft have done all the complicated calculations for you.

Numbers and Currency

This can be quite a confusing subject. In VB 6 formatting a number according to local depends on your computer's setting. You cannot define programmatically that a group separator is a comma or a period. The same goes for the decimal separator. If you used the piece of code

```
X=123,456.78
S=Format ( x, "###,###.###" )
```

you get the string 123,456.78 in the United States, but if your computer is set for Germany you get 123.456,78. The comma and period are swapped.

> **TIP**   *Suppose you use a text box for real number input below 1000. The standard method is to catch each keystroke and verify that it is a digit or a decimal point. Wrong! This works in the United States, but it will not let someone in England input any number other than an integer. You must also allow a comma.*

VS .NET has string-formatting commands built into the numerical data types. Just like the date and time issue, there is no separate function needed in VS .NET to convert a number to a string. Again this is done using the ToString method associated with these objects. By the way, the ToString() method is Unicode-aware.

Let's look at some code to see how the ToString() function works. The first sample shows this function in VB .NET:

```
Dim ThisInt as integer = 12345
Dim MyString as string = ThisInt.ToString( "c" )
MyString = ThisInt.ToString( "d7" )
MyString = ThisInt.ToString( "g" )
```

Here is the C# example:

```
int MyInt = 12345;
String MyString = MyInt.ToString( "c" );
MyString = MyInt.ToString( "d7" );
MyString = MyInt.ToString( "g" );
```

The first MyString would be "$12,345.00".
The second MyString would be "0012345".
The third MyString would be "12345".

As you can see, the format specifier allows you to represent the number in any of several ways. How do you make this internationally aware? The answer is in the System.Globalization.CultureInfo namespace. You can initialize the constructor with a code for a country, and the MyInt.ToString() member swaps the comma and decimal point if appropriate.

The ToString() conversion function for all basic data types is culture-aware. However, if you use a format specifier without a corresponding argument for the culture, the resulting string is formatted according to the culture that your system is set to in the regional settings of the control panel. If you are making a program that will be able to swap languages at runtime then you need to add this extra argument to all your ToString() commands. The following code takes the previous number and currency example and makes it internationally aware. It also allows you to change culture via code, which essentially gives you runtime control over changing languages.

This example is shown here in VB, but it is available for download in C# if you wish.

VB .NET Example:

```vb
Imports System.Globalization
. . .
        Dim mystring As String
        Dim MyCulture As CultureInfo
        Dim thisdate As DateTime = #8/2/2001#
        Dim ThisInt As Integer = 12345

        'The current culture of the computer
        MyCulture = CultureInfo.CurrentCulture
        mystring = thisdate.ToString("d", MyCulture)
        mystring = ThisInt.ToString("c", MyCulture)
        mystring = ThisInt.ToString("d7", MyCulture)
        mystring = ThisInt.ToString("g", MyCulture)

        'The German culture
        MyCulture = New CultureInfo("de-DE")
        mystring = thisdate.ToString("d", MyCulture)
        mystring = ThisInt.ToString("c", MyCulture)
        mystring = ThisInt.ToString("d7", MyCulture)
        mystring = ThisInt.ToString("g", MyCulture)
```

```
'The US culture
MyCulture = New CultureInfo("en-US")
mystring = thisdate.ToString("d", MyCulture)
mystring = ThisInt.ToString("c", MyCulture)
mystring = ThisInt.ToString("d7", MyCulture)
mystring = ThisInt.ToString("g", MyCulture)
```

. . .

Let's describe a little about what is going on here.

The first thing I do is import the System.Globalization namespace. This gives me access to the classes under this namespace without having to resort to using the full name. I could have made a reference to another assembly that imported this namespace and achieved the same thing. After this I set up a variable that will hold the current culture as well as some data variables to work with.

Let's look at this first block of code.

```
'The current culture of the computer
MyCulture = CultureInfo.CurrentCulture
mystring = thisdate.ToString("d", MyCulture)
mystring = ThisInt.ToString("c", MyCulture)
mystring = ThisInt.ToString("d7", MyCulture)
mystring = ThisInt.ToString("g", MyCulture)
```

The current culture is set to U.S. English. For the first block of code the variable mystring will have the following values:

1. "8/2/2001"

2. "$12,345.00"

3. "0012345"

4. "12345"

The next block of code changes the MyCulture object to be German.

```
'The German culture
MyCulture = New CultureInfo("de-DE")
mystring = thisdate.ToString("d", MyCulture)
mystring = ThisInt.ToString("c", MyCulture)
mystring = ThisInt.ToString("d7", MyCulture)
mystring = ThisInt.ToString("g", MyCulture)
```

For this block of code the variable mystring has the following values:

1. "02.08.2001"

2. "12.345,00"

3. "0012345"

4. "12345"

Notice that my code is the same except for changing the culture. The date and currency format changed according to the culture I set.

Notice something interesting about the currency? As of the time I am writing this book the German currency is German Marks. However .NET is anticipating the changeover in 2002 from Marks to Euros.

So what do I do if I want to express money in German Marks? Well as it so happens there is a way to do this by making your own number format class and passing it to the CultureInfo class. Consider this piece of code.

```
'Here is how to represent the old German currency format
Dim OldGermanFormat As New NumberFormatInfo()
OldGermanFormat.CurrencySymbol = " DM"
OldGermanFormat.CurrencyDecimalSeparator = ","
OldGermanFormat.CurrencyGroupSeparator = "."
OldGermanFormat.CurrencyPositivePattern = 1
OldGermanFormat.CurrencyNegativePattern = 1

'The current German culture
MyCulture = New CultureInfo("de-DE")
MyCulture.NumberFormat = OldGermanFormat

mystring = ThisInt.ToString("c", MyCulture)
```

The resulting value of mystring is "12.345,00 DM". Just what I wanted. Let's look at what I did here:

1. I set up an object as a NumberFormatInfo class.

2. I set the decimal separator and group separator to be the same as is used in Germany.

3. I made the CurrencySymbol something that represents the old German Mark. The default for this is the "$."

4. I set the positive and negative pattern for the currency so that the number precedes the symbol.

5. I set the current culture to German. (More than numbers are involved here in a language.)

6. I set the current culture to German. (More than numbers are involved here in a language.)

7. I set the internal number format of the current culture to be OldGermanFormat.

The flexibility included here allows you to pretty much do what you want. Microsoft included just about every known modern culture in the world, but even they can't predict the instability in different regions. By the time this book is published there may be a new country or two to deal with.

How Sort Order Is Affected by Language

There are two basic types of sort orders for strings. The first is ASCII sort order. This is where the strings are sorted according to their letter placement in the ASCII table. Letters are placed in the ASCII table capital letters first. In this case, words that begin with A, b, C would be sorted as A, C, b.

The International sort order is defined as being case-insensitive. So the true sort in the above example would be A, b, C.

There are quite a few other types of sort orders within the international arena. These are all language-based. Some of these are the Czech, Swedish, Danish, Polish, Spanish, French, and so on. Most of these sort orders have different rules for the diacritical marks. Some define a character with a diacritical to come before the same character without, and some are the reverse. Also because some European languages have more letters than English, there are cases where what would seem normal sort order to someone in the United States is totally different to someone in Russia.

Suppose you had the following words sorted in normal International sort order:

- Victory

- Wake

- Woman

- Yak

If you sort them in Finnish sort order they would be arranged like so:

- Wake

- Victory

- Woman

- Yak

In Finland the V is considered the same level as the W. This could really play havoc with your database indexes. Watch out for this.

You can get the sort key string that defines sort order from .NET. It is under the System.Globalization namespace. Look in the SortKey class under OriginalString. The KeyData and OriginalString members can both be overridden to make your own sort order.

Creating International Help Files

Back in the days of DOS, most programmers did not write Help files for their programs. Not much of an issue here. When Windows came along all of a sudden we got context-sensitive Help. Pushing the F1 key while on a field, screen, or even a word would bring up Help that was what you wanted. No more of this pulling up the Help file as a whole and trying to find a topic that addressed your needs.

 NOTE *Full coverage of Help files and how to create them is beyond the scope of this book. Instead I wish to convey some more philosophical aspects of Help file creation.*

Unless your program is the most intuitive in the world, you need a comprehensive Help system. Believe me when I say that the Help file can make or break a good program.

It can also greatly reduce those pesky tech support calls. (But then what is the point because no matter how good the Help is no one ever reads the manual anyway. . .but I digress.)

Make sure to use the same translator, or at least the same translating project manager, for your program strings as well as your Help files. Many English words and phrases can have several meanings in different languages. If you translate a sentence from English to Chinese in your program, make sure that the same sentence in your Help file is translated the same way. If not you run the risk of the Help file adding confusion instead of clarity.

By the same token, have the program and the Help file translated at the same time. Always keep them current with each other. The thought process necessary in converting your text files should be the same one used in converting your Help files. If you decide to translate the Help files six months after the strings then the translator will have probably forgotten some of the nuances involved at the time he or she translated your strings.

As a programmer you probably should not be doing your own Help file. You will instead need to work closely with a tech writer to accomplish this. To summarize, here are a few hints to follow as you work with the designer of your Help system.

- Keep the explanations as free of jargon as you can.

- Make sure that any screen shots can be easily replaced. It is no good translating the Help file while showing screen shots in English.

- Be sure to use the same translating project manager for your program strings as well as your Help files.

- Have the program and the Help file translated at the same time.

Introducing Unicode and Character Sets

What is Unicode? Perhaps you think it is one of those persistent buzzwords that just won't go away. Believe me when I say it is not a buzzword. As far as multilingual computing goes, Unicode is the most important thing to ever come along in the computer business. Unicode is one of those things in the computer industry that is slowly being adopted with hardly any fanfare. In fact, for quite a few programmers, Unicode is largely unseen and unnoticed.

So what is Unicode? Unicode is a way to provide a unique number that identifies every single character in every human language. There is even room left over for Klingon!

Let's back up a step. You have certainly worked with the ASCII table. Consider the following piece of VB code:

```
Dim letter As String
Dim number As Integer

letter = Chr(65)
number = Asc("A")
```

This code converts an ASCII number to its character representation and back again. In ASCII the capital letter A is 65. If you have ever intercepted a key press event from one of the VB controls you have had to use the ASCII conversion routines to see what letter was pressed.

While the ASCII table has 256 character representations, most of us only program with the lower 128. This is mainly because it is enough to write most anything in the English language. If you look at the ASCII table you see that the upper 128 characters are a collection of some foreign characters, punctuation, lines, and blocks.

 NOTE *It was very common in the DOS days to draw menus and graphics on the screen using the upper 128 characters of the ASCII table. In fact quite a few programmers, myself included, could recite most of the ASCII table by heart.*

Code Page Usage

In the days before Unicode Version 1 was fully adopted, programmers used code pages to display characters from different languages. Code pages are still supported in Windows but are only really used for older programs. A code page is a different interpretation of the ASCII character set. Code pages keep the same lower 128 characters intact (mostly) but the upper 128 characters are tailored to a particular language. There are many Windows code pages as well as DOS code pages. This means that the ASCII character for #180 is different for almost every code page. In fact the Cyrillic code page for DOS is different than the Cyrillic code page for Windows. They have all the same characters but the ASCII number is different for both. This was quite a problem for the multilingual programmer always having to keep track of what code page you might be working from. Imagine trying to send a text file that was rendered using a certain code page to someone. Chaos could easily ensue if the person you sent it to was not up on code pages.

I once had to send out English text to be translated into Cyrillic to be used on an embedded system. There were constant phone calls and emails about which code page was being used and how to represent it. The embedded target system used a DOS Cyrillic code page 866 and I got the translations back in a Word doc that used the Windows Cyrillic code page 1251. Do this just once and you understand the need for Unicode.

In Windows 9*x*/2000, code pages could be switched on the fly without having to change language. In DOS you had to change the code page with some DOS commands. Needless to say, using code pages was not the most elegant way of enabling different character sets to be displayed on your screen.

I could go on and make this book quite a bit heavier with code page information. However the preferred method is definitely to use Unicode. Because .NET is totally new and Unicode-based I will not go into any more depth on code pages.

Relating Double Byte Character Sets to Unicode

What about Eastern languages where Chinese for instance has over 5000 characters? A different scheme was invented for this based on the concept of code pages that contain 256 code points. The result is called the Double-Byte Character Set (DBCS).

In DBCS, a pair of code points (a double-byte) represents each character. The first byte of a double-byte set was not considered valid unless it was followed by a second byte defined in the DBCS set. DBCS required code that would treat these pairs of code points as one character. This still disallowed the combination of two languages, for example, Japanese and Chinese, in the same data stream because the same double-byte code points represent different characters depending on the code page. DBCS was used for some time but is now going out of style.

Along comes our saving grace Unicode. Unicode is based on the ASCII table for compatibility but greatly extends it. Instead of being one byte in length Unicode represents characters with 2 bytes. This 16-bit encoding scheme means that codes are available for 64k characters. While this number is sufficient for coding the characters used in the major languages of the world, the Unicode Standard provides the UTF-16 extension mechanism (called surrogates in the Unicode Standard), which allows for the encoding of as many as 1 million additional characters. This is sufficient for all known character encoding requirements, including full representation of all historic scripts of the world. This brings order to the chaotic world of character representation.

The first 128 characters of Unicode are the normal Latin ASCII character set. These characters go from 0000 to 007F hex. In Unicode the word "dog" would be represented by 0064006F0067. This plays havoc with C code because in C a string is terminated with a NULL character, which is 00. As you can see Unicode is not compatible with normal C strings.

To reiterate, Unicode assigns a unique letter for every character without regard to:

- Language

- Computing platform

- Program

This is quite an accomplishment considering all the disparate computing systems in the world.

Programming with Unicode

> **NOTE** *This is just a scant introduction to Unicode. Many pounds of books have been written about Unicode. I suggest you get the Unicode 3.0 book put out by the Unicode consortium. It is a valuable reference.*

 If you are a VB programmer you have been using Unicode since Version 5. All Visual Basic strings are represented internally in Unicode. VB has been ready, willing, and able to help

in localization for years.. How can you tell that your string is represented in Unicode? Try the following VB example.

```
x = Len("Unicode")
x = LenB("Unicode")
```

The first line sets *x* to 7, the number of letters in the word Unicode. The second line sets *x* to 14. This is the number of bytes needed to store the word Unicode. In ASCII 7 bytes would be enough. For you C lovers, an 8th byte would be needed to store the null terminator.

Visual Basic always did the Unicode to ANSI translation for you transparently. Windows NT and higher operating systems from Microsoft are fully Unicode compliant. Visual Studio .NET is fully Unicode compliant. You now have a great basis for writing programs in .NET that will work anywhere in the world.

So how can you see the power of Unicode? There is a great Unicode editor called `UniEdit`. This program was developed in conjunction with Duke University. There is currently a free trial version of UniEdit available at `http://www.humancomp.org/uniintro.htm`. The cost for buying it is minimal and its usefulness is infinite.

> **NOTE** *I have occasional need to reference the official Unicode book. I often find it fascinating to flip though and look at other writing systems. A 2-minute lookup may take me $\frac{1}{2}$ hour. I am the same way with the dictionary.*

How do you know that .NET is Unicode just by glancing at the documentation? Look at the documentation concerning data types. A Char is now two bytes. It is big enough to hold a UTF-16 Unicode character. Traditionally it had always been one byte.

NOTE *I can't tell you how many programs I have written (embedded and DOS) that counted on the fact that a char was one byte. So many algorithms that involved counting were based on this fact.*

Summary

This chapter dealt with some of the more prevalent concepts surrounding localization. I talked about what is necessary to properly format and display your information to the user. Data presentation is arguably the most important aspect of a program.

I ended up this chapter with a short discussion of Unicode and how prevalent it is in both programming languages and in the operating system itself.

Some things to remember are:

- Make sure your text boxes are able to handle translated strings that can be anywhere from 20 to 100 percent of the original English size.

- Make sure that numeric input allows the interchange of a comma with a period as demarcation identifiers.

- Allow for growth in the size of dialog boxes, message boxes, and menus.

- .NET is Unicode aware. Learn what Unicode is and use it to your advantage.

- Be aware of different time, date, and numeric formats for different cultures.

- Do not depend on the U.S.'s standard sort order. Some cultures sort strings in a different order. Make sure your program takes this into account.

- Do not forget the Help files. Translating them in synch with the program strings can avoid confusion between different translations of the same phrases.

There are many of you who will spend some time in between programming languages as you slowly migrate to .NET. In Chapter 3 I cover how to use multiple resource files in VB 6. I also show you how to manage these resource files in a manner similar to .NET.

Using Multiple Resource Files in VB 6

BEFORE WE GET INTO the nitty-gritty of localizing code written in VS .NET I want to take a bit of time to explain how to simulate some of the .NET resource file features from within VB 6. (I used this method about a year before I knew what .NET was.) After all, there is quite a bit of VB 6 code that works, and you will not want to port it all. VB 6 will be around for some time to come.

In this chapter, I cover resource files in depth from the perspective of VB 6. By the end of this chapter you should know quite a lot about VB 6 resource files, their faults, and how to overcome them.

- I show you how to set up and write resource files for easy maintenance.

- I show you how to use the WIN32 API to load resource DLLs at runtime.

- I show you how to load another languages on the fly without the program having any prior knowledge of it.

- Finally, I show you a fallback method of loading resources similar to .NET.

All the code for this chapter can be downloaded from the Apress web site at http://www.apress.com. Often when I read a programming book I prefer to enter code myself. It is like riding a bicycle to work instead of driving. You tend to notice so much more. If you are not doing any VB coding then perhaps you might want to "take the car" and just download the code to see how it works. However, if you are still programming in VB 6 I encourage you to "ride your bike" a little. By the way, the methods used in this chapter appeared in an article I wrote for *Multilingual Magazine* last year.

VB 6 Resource File Overview

The reason I developed this method of using resource files in VB is that I found the resource files lacking in many ways. Resource files were a great boon to me as an international programmer but after working with them for some time I wished they had more functionality.

VB 6 allows only one resource file per project, and it cannot be external to the program. This forces you to recompile an entire project whenever you make a change to your resource file. VB links the resource file during compilation. Internalizing the resource file makes for quicker loads and fewer files to deploy, but the loss of flexibility is not worth it.

One of the samples that VB 6 comes with is an ATM example that is supposed to illustrate how to use a resource file. It is very basic at best. This example makes use of a resource file that has several translations of strings used in a hypothetical ATM. The user is given the opportunity to press a button to instantly change the display to one of several languages. This code uses the resource editor add-in for VB to create the resource file. There are several problems with this method of using resource files in VB, which I detail in the following section.

What VB 6 Resource Files Lack

First, the resource editor makes a compiled binary resource file directly. There is no intermediate text file generated. How do you get a few thousand strings translated using this method? This would be very difficult, user-intensive, and prone to error.

The next problem is one of syntax. The resource file mechanism in VB is number-driven. This means that you can only refer to a string resource by its number. As I have said in Chapter 2, it is much better and more maintainable to refer to a resource by a literal constant. As all good programmers know (and I know you are all good programmers), using hard-coded numbers as references is not good programming practice. If the ATM example is followed for a large program, it would soon be impossible to maintain.

The third problem is one of quantity. Since the resource file must be linked to your program during compile, there can only be one. If you want multiple languages then you need to put them all into the same resource file. This is a maintenance nightmare. To add a language you would need to touch the original debugged resource file. I have said it before, and it bears saying again, whenever you touch code you greatly increase the chance of introducing bugs. The more compartmentalized and modularized your code is (include external files) the better off you are.

These problems can be overcome with a little work and know-how. First of all there is the problem of the included resource editor. You need a file that you can send to a translator, then get back the same file but with strings translated. Fortunately VB comes with a resource compiler called RC.exe to help with this.

External Resource Compiler

This external resource compiler allows you to make a resource file with a simple text editor like NotePad. If the resource file you make is in the correct format you can pass it through the resource compiler and get a binary .res file.

The resource compiler directory on the disk has several files associated with it. They are: Resource.txt, Rcdll.dll, Rc.exe, Rc.hlp. The rc.exe file is the actual resource compiler executable. It is best to put these files in your path somewhere. The resource compiler has quite a few options available to the programmer. Consult the rc.hlp file and the resource.txt file for an explanation of all the things you can do inside a resource file.

Here are the steps necessary to make an external resource file.

1. Open a text file called myresource.rc.

2. Edit the file and put in the following code:

```
#define STR_OK    100

STRINGTABLE
BEGIN
        STR_OK,    "&OK"
END
```

3. Save this file and run `rc.exe /r myresource.rc`.

The result of these three steps is a compiled resource file called `myResource.res`.

The external resource compiler solves several of the problems I detailed in the previous section. It allows you to make many resource files that can all contain the translated strings for just one language each. Also when you send out a copy of the original file to be translated you get back only the translated copy. You do not need to touch or recompile the original resource file. You have now compartmentalized the external files.

There are several other things we would like to do as well to make the method complete.

*   Use literal constants as keys for string retrieval.

*   Keep the resource files external to the program so you can have multiple resource files. You need to be able to access the resources in external files.

*   Have a fallback mechanism for strings that are not found in the translated files.

*   Load a new unknown language at runtime.

All this is achievable and is shown in the example in the following section.

A More Readable Resource File

First, let me explain a method to replace the numerical key with a constant. I use a module called strdef.bas, which contains constants that resolve to keys in the resource file. In this module I put all my string definitions such as: const STR_LANG = 1000. It is much easier to read code that uses LoadResString(STR_LANG) rather than LoadResString(1000). I immediately know what the programmer (usually myself) meant to do.

What about the resource file? Now that I have some constants in my code that refers to resources can I do the same in the resource file itself? The resource file structure for VB looks like this.

```
STRINGTABLE
BEGIN
    . . .
1000 "French"
. . .
END
```

You could leave the resource file like this, and the line LoadResString(STR_LANG) would work. However you also want your resource file to be readable and maintainable. To achieve this you need to duplicate the constants defined in the program, in the resource file as well. Your resource file will look like this.

```
#define STR_LANG    1000
. . .
. . .
STRINGTABLE
BEGIN
    . . .
STR_LANG        "French"
. . .
END
```

This takes some discipline but it will be worth it to the next programmer who comes along and needs to read your code. I know I am duplicating the definitions in two places, but being the smart programmer you will probably want to make a small VB add-in that takes your strdef.bas module and writes out the definitions to your external resource file. This is not rocket science, but making a VB 6 add-in is out of the scope of this book.

Making an External Resource File

Okay, now you know how to make an external resource file. You now need to tackle the problem of keeping the files external so you can use as many resource files as necessary in the program. This is a three-step process. It involves making a resource file with a text editor, compiling it into a .res file, and making a DLL out of the resource file. I have shown you how to use a text editor to make a resource file and also how to use the RC program to compile the text file into a binary resource file. The final step as far as the resource file is concerned is to make the DLL necessary to contain the resource file.

There are several ways to make a DLL to contain your resource file. You will concentrate on using VB to generate the necessary file. Why a DLL? You need to use the Win32API command LoadLibrary(). This API command takes for an argument either a DLL or an EXE. I chose a DLL over an EXE because the code is smaller and I do not want anyone to think they can just click on the EXE name and have something happen.

NOTE   *I also use a DLL for another reason. If you follow and understand all the steps in this VB project you will realize that I am doing by hand what .NET appears to be doing behind the scenes. When I go through the .net example for satellite resource files it will become clear.*

The first thing you need is a compiled resource file. Let's say the resource file contains Spanish translations of an original English resource file. The resource file should be called es-ES.res. This convention is based on the two-letter ISO abbreviation for a country.

Put this resource file in a directory where you will make your new DLL. Open up VB and chose a new ActiveX DLL project. VB does not let you make a plain DLL where you can export functions. Rename the project to es-ES and rename the class to NoShow. On the VB menu click on Project-Add File. Choose the resource file and add it to the project. You are now done. It is that easy. The empty class is a requirement of VB when making an ActiveX DLL. The only thing you use in this DLL is the resource file.

Save and compile the project. The file produced will be es-ES.dll. It will contain essentially nothing but the resource file. It is interesting to note that this is a COM object. However, you will not use it as such so there is no need to register it.

One of the keys to making the most out of resource files is being able to make, edit, and compile the resource file external to the VB IDE as I have already shown you. By being able to create an external resource file you will then be able to make a resource DLL. Making a resource DLL is crucial to being able to use

external resources. It is the resource DLL that your new project will load. When
the resource DLL is loaded you can then access any of the strings with the new
function I am about to describe. It is important to note here that any resource
DLL you make for a particular project should have the same constants associated
with the particular strings. For example, in English I would have:

```
#define str_fr    500
. . .
STRINGTABLE
BEGIN
     Str_fr    "French"
END
```

If translated to French this would be inside the French resource file.

```
#define str_fr    500
. . .
STRINGTABLE
BEGIN
     Str_fr    "Francais"
END
```

If done this way then any translated string resource file could replace the
original resource file with no code changes. I could have LoadResString(Str_fr) in
my code, and I would get the correct string no matter what language I use.

There are several Windows API functions associated with localization of
applications. I examine two of them. I also describe a way to wrap these API calls
inside some VB functions. One of these functions replaces the LoadResString()
function. The LoadResString() function that VB provides returns a string from the
embedded resource file if you provide it with a numerical argument that identifies the string.

Loading Resources at Runtime

This is all fine for making and using resource files. How do you put this all
together so you can change resource files, and therefore languages, at runtime?
The answer lies in using the Windows API. The API functions you use are
LoadLibrary() and LoadString().

In order to use these functions you need to load the API viewer add-in.
Choose Add-ins from the VB IDE menu and then click API Viewer. To use the
API viewer, first you need to load the Windows API text file. While in the Viewer
click File then Load Text File to bring up the list of API text files available to you.

Choose Win32API.txt. The "Available Items" box is populated by windows API functions.

Add the LoadLibrary and LoadString functions to the Selected Items box; then click the Insert button. The API declarations are automatically copied to the current open form. This is all the preparation needed to use these two Windows API functions.

The GetStrings.bas Module

Let's make a module that has three functions in it that allow us to change languages between English and, for simplicity's sake, one other language. However the idea can be expanded to include any number of languages. For this example the DLL filename will be es-ES.dll. Included in this module are the Windows API function declarations LoadLibrary and LoadString. You use this module in your example project. This module is self-contained in that it can be used in any project with no code change. It is called GetStrings.bas. The code for this module in its entirety is in Listing 3-1.

Listing 3-1. The GetString.bas example

```
Option Explicit

Public Declare Function LoadLibrary Lib "kernel32" Alias "LoadLibraryA" _
(ByVal lpLibFileName As String) As Long
Public Declare Function LoadString Lib "user32" Alias "LoadStringA" _
(ByVal hInstance As Long, ByVal wID As Long, ByVal lpBuffer As String, _
ByVal nBufferMax As Long) As Long

Private STRING_RESOURCE As Long
Private UseEnglish As Boolean

Public Function LoadStringRes(wID As Long) As String
    Dim Buff As String * 80
    Dim BytesCopied As Long

    BytesCopied = 0
    If Not UseEnglish Then
        BytesCopied = LoadString(STRING_RESOURCE, wID, Buff, Len(Buff))
    End If

    If BytesCopied Then
        LoadStringRes = Buff
```

```
        Else
            LoadStringRes = LoadResString(wID)
        End If

End Function

Public Function LoadAltLanguage() As Boolean

On Error GoTo BadDLL
    If STRING_RESOURCE = 0 Then
        STRING_RESOURCE = LoadLibrary(InstallDirectory & "\es-ES.dll")
    End If

    If STRING_RESOURCE Then
        LoadAltLanguage = True
        UseEnglish = False
    Else
        LoadAltLanguage = False
    End If

    Exit Function

BadDLL:
    Dim s As String
    s = "Error loading DLL." & vbCrLf
    s = s & "InstallDirectory not defined" & vbCrLf
    s = s & "Or missing es-ES.dll"

    MsgBox s, vbCritical

End Function

Public Sub UseEnglishLanguage()
    UseEnglish = True
End Sub
```

Listing 3-2 is an excerpt from the code in Listing 3-1. It is a replacement for the VB function LoadResString(). It is called LoadStringRes().

Listing 3-2. Replacing LoadResString() with LoadStringRes()

```
. . .
Public Function LoadStringRes(wID As Long) As String
    Dim Buff As String * 80
    Dim BytesCopied As Long

    BytesCopied = 0
    If Not UseEnglish Then
        BytesCopied = LoadString(STRING_RESOURCE, wID, Buff, _
Len(Buff))
    End If

    If BytesCopied Then
        LoadStringRes = Buff
    Else
        LoadStringRes = LoadResString(wID)
    End If
End Function
```

Notice that this function returns a string from either the embedded resource file or from the resource DLL you previously loaded. This is important to note because it provides your fallback mechanism. If you do not find the requested string in the external resource file then you will find it in the embedded resource file. The nature of the LoadString API is that it will return a zero if the file is not found (essentially when STRING_RESOURCE = 0). This is another type of fallback. When you get to the .NET examples you will see that this is a major part of the .NET method of handling resource files.

The LoadString() Call

Let's take a minute to explain the arguments to the LoadString() call. The first argument STRING_RESOURCE, is a handle to the loaded DLL. If the DLL is not loaded, this handle is zero and the call fails to return zero bytes copied into the buffer. The second argument is the string identifier. The third argument is a fixed-length buffer where the string is copied. The last argument is the maximum number of characters to be copied. Note that I set this for 80 characters.

Before you ask, I can say that, yes, it does work for Unicode resource strings. This means that you can have a resource file with Korean strings and all works well. Remember that VB stores strings internally in two-byte Unicode fashion. Setting the string length for 80 characters actually uses 160 bytes. Also I use the len() function to determine string length. This function is Unicode-aware.

If the LoadString() call fails, or English is chosen as a language, then the normal VB LoadResString() function is called to return the string to the user. This wrapper works with or without an external resource file loaded. It can be used as a drop-in replacement for the normal LoadResString() function that VB provides.

There is a function in the GetStrings.bas module called LoadAltLanguage(). This function loads the DLL into memory and assigns the handle to the STRING_RESOURCE variable. The code for this subroutine is shown in Listing 3-3.

Listing 3-3. Loading an alternate language

```
Public Function LoadAltLanguage() As Boolean

    ' If not 0 then you have already loaded it.
    If STRING_RESOURCE = 0 Then
        STRING_RESOURCE = LoadLibrary(App.Path & "\es-ES.dll")
    End If

    If STRING_RESOURCE Then
        LoadAltLanguage = True
        UseEnglish = False
    Else
        LoadAltLanguage = False
    End If
End Function
```

This function uses the LoadLibrary() API function to load your language DLL into memory. The return value from this call is the handle to the DLL. Notice that successful loading of the DLL automatically puts the program in the alternate language mode.

Last, a small but necessary subroutine is also included. You need to somehow change from your alternate language to English. Here it is:

```
Public Sub UseEnglishLanguage()
    UseEnglish = True
End Sub
```

Other than declaring the API functions, this is all there is to changing languages in VB.

The Full Example

The example project is a simple one that has several controls on the screen. These controls all have text associated with them. There are also three buttons. One changes text to English, one changes text to Spanish, and the last is a quit button to exit the application. This project has one form, two BAS modules, and an embedded resource file. The screen shot of the GUI form is shown in Figure 3-1.

Listing 3-4 shows the complete code for the sample. Not much here, is there?

Listing 3-4. Calling the code

```
Option Explicit

Private Sub cmdEnglish_Click()
    Call UseEnglishLanguage
    Call LoadStrings
End Sub

Private Sub cmdQuit_Click()
    End
End Sub

Private Sub cmdSpanish_Click()
    Call LoadAltLanguage
    Call LoadStrings
End Sub

Private Sub Form_Load()
    Call LoadStrings
End Sub

Private Sub LoadStrings()
    Caption = LoadStringRes(STR_DYNAMICRESOURCE)
    lblHeader.Caption = LoadStringRes(STR_LANGUAGE)
    lblLabel.Caption = LoadStringRes(STR_BORDERLABEL)
    cmdEnglish.Caption = LoadStringRes(STR_ENGLISH)
    cmdSpanish.Caption = LoadStringRes(STR_SPANISH)
    cmdQuit.Caption = LoadStringRes(STR_QUIT)
    txtText.Text = LoadStringRes(STR_NORMALTEXTBOX)
    chkCheck.Caption = LoadStringRes(STR_CHECKBOX)
End Sub
```

Making the String Definition File

The first thing you need to do is start a new project and then make a string definition file. This module file will hold named constants that resolve to integers. Integer keys are the formats necessary for identifying resources in VB 6.

1. Make a new standard project in the same directory as the DLL project. Call it MultiResource.

2. Name the first form "GUI".

3. Add a module called strings.bas. This module contains all the string definitions used in this project.

4. Add the code shown in Listing 3-5 to the strings.bas module.

Listing 3-5. Adding constants that refer to the resource file

```
Public Const STR_LANGUAGE = 1000
Public Const STR_ENGLISH = 1001
Public Const STR_SPANISH = 1002
Public Const STR_BORDERLABEL = 1003
Public Const STR_NORMALTEXTBOX = 1004
Public Const STR_CHECKBOX = 1005
Public Const STR_QUIT = 1006
Public Const STR_DYNAMICRESOURCE = 1007
```

Next, add the module called GetStrings.bas. This module is where you add all the code I described previously to load and retrieve strings.

Make the Form

The next thing to do is populate the form with the controls shown in Figure 3-1.

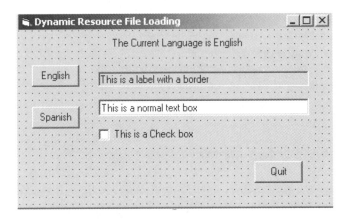

Figure 3-1. Resource file test form

Open this form and in the load procedure add the code in Listing 3-6.

Listing 3-6. Loading the strings

```
Private Sub Form_Load()
    Call LoadStrings
End Sub

Private Sub LoadStrings()
    Caption = LoadStringRes(STR_DYNAMICRESOURCE)
    lblHeader.Caption = LoadStringRes(STR_LANGUAGE)
    lblLabel.Caption = LoadStringRes(STR_BORDERLABEL)
    cmdEnglish.Caption = LoadStringRes(STR_ENGLISH)
    cmdSpanish.Caption = LoadStringRes(STR_SPANISH)
    cmdQuit.Caption = LoadStringRes(STR_QUIT)
    txtText.Text = LoadStringRes(STR_NORMALTEXTBOX)
    chkCheck.Caption = LoadStringRes(STR_CHECKBOX)
End Sub
```

This code populates the text fields of all the controls with the correct strings. Note that you use your new string function. Add some code to the buttons to change languages and to exit the program when done. The code for this is shown in Listing 3-7.

Listing 3-7. Switching languages

```
Private Sub cmdEnglish_Click()
    Call UseEnglishLanguage
    Call LoadStrings
End Sub

Private Sub cmdSpanish_Click()
    Call LoadAltLanguage
    Call LoadStrings
End Sub

Private Sub cmdQuit_Click()
    End
End Sub
```

Creating Multilingual Resource Files

The last thing you do is to create two resource files. One contains the English strings and the other contains the Spanish strings. Call the one with the English strings "strings.res." Once the resource files are compiled you need to make a DLL out of the Spanish resource file. Remember to call the DLL es-ES.dll.

Put the code shown in Listings 3-8 and 3-9 in your two resource files.

Listing 3-8. English resource file called strings.rc

```
#define STR_LANGUAGE          1000
#define STR_ENGLISH           1001
#define STR_SPANISH           1002
#define STR_BORDERLABEL       1003
#define STR_NORMALTEXTBOX     1004
#define STR_CHECKBOX          1005
#define STR_QUIT              1006
#define STR_DYNAMICRESOURCE   1007


STRINGTABLE
BEGIN
    STR_LANGUAGE          "The Current Language is English"
    STR_ENGLISH           "English"
    STR_SPANISH           "Spanish"
    STR_BORDERLABEL       "Label: embedded resoure file"
    STR_NORMALTEXTBOX     "Text: embedded resoure file"
    STR_CHECKBOX          "Check box: embedded resoure file"
    STR_QUIT              "Quit: embedded"
    STR_DYNAMICRESOURCE   "Dynamic Resource File Loading"
END
```

Listing 3-9. Spanish resource file called es-ES.rc

```
#define STR_LANGUAGE          1000
#define STR_ENGLISH           1001
#define STR_SPANISH           1002
#define STR_BORDERLABEL       1003
#define STR_NORMALTEXTBOX     1004
#define STR_CHECKBOX          1005
#define STR_QUIT              1006
#define STR_DYNAMICRESOURCE   1007
```

```
STRINGTABLE
BEGIN
    STR_LANGUAGE              "The Current Language is Spanish"
    STR_ENGLISH               "English"
    STR_SPANISH               "Spanish"
    STR_BORDERLABEL           "Label: Satellite resource file"
    STR_NORMALTEXTBOX         "Text: Satellite resource file"
    STR_CHECKBOX              "Check box: Satellite resource file"
    STR_QUIT                  "Quit: Satellite"
    STR_DYNAMICRESOURCE       "Dynamic Resource File Loading"
END
```

Finish It Off

Jump back into your VB project and add the English resource file to the project. To do this click on Project-Add File, and then choose the resource file. You should now have a project with one form, two .bas modules, and one resource file. At this point you can run the program. Figure 3-2 shows how your project should look.

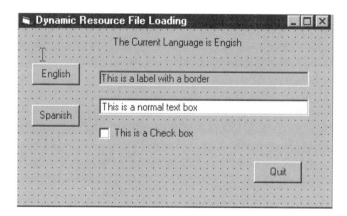

Figure 3-2. All your project files

Click the English button to see the text in English, and click on the Spanish button to see the text in Spanish.

Adding a New Language

Now you modify the program a little to allow adding a new language at runtime without changing any code on the target machine. What do I mean by this?

Suppose you had a program that needed to run 24x7 and you needed another language that was not included with your installation. I show you how to handle this. I am going to change the example somewhat to allow the program to keep running. I provide a new combo box that detects any new language that has been put on the system. When you choose the new language all the strings are replaced. You (the user) never had to do a thing. Keep in mind that this is a somewhat simplistic model and lacks some robustness for the sake of clarity. Listing 3-10 is the new GetStrings.bas module.

NOTE *Some countries that speak the same language have major regional differences in words or phrases. Be safe and put everything in a resource file and get it translated.*

Listing 3-10. New GetStrings() module

```
Option Explicit

Public Declare Function LoadLibrary Lib "kernel32" Alias "LoadLibraryA" _
(ByVal lpLibFileName As String) As Long
Public Declare Function LoadString Lib "user32" Alias "LoadStringA" _
  (ByVal hInstance As Long, ByVal wID As Long, ByVal lpBuffer As String, _
ByVal nBufferMax As Long) As Long
Public Declare Function FreeLibrary Lib "kernel32" _
  (ByVal hLibModule As Long) As Long


Public Type ResourceFiles
    fname    As String
    lang     As LANGUAGES_tag
End Type
'This tag is used to index into the embedded resource file
Enum LANGUAGES_tag
    ln_FIRSTLANG = 500
    ln_AUSTRALIAN
    ln_NEWZEALAND
    ln_ENGLAND
    ln_USA
    ln_SPAIN
    ln_MEXICO
    ln_FRENCHCANADIAN
    ln_FRENCH
    ln_LASTLANG
```

```vb
End Enum
Public ResFileName(ln_LASTLANG - ln_FIRSTLANG - 1) As ResourceFiles
Public LangDLL  As String


Private STRING_RESOURCE As Long

Public Function LoadStringRes(wID As Long) As String
    Dim Buff As String * 80
    Dim BytesCopied As Long

    BytesCopied = LoadString(STRING_RESOURCE, wID, Buff, Len(Buff))

    If BytesCopied Then
        LoadStringRes = Buff
    Else
        LoadStringRes = LoadResString(wID)
    End If

End Function


Public Sub FreeResources()
    If STRING_RESOURCE Then FreeLibrary (STRING_RESOURCE)
End Sub

Public Function LoadAltLanguage() As Boolean

    Call FreeResources
    STRING_RESOURCE = LoadLibrary(LangDLL)
    If STRING_RESOURCE Then
        LoadAltLanguage = True
    Else
        LoadAltLanguage = False
    End If

End Function

Public Sub InitResArray()
    Dim rf  As ResourceFiles

    rf.fname = "en-US"
    rf.lang = ln_USA
    ResFileName(0) = rf
```

```
        rf.fname = "es-ES"
        rf.lang = ln_SPAIN
        ResFileName(1) = rf

        rf.fname = "en-GB"
        rf.lang = ln_ENGLAND
        ResFileName(2) = rf

        rf.fname = "en-AU"
        rf.lang = ln_AUSTRALIAN
        ResFileName(3) = rf

        rf.fname = "en-NZ"
        rf.lang = ln_NEWZEALAND
        ResFileName(4) = rf

        rf.fname = "es-MX"
        rf.lang = ln_MEXICO
        ResFileName(5) = rf

        rf.fname = "fr-CA"
        rf.lang = ln_FRENCHCANADIAN
        ResFileName(6) = rf

        rf.fname = "fr-FR"
        rf.lang = ln_FRENCH
        ResFileName(7) = rf

End Sub
```

I have added a type, an enum, and an array at the top. I also added a type variable that defines the DLL to load.

```
Public Type ResourceFiles
    fname   As String
    lang    As LANGUAGES_tag
End Type
```

This new type is used to hold the file name of the resource file and a number that will resolve to a string in the embedded resource file. The enum is defined in Listing 3-11.

Listing 3-11. Language enumeration

```
Enum LANGUAGES_tag
    ln_FIRSTLANG = 500
    ln_AUSTRALIAN
    ln_NEWZEALAND
    ln_ENGLAND
    ln_USA
    ln_SPAIN
    ln_MEXICO
    ln_FRENCHCANADIAN
    ln_FRENCH
    ln_LASTLANG
End Enum
Public ResFileName(ln_LASTLANG - ln_FIRSTLANG - 1) As ResourceFiles
```

The enum defines the languages I consider possible in my program. For production purposes I would include all the ISO languages. Note that I have added a sentinel to the end of the enum. Keep it there. If you want to add languages then add them before the ln_LASTLANG sentinel The ResFileName array is sized to fit the number of languages and will hold variables of the new type you just made.

The InitResArray() function in this module fills the ResFileName array with all the necessary information to use any of these languages. See Listing 3-12.

Listing 3-12. Loading a new language

```
Public Sub FreeResources()

    If STRING_RESOURCE Then FreeLibrary (STRING_RESOURCE)

End Sub

Public Function LoadAltLanguage() As Boolean

    Call FreeResources

    STRING_RESOURCE = LoadLibrary(LangDLL)

    If STRING_RESOURCE Then
        LoadAltLanguage = True
    Else
        LoadAltLanguage = False
    End If

End Function
```

In Listing 3-12 I have added the FreeResources routine in the hope that it will actually unload the DLL when I'm finished with it. The LoadAltLanguage() routine now has no error message if it cannot load a resource DLL. This was taken out because no errors should be thrown unless all avenues of resource searching are completed. This means that an error is raised only if after searching for the proper resource the program does not find it in the embedded resource file.

NOTE   *There is no such thing as UseEnglish anymore and there is no UseEnglish() routine either. You should not count on English as being in the embedded resource file. You are, after all, global. If you want English as a language you need to supply it as a satellite resource like all the rest.*

I have made some changes in the GUI portion of this project as well. The screen now looks like Figure 3-3.

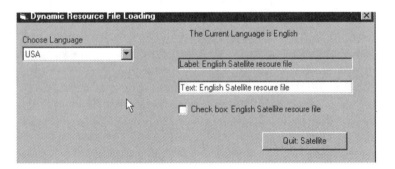

Figure 3-3. New resource GUI screen

I have added a combo box and taken away the Spanish and English buttons. Listing 3-13 is the code for the new screen.

Listing 3-13. New GUI code to change languages

```
Option Explicit

Private Sub cmbLanguage_Click()
    Dim k As Integer

    For k = LBound(ResFileName) To UBound(ResFileName)
```

```
            If ResFileName(k).lang = cmbLanguage.ItemData(cmbLanguage.ListIndex) Then
                LangDLL = App.Path & "\" & ResFileName(k).fname & _
                          "\" & ResFileName(k).fname & ".dll"
            End If
        Next

        Call LoadAltLanguage
        Call LoadStrings

End Sub

Private Sub cmbLanguage_GotFocus()

    Call FindLanguages

End Sub

Private Sub cmdQuit_Click()

    Unload Me

End Sub

Private Sub Form_Load()

    Call InitResArray
    Call LoadStrings
    Call FindLanguages

End Sub

Private Sub Form_Unload(Cancel As Integer)

    Call FreeResources

End Sub

Private Sub LoadStrings()
    Caption = LoadStringRes(STR_DYNAMICRESOURCE)
    lblHeader.Caption = LoadStringRes(STR_LANGUAGE)
    lblLabel.Caption = LoadStringRes(STR_BORDERLABEL)
    cmdQuit.Caption = LoadStringRes(STR_QUIT)
```

```
        txtText.Text = LoadStringRes(STR_NORMALTEXTBOX)
        chkCheck.Caption = LoadStringRes(STR_CHECKBOX)
End Sub

Private Sub FindLanguages()
    Dim LangFile    As String
    Dim k           As Integer

    cmbLanguage.Clear
    For k = LBound(ResFileName) To UBound(ResFileName)
        'form subdirectories with the array names
        LangFile = App.Path & "\" & ResFileName(k).fname & _
                    "\" & ResFileName(k).fname & ".dll"

        If Dir(LangFile) <> "" Then
            cmbLanguage.AddItem LoadStringRes(ResFileName(k).lang)
            cmbLanguage.ItemData(cmbLanguage.NewIndex) = ResFileName(k).lang
        End If
    Next

    If cmbLanguage.ListCount Then cmbLanguage.ListIndex = 0

End Sub
```

When the program starts I call a function called FindLanguages(). As can be seen in Listing 3-13, this function searches a particular path for any resource file that matches the list I created in the ResFileName array. This path corresponds with the search path, directory name, and filename conventions in .NET. As you can see, you are getting closer to what .NET does for you without all this hassle. Figure 3-4 shows the directory structure necessary for this to work. The GUI directory is the executable directory.

Figure 3-4. Directory tree showing language subdirectories

Notice that all my subdirectories are named according to the ISO culture specification.

Here is how I set up the program.

```
Private Sub Form_Load()

    Call InitResArray
    Call LoadStrings
    Call FindLanguages

End Sub
```

The form_load needs to first set up the resource array, and then load whatever strings are in the embedded resource file, and find all the available languages. The program is now running.

Start the Program

Choose a language from the combo box, and the strings will change in the controls. This is done with the code in Listing 3-14.

Listing 3-14. Choosing a new language

```
Private Sub cmbLanguage_Click()
    Dim k As Integer

    For k = LBound(ResFileName) To UBound(ResFileName)

        If ResFileName(k).lang = cmbLanguage.ItemData(cmbLanguage.ListIndex) Then
            LangDLL = App.Path & "\" & ResFileName(k).fname & _
                    "\" & ResFileName(k).fname & ".dll"
```

```
        End If
    Next

    Call LoadAltLanguage
    Call LoadStrings

End Sub
```

I have previously assigned the language to each item in the combo box. In this routine I search through the resource-file-name-array to get the file name that is associated with that language. I then load the LangDLL variable with the path and filename of the resource DLL. Finally I load the DLL and then load the strings.

Detecting a New Language

The following code snippet shows how to detect a new language. All I need to do is capture the got-focus event of the language combo box.

```
Private Sub cmbLanguage_GotFocus()

    Call FindLanguages

End Sub
```

One line in the GotFocus event for the combo box is all that is necessary. I call the FindLanguage routine, which goes out and fills the combo box with any new languages.

Before compiling and running this program you need to change all the resource files. See Listings 3-15 through 3-18. They are the resource files for all the languages we are using in this example.

Listing 3-15. New resource file Strings.rc

```
#define STR_LANGUAGE              1000
#define STR_ENGLISH               1001
#define STR_SPANISH               1002
#define STR_BORDERLABEL           1003
#define STR_NORMALTEXTBOX         1004
#define STR_CHECKBOX              1005
#define STR_QUIT                  1006
#define STR_DYNAMICRESOURCE       1007
```

```
STRINGTABLE
BEGIN
    501                         "Australian"
    502                         "New Zealand"
    503                         "England"
    504                         "USA"
    505                         "Spain"
    506                         "Mexico"
    507                         "French Canadian"
    508                         "French"
END


STRINGTABLE
BEGIN
    STR_LANGUAGE                "The Current Language is English"
    STR_ENGLISH                 "English"
    STR_SPANISH                 "Spanish"
    STR_BORDERLABEL             "Label: embedded resource file"
    STR_NORMALTEXTBOX           "Text: embedded resource file"
    STR_CHECKBOX                "Check box: embedded resource file"
    STR_QUIT                    "Quit: embedded"
    STR_DYNAMICRESOURCE         "Dynamic Resource File Loading"
END
```

Listing 3-16. Spanish resource file es-ES.rc

```
#define STR_LANGUAGE            1000
#define STR_ENGLISH             1001
#define STR_SPANISH             1002
#define STR_BORDERLABEL         1003
#define STR_NORMALTEXTBOX       1004
#define STR_CHECKBOX            1005
#define STR_QUIT                1006
#define STR_DYNAMICRESOURCE     1007


STRINGTABLE
BEGIN
    STR_LANGUAGE                "The Current Language is Spanish"
    STR_ENGLISH                 "English"
    STR_SPANISH                 "Spanish"
    STR_BORDERLABEL             "Label: Spanish Satellite resource file"
    STR_NORMALTEXTBOX           "Text: Spanish Satellite resource file"
    STR_CHECKBOX                "Check box: Spanish Satellite resource file"
```

```
        STR_QUIT                        "Quit: Satellite"
        STR_DYNAMICRESOURCE             "Dynamic Resource File Loading"
END
```

Listing 3-17. USA resource file en-US.rc

```
#define STR_LANGUAGE              1000
#define STR_ENGLISH               1001
#define STR_SPANISH               1002
#define STR_BORDERLABEL           1003
#define STR_NORMALTEXTBOX         1004
#define STR_CHECKBOX              1005
#define STR_QUIT                  1006
#define STR_DYNAMICRESOURCE       1007
STRINGTABLE
BEGIN
        STR_LANGUAGE              "The Current Language is English"
        STR_ENGLISH              "English"
        STR_SPANISH              "Spanish"
        STR_BORDERLABEL          "Label: English Satellite resource file"
        STR_NORMALTEXTBOX        "Text: English Satellite resource file"
        STR_CHECKBOX             "Check box: English Satellite resource file"
        STR_QUIT                 "Quit: Satellite"
        STR_DYNAMICRESOURCE      "Dynamic Resource File Loading"
END
```

Listing 3-18. French resource file fr-FR.rc

```
#define STR_LANGUAGE              1000
#define STR_ENGLISH               1001
#define STR_SPANISH               1002
#define STR_BORDERLABEL           1003
#define STR_NORMALTEXTBOX         1004
#define STR_CHECKBOX              1005
#define STR_QUIT                  1006
#define STR_DYNAMICRESOURCE       1007
STRINGTABLE
BEGIN
        STR_LANGUAGE              "The Current Language is French"
        STR_ENGLISH              "English"
        STR_SPANISH              "French"
        STR_BORDERLABEL          "Label: FrenchSatellite resource file"
        STR_NORMALTEXTBOX        "Text: FrenchSatellite resource file"
```

```
STR_CHECKBOX              "Check box: FrenchSatellite resource file"
STR_QUIT                  "Quit: Satellite"
STR_DYNAMICRESOURCE       "Dynamic Resource File Loading"
END
```

Compile all these resource files in their proper directories and make them into DLLs. Once you do this, you can see if you can make this program work. Try these steps.

1. Make the directory structure as I have done with English, Spanish, and French resource subdirectories under the executable directory.

2. Make each of the resource file DLLs properly in each of these directories. Use the correct naming convention and so on.

3. Rename the French DLL to something else.

4. Run the program. You should see only USA and Spain in the combo box, and you should be able to see the new strings as you switch between them.

5. While the program is running, rename the French DLL to its proper name.

6. Click on the combo box again and, voila, you will see French as a choice. Choose French and you will see the strings from the French resource file appear.

You have managed to add the French language at runtime.

In case you did not catch it you should notice that I have more strings in the embedded strings.rc resource file than in the others. In the FindLanguage() routine I have this piece of code.

```
If Dir(LangFile) <> "" Then
    cmbLanguage.AddItem LoadStringRes(ResFileName(k).lang)
    cmbLanguage.ItemData(cmbLanguage.NewIndex) = ResFileName(k).lang
```

Note that I am getting the names of the languages from a resource file and filling the combo box with them. I am forcing a fallback to the embedded resource file to get these strings. At start-up the embedded resource file is all there is, so this is the logical place for them. Once I have loaded an external string resource DLL this line of code tries to get the string from that other resource file. It will fail and fallback to the embedded resource file.

The fallback mechanism works!

NOTE *You may get an error making a DLL after you have run the main program. The error will say, "Permission denied." If this happens you find that you need to exit VB completely between editing and running the main program and compiling any of the DLLs. The reason for this is that once you run the main program and load a DLL VB keeps hold of it. If you then swap projects in VB without exiting and reentering VB you get an error when you try to compile the DLL. The program does use the FreeLibrary() API but sometimes this does not work.*

Summary

What I have shown you with this example is a way to make VB use external resource files with a fallback mechanism. Let's review the steps in doing this.

1. Make a generic bas module that contains the code necessary to pull in resource files from external resource DLLs. This code also has a fallback mechanism to load a string from the embedded resource file if it is not found in the external one.

2. Generate a resource file to include in the project. This resource file will be embedded in the executable during linking. This resource file should be the native language.

3. Generate external resource files for as many languages as needed. Name these resource files according to the ISO specification.

4. Compile the external resource files and make them into DLLs. Put the resource DLLs into a searchable directory.

5. Make a program that uses the methods in the bas module to retrieve string.

You now have a resource file mechanism similar to that in .NET. A lot of work isn't it? Well your program is now very flexible. It also allows you to add or delete a language at runtime. As you move on you will see that all that I have done here is internal to .NET.

The next chapter gets into the heart of the .NET localization capability. I discuss the System.Globalization namespace. You also see many examples in both VB .NET and C#

CHAPTER 4

The Globalization Namespace

THIS CHAPTER INTRODUCES you to the .NET way of doing things and explains all the classes, interfaces, and important methods involved in localizing a .NET application using the System.Globalization namespace. There is quite a lot to learn in this chapter. The globalization features of .NET are very comprehensive indeed.

.NET is fully object-oriented and as such takes advantage of polymorphism whenever possible. The globalization features are no different. Before you delve too deeply into this and the next two chapters, let's do a little review on interfaces and classes.

Interfaces and Classes

An interface can be described as a class with no implementation details. Like classes, interfaces define a set of methods, properties, and events. Interfaces do not define any data. In some ways, an interface can be thought of as a class with pure virtual functions.

Other classes can inherit from a base class with pure virtual functions. One of the differences between a virtual base class and an interface is that when you inherit from an interface you are required to implement all the interface's functionality. A derived class is not required to override a base class' methods. (You can force this, but it is an option and not inherent in the definition of a class.)

Class inheritance is often used in place of interface inheritance. It is, however, often used incorrectly. A class should inherit from another class only if it needs to extend the functionality of that class. A class should inherit an interface if that class has only a loose relationship with that interface. Let's take a small example—a dog.

You could have a base class called Dog that has methods that are common to all dogs. You could have an interface called *mouth* that has methods and properties that are common to all mouths. You now want to create a beagle. Your beagle would inherit from the base class of Dog because it is a dog. You want all the functionality of a dog except that you want to extend this functionality with something particular to a beagle such as baying all night and keeping the neighbors awake. Your beagle also needs a mouth. You would implement the mouth interface. Your beagle *is a* dog, but it is not a mouth. It *has a* mouth. See the difference? Your little sister would not inherit from a dog (hopefully), but she would implement the mouth interface.

Don't you hate it when books talk about polymorphism in terms of animals? How are you supposed to transfer that to a program?

Well, here's a more practical example of a class vs. an interface. Your company makes printers. Your job is to write printer drivers. You make a base class called Printer, which includes software that takes care of functions that are common to all printers whether they are LaserJet printers or inkjet printers. Such functions include communications methods, paper-sensing, power-on sequence, and so forth. Now you derive classes from this base class that extends the functionality to be specific to LaserJet printers and specific to inkjet printers. An inkjet printer *is a* printer. A LaserJet printer *is a* printer. You would add a function to the LaserJet printer such as LowTonerDetect(). You would add a function to the inkjet printer such as CarriagePosition(). You have extended the base class.

Some of your high-end printers have an envelope feature. What you do is make an interface called HandleEnvelope. Here you would have methods called DetectEnvelope(), TurnOffPaperBin(), WriteSideways(), and so on. All these methods are necessary for any printer you make that handles envelopes. It is just that each printer needs a slightly different implementation. In one of your derived LaserJet printer classes you inherit this interface. A LaserJet printer is a printer, but it has a feature to handle envelopes.

You could have made the envelope features virtual functions in the base class and override them when necessary, but you would not be forced to do so. An interface forces you to implement all its functionality. You would also start to drift from the true meaning of class vs. interface.

.NET has several classes and interfaces that have to do with globalization. Keep this very brief review of the differences between classes and interfaces in mind when I go over the globalization classes and interfaces. It will make it easier to understand why they exist and when to use one or the other.

All the examples in this chapter are provided in both VB .NET and in C#. While they are much the same, there are some differences. Since there is an opportunity in .NET to make a program that has a mix of programming languages, it only seems right.

System.Globalization Namespace

System.Globalization namespace is the mother of all namespaces that has to do with globalization in .NET; hence the name. This namespace includes all the classes necessary to distinguish one culture from another and to describe each culture in detail. It also has classes that let you make a new culture from scratch.

As a namespace, it does not do anything. It just allows you to refer to any of the classes within it by direct name instead of by the fully qualified name. The classes and enumerations this namespace contains are what do the real work.

Calendar Class

Calendar class has implementations for several of the most popular calendars in use today. Table 4-1 lists these calendar implementations.

Table 4-1. Calendar Implementations

CALENDAR	USE
Gregorian	World standard since 1500s.
Julian	Rarely used. Was replaced by Gregorian. Still used by some monks.
Hebrew	Official calendar of Israel. Used for religious purposes.
Japanese	Lunar calendar still used to plan some events.
Hijri	Official calendar of some Islamic countries. Used for religious purposes.
Korean	Lunar calendar still used for festivities.
Taiwan	Same as Gregorian except year and era are different.
ThaiBuddhist	Same as Gregorian except year and era are different.

To use these calendars properly you need to be able to manipulate time within them. There is a rich set of functions to do just this. For instance, it is possible to add any time frame to a particular date from milliseconds to years. Let's look at a small console project that defines a calendar and manipulates dates (see Listing 4-1).

Listing 4-1. Calendar output

VB .NET

```
Imports System
Imports System.Globalization

Module Module1
```

```vbnet
Sub Main()
    Dim MyCalendar As Calendar = New GregorianCalendar()
    Dim MyDate As New DateTime(2001, 8, 22, 15, 30, 0, 0)
    'Dim MyCalendar As Calendar = New HebrewCalendar()
    Dim MyCulture As CultureInfo = New CultureInfo("es-ES")

    'ToDateTime is not culture aware
    Console.WriteLine(MyCalendar.ToDateTime(MyDate.Year, _
                MyDate.Month, MyDate.Day, MyDate.Hour, _
                MyDate.Minute, 0, 0))

    'Remeber these are objects so use the ToString() method
    'to make it culture aware
    Console.WriteLine(MyCalendar.AddMinutes(MyDate, _
                        15).ToString("G", MyCulture))

    'See what the last 2 digit year is you can use to represent
    'this century
    Console.WriteLine(MyCalendar.TwoDigitYearMax)
    'This should be 1932 in Gregorian
    Console.WriteLine(MyCalendar.ToFourDigitYear(32))
    'This should be 2028 in Gregorian
    Console.WriteLine(MyCalendar.ToFourDigitYear(28))

    Console.ReadLine()
End Sub

End Module
```

C# .NET

```csharp
using System;
using System.Globalization;

namespace Calendar_Console_in_C_Sharp
{
    /// <summary>
    /// Summary description for Class1.
    /// </summary>
    class Class1
    {
        static void Main(string[] args)
        {
```

```
Calendar MyCalendar = new  GregorianCalendar();
CultureInfo MyCulture = new CultureInfo("es-ES");
DateTime MyDate = new DateTime(2001,8,22,15,30,0,0);

//ToDateTime is not culture aware
Console.WriteLine(MyCalendar.ToDateTime(MyDate.Year,
                        MyDate.Month,
                        MyDate.Day,
                        MyDate.Hour,
                        MyDate.Minute,
0, 0));

//Remember these are objects, so use the ToString()
//method to make it culture aware
Console.WriteLine(MyCalendar.AddMinutes(MyDate, 15).
                        ToString("G",
                        MyCulture));

//See what the last 2 digit year is you can use to
//represent this century
Console.WriteLine(MyCalendar.TwoDigitYearMax);
//This should be 1932 in Gregorian
Console.WriteLine(MyCalendar.ToFourDigitYear(32));
//'This should be 2028 in Gregorian
Console.WriteLine(MyCalendar.ToFourDigitYear(28));

Console.ReadLine();
    }
  }
}
```

The output of this code is:

```
8/22/2001 15:30:00
22/08/2001 15:45:00
2029
1932
2028
```

NOTE *My development machine is set for military time. If your machine is set to display time in a 12 hr clock you would get 3:30:00 PM instead of 15:30:00.*

NOTE *I have been using a program from a company in Germany that is only half localized. There are strings in English and in German. There are date fields that only show dates in 24 hr format. My machine was set up to display dates in AM/PM format. The program blows up if I do not have the machine date settings set for 24 hr time. This is a perfect example of how NOT to localize your software.*

First I define a new calendar as a Gregorian calendar. I then define a new culture as Spanish. The first line of console output comes from stringing together all the integers that make up a date. The second line of console output takes advantage of the new Spanish culture I defined and formats the output correctly using this culture. For any kind of conversion output the ToString() member of any object is a powerful tool. Notice that I am also adding 15 minutes to the current time using the overridden AddMinutes() member of this derived calendar class.

The third line is where you can see what happens with the Y2K bug if it is still around. All the derived calendars have defined a 2-digit year that represents the last 2-digit year you can use in the current century. For the Gregorian calendar it is 29. You can see that when I subtract 4 years from the 2-digit year I advance 96 years in the future. The TwoDigitYearMax() member can be very handy when you are getting prepared to read in dates from a file. If you happen to have a file that contains birth dates in mm/dd/yy format then anyone born in 1927 have a birth date in 2027. The TwoDigitYearMax() number is different for different calendars, as it should be.

Change the program a little, and instead of defining a Gregorian calendar define a Hebrew calendar. This causes an unhandled exception error when you run it. This is okay, as you will see.

Change this:

```
Dim MyCalendar As Calendar = New GregorianCalendar()
```

to this:

```
Dim MyCalendar As Calendar = New HebrewCalendar()
```

Now run the program again. You get an error on the first console.writeline() function. This is because the Hebrew calendar in .NET only recognizes dates between 5343 and 6000.

Comment this line out and you get the following output.

```
22/08/2001 15:45:00
5790
5732
5728
```

Notice the TwoYearMax() is now 90 and the last two lines show what the casual observer would expect.

CultureInfo Class

CultureInfo class is the class that makes the necessary adjustments as you go from one culture to another. It includes information about any culture such as language, number format, and date format, how to sort strings, what calendar is used, and so forth. This is a very important class and is probably the most used class in this namespace. It is crucial that you understand this class and how to use it.

Before you get deep into this class you need to go behind the scenes a bit and look at the basis for the culture identification convention. There are two ways that .NET identifies a culture.

This first is called the LCID. This value corresponds to the National Language Support (NLS) locale identifier. The LCID is composed of three parts: a primary language identifier, a sublanguage identifier, and a sort ID.

The second and more descriptive way to identify a culture is via a string. The string used is made up of two parts. The first part is the two-letter language code derived from the ISO 639-1 standard. The second part is a two-letter country/region code derived from the ISO 3166 standard. The string looks like "es-ES" or "en-US," and so on.

The <language> - <country/region> string method is the method used by Microsoft to determine the directory search path for resource files. I showed you this method in the VB 6 sample, and it will pop up again when you do resource files under .NET. Table 4-2 lists the LCIDs and string representations of all the cultures that Windows knows about.

Table 4-2. Culture Identifiers

LOCALE	ISO COUNTRY – REGION STRING VALUE	LCID HEX VALUE	LCID DECIMAL VALUE
Afrikaans	af	0x0436	1078
Albanian	sq	0x041C	1052
Arabic - U.A.E.	ar-ae	0x3801	14337
Arabic - Bahrain	ar-bh	0x3C01	15361
Arabic - Algeria	ar-dz	0x1401	5121
Arabic - Egypt	ar-eg	0x0C01	3073
Arabic - Iraq	ar-iq	0x0801	2049
Arabic - Jordan	ar-jo	0x2C01	11265
Arabic - Kuwait	ar-kw	0x3401	13313
Arabic - Lebanon	ar-lb	0x3001	12289
Arabic - Libya	ar-ly	0x1001	4097
Arabic - Morocco	ar-ma	0x1801	6145
Arabic - Oman	ar-om	0x2001	8193
Arabic - Qatar	ar-qa	0x4001	16385
Arabic - Saudi Arabia	ar-sa	0x0401	1025
Arabic - Syria	ar-sy	0x2801	10241
Arabic - Tunisia	ar-tn	0x1C01	7169
Arabic - Yemen	ar-ye	0x2401	9217
Basque	eu	0x042D	1069
Belarusian	be	0x0423	1059
Bulgarian	bg	0x0402	1026
Catalan	ca	0x0403	1027
Chinese - PRC	zh-cn	0x0804	2052
Chinese - Hong Kong S.A.R.	zh-hk	0x0C04	3076
Chinese - Singapore	zh-sg	0x1004	4100
Chinese - Taiwan	zh-tw	0x0404	1028
Croatian	hr	0x041A	1050
Czech	cs	0x0405	1029
Danish	da	0x0406	1030
Dutch	nl	0x0413	1043
Dutch - Belgium	nl-be	0x0813	2067
English - Australia	en-au	0x0C09	3081

Table 4-2. Culture Identifiers (continued)

LOCALE	ISO COUNTRY - REGION STRING VALUE	LCID HEX VALUE	LCID DECIMAL VALUE
English - Belize	en-bz	0x2809	10249
English - Canada	en-ca	0x1009	4105
English - Ireland	en-ie	0x1809	6153
English - Jamaica	en-jm	0x2009	8201
English - New Zealand	en-nz	0x1409	5129
English - South Africa	en-za	0x1C09	7177
English - Trinidad	en-tt	0x2C09	11273
English - United Kingdom	en-gb	0x0809	2057
English - United States	en-us	0x0409	1033
Estonian	et	0x0425	1061
Farsi	fa	0x0429	1065
Finnish	fi	0x040B	1035
Faeroese	fo	0x0438	1080
French - Standard	fr	0x040C	1036
French - Belgium	fr-be	0x080C	2060
French - Canada	fr-ca	0x0C0C	3084
French - Luxembourg	fr-lu	0x140C	5132
French - Switzerland	fr-ch	0x100C	4108
Gaelic - Scotland	gd	0x043C	1084
German - Standard	de	0x0407	1031
German - Austrian	de-at	0x0C07	3079
German - Lichtenstein	de-li	0x1407	5127
German - Luxembourg	de-lu	0x1007	4103
German - Switzerland	de-ch	0x0807	2055
Greek	el	0x0408	1032
Hebrew	he	0x040D	1037
Hindi	hi	0x0439	1081
Hungarian	hu	0x040E	1038
Icelandic	is	0x040F	1039
Indonesian	in	0x0421	1057
Italian - Standard	it	0x0410	1040
Italian - Switzerland	it-ch	0x0810	2064

Table 4-2. Culture Identifiers (continued)

LOCALE	ISO COUNTRY – REGION STRING VALUE	LCID HEX VALUE	LCID DECIMAL VALUE
Japanese	ja	0x0411	1041
Korean	ko	0x0412	1042
Latvian	lv	0x0426	1062
Lithuanian	lt	0x0427	1063
Macedonian	mk	0x042F	1071
Malay - Malaysia	ms	0x043E	1086
Maltese	mt	0x043A	1082
Norwegian - Bokmål	no	0x0414	1044
Polish	pl	0x0415	1045
Portuguese - Standard	pt	0x0816	2070
Portuguese - Brazil	pt-br	0x0416	1046
Raeto-Romance	rm	0x0417	1047
Romanian	ro	0x0418	1048
Romanian - Moldova	ro-mo	0x0818	2072
Russian	ru	0x0419	1049
Russian - Moldova	ru-mo	0x0819	2073
Serbian - Cyrillic	sr	0x0C1A	3098
Setsuana	tn	0x0432	1074
Slovenian	sl	0x0424	1060
Slovak	sk	0x041B	1051
Serbian	sb	0x042E	1070
Spanish - Standard	es	0x040A	1034
Spanish - Argentina	es-ar	0x2C0A	11274
Spanish - Bolivia	es-bo	0x400A	16394
Spanish - Chile	es-cl	0x340A	13322
Spanish - Colombia	es-co	0x240A	9226
Spanish - Costa Rica	es-cr	0x140A	5130
Spanish - Dominican Republic	es-do	0x1C0A	7178
Spanish - Ecuador	es-ec	0x300A	12298
Spanish - El Salvador	es-sv	0x440A	17418
Spanish - Guatemala	es-gt	0x100A	4106

Table 4-2. Culture Identifiers (continued)

LOCALE	ISO COUNTRY – REGION STRING VALUE	LCID HEX VALUE	LCID DECIMAL VALUE
Spanish - Honduras	es-hn	0x480A	18442
Spanish - Mexico	es-mx	0x080A	2058
Spanish - Nicaragua	es-ni	0x4C0A	19466
Spanish - Panama	es-pa	0x180A	6154
Spanish - Paraguay	es-py	0x3C0A	15370
Spanish - Peru	es-pe	0x280A	10250
Spanish - Puerto Rico	es-pr	0x500A	20490
Spanish - Uruguay	es-uy	0x380A	14346
Spanish - Venezuela	es-ve	0x200A	8202
Sutu	sx	0x0430	1072
Swedish	sv	0x041D	1053
Swedish - Finland	sv-fi	0x081D	2077
Thai	th	0x041E	1054
Turkish	tr	0x041F	1055
Tsonga	ts	0x0431	1073
Ukranian	uk	0x0422	1058
Urdu - Pakistan	ur	0x0420	1056
Vietnamese	vi	0x042A	1066
Xhosa	xh	0x0434	1076
Yiddish	ji	0x043D	1085
Zulu	zu	0x0435	1077

CultureInfo Class Members

The CultureInfo class is at the crux of any localization effort in .NET. This class has members that allow you to manipulate the culture you are using and any aspect of that culture. Such aspects would be how the date and time are displayed, and how numbers and currency are displayed. You can also get and control aspects of the region that are associated with the culture. The following members serve important functions in this class.

CurrentCulture, CurrentUICulture, InstalledUICulture, InvariantCulture

What are all these? Why so many of them? They are basically a way of getting information from the culture you have created. All of them give you the same type of information but from a slightly different source. Suppose you create an object of a culture that defines Spain.

In VB you would define it as such:

```
Dim MyCulture as new CultureInfo("es-ES")
```

In C# it would be:

```
CultureInfo MyCulture = new CultureInfo("es-ES")
```

If this is the culture you work with throughout your program you may want to find information as to how the resource manager will look up strings. Perhaps you want to find out what operating system language was installed on the current machine? You could also find out what language is supposed to be used by your program at startup.

CultureInfo.CurrentCulture

CurrentCulture refers to the culture being used by the current thread. In essence this is the culture that your program thinks it is running. To see what this culture is you could use the following line of code:

VB

```
MyCulture.CurrentCulture.EnglishName
```

C#

```
(What VB said but with a semicolon at the end.)
```

This code would display the English name of the current threads culture. The CurrentCulture instance is rather redundant. If you want to know the CurrentCulture of the current thread, just ask it. These two lines of code give you the same result.

VB

```
MyCulture.CurrentCulture.EnglishName
Thread.CurrentThread.CurrentCulture.EnglishName
```

C#

```
Ditto with an ending semi.
```

Of course, in order to get at the thread class you need to import the System.Threading namespace. More on that later.

CultureInfo.CurrentUICulture

CurrentUICulture refers to the culture that the resource manager uses to get resources from a resource file. This one is very important.

If your resource has not been localized to a specific culture then the resource returned is the best match. The resource manager accomplishes this by looking at this class.

The resource manager has quite a few methods to retrieve resources. Consider the GetString() method of the resource manager. If the CurrentUICulture.Name was "es-mx" the resource manager would look in the es-mx directory for an es-mx.dll resource file from which to get its resources. This is where it looks first by default.

The GetString() method also has an overloaded version that allows you to force it to get strings from the culture of your choice. You can tell it which culture to use when looking for resources. More on that later as well.

CultureInfo.InstalledUICulture

InstalledUICulture is the culture that your whole computer is operating under. If you installed Windows 2000 for German on your machine, this is your installed UI culture. So what? What can you use it for? Well this culture is what the resource manager looks to as a final default when it tries to get resources. Consider this scenario:

- Your machine is Ukrainian.

- Your Current Thread is in German.

- You have the subdirectories "de-DE" and "uk".

- You put a string in the "uk" directory resource file that is not in the "de-DE" directory resource file.

If you use the GetString() method to get this string, the resource manager searches the culture defined by CurrentUICulture. It looks in the "de-DE" resource file first. Not being able to find it the resource manager then searches the culture defined by InstalledUICulture. In this case it looks in the "uk" resource file. The InstalledUICulture is used by the resource manager in its fallback scheme. It must be noted that this is only true if you did not specify a culture when looking for the resource.

CultureInfo.InvariantCulture

The InvariantCulture is used by the resource manager to determine the fallback scheme for obtaining resources. It represents the neutral culture. For instance you could have a culture called "de-DE" to represent Germany. The parent of this culture is "de" which is language-specific but not culture-specific. The parent culture of "de" is the InvariantCulture, which in my case is "en-US." The resources for the invariant culture are usually bound in the assembly as the last fallback culture.

The InvariantCulture is also the culture you use when you want to perform a function that is culture-independent. There are some methods in the System namespace that require a culture. If you want to invoke one of these methods but did not want a localized result you would pass this culture to it.

Can't think of a method you would use this for? How about using event logging? Suppose you have a very flexible internationalized program where you allowed the culture to be changed at will. As a flexible programmer, you also have some code in several places to log various error events. All the entries in the error log should look the same to the person who reads it. It would not do to have entries in your log that are formatted according to the language the user was using at the time. You would end up with a confusing muddle of entries. To write all the events in a consistent manner, use something like this:

```
. . .
Mylog.WriteEntry(MyDate.ToString("d", MyCulture.InvariantCulture))
. . .
```

This way no matter what language or culture your program was in at the time, you would write the date in the same format.

The DateTimeFormatInfo class and the NumberFormatInfo class when constructed are culture-independent. You get into these classes next.

CultureInfo.DateTimeFormat

The CultureInfo.DateTimeFormat read/write property is used to determine how dates and times are output. It actually gets or sets a class of DateTimeFormatInfo. It is possible using this property to not only see how dates and times are formatted in your culture, but you can also use this property to change the format of the dates and times of another culture. The data type that is affected by this is the DateTime type.

If you have a DateTime variable, you can display the value in several ways. Each of the following methods gets the formatting information from the DateTimeFormatInfo class returned by the DateTimeFormat member in the CultureInfo class:

DateTime.ToLongDateString(). Uses the "D" specifier

DateTime.ToLongTimeString(). Uses the "T" specifier

DateTime.ToShortDateString(). Uses the "d" specifier

DateTime.ToShortTimeString(). Uses the "t" specifier

It is the specifiers that are changed by the DateTimeFormatInfo class. Normally you leave this class alone unless you want to actually change the format of a particular culture. By the way, it is entirely possible to make your own culture at which point you would want to change the DateTimeFormat specifiers to whatever is appropriate.

As with most things, there are other ways to get the same formatted answer in .NET to a formatted DateTime variable. The following two lines of code are identical.

```
Console.WriteLine(DateTime.LongDateString())
Console.WriteLine(DateTime.ToString("D")
```

Which one is easier to read? I used to pride myself on my knowledge of all the arcane printf() specifiers in the languageC ; however, for readability, the first one is more intuitive. Table 4-3 shows the date and time format specifiers.

Table 4-3. The Date and Time Format Specifiers

CHARACTER	FORMAT PATTERN	ASSOCIATED PROPERTY/DESCRIPTION
d	MM/dd/yyyy	ShortDate Pattern
D	dddd, dd MMMM yyyy	LongDatePattern
f	dddd, dd MMMM yyyy HH:mm	Full date and time (long date and short time)
F	dddd, dd MMMM yyyy HH:mm:ss	FullDateTimePattern(long date and long time)
g	MM/dd/yyyy HH:mm	General (short date and short time)
G	MM/dd/yyyy HH:mm:ss	General (short date and long time)
m, M	MMMM dd	MonthDayPattern
r, R	ddd, dd MMM yyyy HH':'mm':'ss 'GMT'	RFP1123Pattern
s	yyyy'-'MM'-'dd'T'HH':'mm':'ss	SortableDateTimePattern (based on ISO 8601) using local time
t	HH:mm	ShortTimePattern
T	HH:mm:ss	LongTimePattern
u	yyyy'-'MM'-'dd HH':'mm':'ss'Z'	UniversalSortableDateTimePattern (based on ISO 8601) using universal time
U	dddd, dd MMMM yyyy HH:mm:ss	Sortable date and time (long date and long time) using universal time
y, Y	yyyy MMMM	YearMonthPattern

I go over the DateTimeFormatInfo class later in this chapter.

Listing 4-2. Code showing ToLongDate functions

VB

```
Imports System
Imports System.Globalization
Imports System.Threading
Module Module1

    Sub Main()

        Dim MyCulture As CultureInfo = New CultureInfo("fr-FR")
        Dim MyDate As DateTime = Now()
        Dim dtf As DateTimeFormatInfo

        Thread.CurrentThread.CurrentCulture = MyCulture
```

```
        Console.WriteLine(MyDate.ToLongDateString())
        Console.WriteLine(MyDate.ToLongTimeString())
        Console.WriteLine(MyDate.ToShortDateString())
        Console.WriteLine(MyDate.ToShortTimeString())

        dtf = MyCulture.DateTimeFormat
        'Change date and time separator
        dtf.DateSeparator = "\"
        dtf.TimeSeparator = "&"

        Console.WriteLine()
        Console.WriteLine(MyDate.ToLongDateString())
        Console.WriteLine(MyDate.ToLongTimeString())
        Console.WriteLine(MyDate.ToShortDateString())
        Console.WriteLine(MyDate.ToShortTimeString())

        Console.ReadLine()
    End Sub

End Module
```

C#

```csharp
using System;
using System.Globalization;
using System.Threading;
namespace CH7DateTimeFormatFrench_C
{
    /// <summary>
    /// Summary description for Class1.
    /// </summary>
    class Class1
    {
        static void Main(string[] args)
        {
CultureInfo MyCulture = new CultureInfo("fr-FR");
        DateTime MyDate = System.DateTime.Now;
        DateTimeFormatInfo dtf;

        Thread.CurrentThread.CurrentCulture = MyCulture;

        Console.WriteLine(MyDate.ToLongDateString());
        Console.WriteLine(MyDate.ToLongTimeString());
```

```
            Console.WriteLine(MyDate.ToShortDateString());
            Console.WriteLine(MyDate.ToShortTimeString());

            dtf = MyCulture.DateTimeFormat;
            //Change date and time separator
            dtf.DateSeparator = "\\";
            dtf.TimeSeparator = "&";

            Console.WriteLine();
            Console.WriteLine(MyDate.ToLongDateString());
            Console.WriteLine(MyDate.ToLongTimeString());
            Console.WriteLine(MyDate.ToShortDateString());
            Console.WriteLine(MyDate.ToShortTimeString());

            Console.ReadLine();


        }
    }
}
```

The output of this program is:

```
mercredi 26 septembre 2001
19:33:19
26/09/2001
19:33
mercredi 26 septembre 2001
19&33&19
26\09\2001
19:33
```

As you can see it is an easy task to change some of the date separators to anything that you want.

CultureInfo.NumberFormat

The CultureInfo.NumberFormat read/write property is used to determine how numbers are output. By numbers I mean things such as integers, decimals, currency, and negative numbers. Any time you want to print a number that is culturally-aware this member is involved.

This property actually gets or sets a class of NumberFormatInfo. It is possible using this property to not only see how numbers are formatted in your culture but you can also use this property to change the format of the numbers of another culture. The data type that is affected is any numeric type.

As with the DateTime type you can print out a number using the ToString() member.

```
Console.Writeline(123456.ToString("D"));
```

Does this seem strange to you? It does to me. Numbers derive from objects, and objects have a ToString() method. So, 123456.ToString() is valid within .NET. It takes some getting used to, but you will find that all basic types are much more versatile than they were. The output of the preceding code line would be 123,456.0.

Table 4-4 shows the number format specifiers used in .NET.

Table 4-4. .NET Number Format Specifiers

FORMAT CHARACTER	DESCRIPTION
C, c	Currency
E, e	Scientific
D, d	Decimal
F, f	Fixed point
G, g	General
N, n	Number format
R, r	Round Trip format
X, x	Hex

I go over the NumberFormatInfo class later in this chapter.

CultureInfo.Calendar

The CultureInfo.Calendar read-only property gets the calendar used by the current culture. This property is read-only and as such you cannot change the current culture's calendar. The calendars available for use by a .NET culture were defined earlier in this chapter.

CultureInfo.DisplayName

The CultureInfo.DisplayName read-only property gets the name of the culture in the format <Language> (country). The language used is the language to which the computer was set. If your computer was set to display Spanish and your culture is "en-US" this property returns "Ingles (Estados Unidos)."

CultureInfo.EnglishName

The CultureInfo.EnglishName read-only property is the same as the DisplayName except that the name returned is always displayed in English. The preceding example would return "English (United States)" no matter what the computer was set to.

CultureInfo.LCID

The CultureInfo.LCID property returns the NLS identifier. The NLS identifier is a number that identifies a language/country. What is the point of this? Well there are many overloaded constructors in the System.Globalization namespace that take either a string or the LCID. The following two lines of code are the same:

VB

```
Dim ThisCulture As New CultureInfo(1078)        'LCID
Dim ThisCulture As New CultureInfo("af-ZA")     'Name
```

C#

```
CultureInfo ThisCulture = new CultureInfo(1078);     //LCID
CultureInfo ThisCulture = new CultureInfo("af-ZA");  //Name
```

The EnglishName result of this would be "Afrikaans (South Africa)." To my mind using the LCID is neither here nor there. The only reason I can see for using the LCID instead of the name is that a number takes less memory and is thus quicker to marshal between processes. It is certainly not intuitive as to which country is referenced.

CultureInfo.Name

The CultureInfo.Name property is the same as the LCID in that it returns the culture identifier. However, instead of returning the LCID it returns the string. The name in the preceding example is "af-ZA." This is a better argument for a constructor than the LCID. It makes your code much more readable.

CultureInfo.TextInfo

The CultureInfo.TextInfo property gets or sets the TextInfo object that is associated with the Culture. The TextInfo object contains information about the following items:

- The ANSI Code page used.

- The EBCDIC code page used.

- The MacCodePage used for Apple Macintosh computers.

- The OEM code page used.

- The List separator that is the delimiter used in lists of items. The default is the comma.

This object also has the following text-conversion routines:

- ToUpper.

- ToLower.

- ToString.

- ToTitleCase. In English, title case refers to capitalizing the first letter of each word in a string. This may be different for different cultures.

The text conversion routines are very handy. If you have a string resource that is lowercase Cyrillic, you may want at some time to capitalize it. There are quite a few languages, including English that do not have capital letters that look like their lowercase counterparts. Instead of going out and translating each string or word into its uppercase (capital) and lowercase versions you can just use the ToUpper() method.

TIP   *Do not be tempted to just add or subtract 32 from each character to go between lowercase and uppercase letters. This only works in the basic ASCII table. You could end up with some strange strings if you did this.*

NOTE   *How I long for the good old days of manipulating strings as arrays and depending on the ASCII table format to speed up my code. <Sigh>.*

ThreeLetterISOLanguageName, TwoLetterISOLanguageName, ThreeLetterWindowsLanguageName

What is all this? There are several standards that refer to the language of the culture you are in.

Table 4-5. Language Standards

STANDARD	MEMBER NAME	EXAMPLE
ISO 639-2	ThreeLetterISOLanguageName	English = "eng"
ISO 639-1	TwoLetterISOLanguageName	English = "en"
Windows	ThreeLetterWindowsLanguageName	English = "enu"

CultureInfo.GetFormat, CultureInfo.GetType

The GetFormat method returns an instance of the NumberFormat or DateTimeFormat type. Yes, I know you can get the NumberFormatInfo and DateTimeFormatInfo directly. You must be wondering why you need the GetFormat() method. Well, it is used for reflection. It allows you to use one method to return either a NumberFormatInfo or a DateTimeFormatInfo instance depending on the type argument.

A long explanation of reflection is a little out of the scope of this book but I thought I would let you know why you would want to do this.

Reflection is a way a program finds out everything about itself. It is also used to enable one program to query another .NET program for its metadata. It is a sort of decompiler. Reflection exposes metadata associated with an object. It is possible to walk the list of objects in an assembly and make a tree showing exactly what is going on in a program at any time. The GetFormat method uses reflection to obtain information about the NumberFormatInfo or DateTimeFormatInfo objects in the culture.

To use the GetFormat method you need to know the type of the object. The only types supported by this GetFormat method are the NumberFormat and DateTimeFormat types. If you want to get the type of an object you can use the GetType method. The GetType method is used extensively in reflection.

Consider this code fragment.

VB .NET

```
Dim MyObj As Object
Dim fmt As New NumberFormatInfo()
MyObj = MyCulture.GetFormat(fmt.GetType)
mystring = MyObj.ToString()
```

C#

```
Object MyObj;
CultureInfo MyCulture = new CultureInfo("es-ES");
NumerFormatInfo fmt = new NumberFormatInfo();
MyObj = MyCulture.GetFormat(fmt.GetType());
Console.WriteLine(MyObj.ToString());
```

Here I use the GetFormat method to get an instance of the object referred to by the GetType method. This is reflection at work.

The mystring variable will be set to:
"System.Globalization.NumberFormatInfo."

DateTimeFormatInfo Class

The DateTimeFormatInfo class is used to define the date and time formats that are used during a DateTime.ToString() call. It is possible to get and set various flavors of date and time formats through properties of this class.

You have already gone over some of the uses of the DateTimeFormatInfo class while looking at the CultureInfo class. As you can see, most of these classes are intertwined. Here are some of the more important properties of this class.

DateTimeFormatInfo.CurrentInfo

I know you thought you just read CultureInfo so read it again. It is CurrentInfo. This property gets an instance of the DateTimeFormatInfo class that is being used by the CultureInfo instance defined by the current thread.

VB .NET

```
Dim MyCulture As New CultureInfo("es-ES")
Dim Myfmt As DateTimeFormatInfo
Dim fmt1 As DateTimeFormatInfo

Myfmt = MyCulture.DateTimeFormat
fmt1 = DateTimeFormatInfo.CurrentInfo

Console.WriteLine(Myfmt.GetMonthName(12))
Console.WriteLine(fmt1.GetMonthName(12))
Console.WriteLine(Thread.CurrentThread. _
CurrentCulture. _
DateTimeFormat. _
GetMonthName(12))
```

C#

```
CultureInfo MyCulture = new CultureInfo("es-ES");
DateTimeFormatInfo Myfmt;
DateTimeFormatInfo fmt1;

Myfmt = MyCulture.DateTimeFormat;
fmt1  = DateTimeFormatInfo.CurrentInfo;

Console.WriteLine(Myfmt.GetMonthName(12));
Console.WriteLine(fmt1.GetMonthName(12));
Console.WriteLine(Thread.CurrentThread.
            CurrentCulture.
            DateTimeFormat.
            GetMonthName(12));
```

The output is as follows:

```
diciembre
December
December
```

The GetMonthName() property gets the month's name according to the current threads culture. The last console line shows this.

What is nice about the CurrentInfo property is that you can get it directly from the data type itself without needing to create an instance. Consider the C# program, which has the following two lines of code:

```
fmt1   = DateTimeFormatInfo.CurrentInfo;
Console.WriteLine(fmt1.GetMonthName(12));
```

I created an instance of the DateTimeFormatInfo class and then obtained the CurrentInfo from it. This is not strictly necessary as you can do the following:

```
Console.WriteLine(DateTimeFormatInfo.
CurrentInfo.
GetMonthName(12));
```

No instance of the DateTimeFormatInfo class was explicitly created. No classes were harmed during the testing of this code.

DateTimeFormatInfo.InvariantInfo

The DateTimeFormatInfo.InvariantInfo property is identical in use to the CurrentInfo property with the following exception: It gets an instance of the DateTimeFormat for the Invariant culture, which is based on English.

If you want to see this in action just take the CurrentInfo example and replace CurrentInfo with InvariantInfo then run it. See what you get.

Patterns

The following is a list of format patterns supported by this DateTimeInfo class.

- LongDatePattern

- ShortDatePattern

- LongTimePattern

- ShortTimePattern

- MonthDayPattern

- YearMonthPattern

All these properties are read/write. They either return a string that indicates the associated pattern or they are set using a string. How do you know what characters to use to set a pattern? You must use the custom pattern specifiers. Table 4-6 shows these custom pattern specifiers.

Table 4-6. DateTimeInfo Pattern Specifiers

PATTERN SPECIFIER	DESCRIPTION
d	Day of Month. Single-digit days have no leading zero
dd	Day of Month. Single digit days have a leading zero
ddd	Abbreviated name for the day of the week
dddd	Full name for the day of the week
M	Numeric month. Single-digit month has no leading zero
MM	Numeric month. Single-digit month has a leading zero
MMM	Abbreviated month name
MMMM	Full month name
y	Year with no century. Single-digit years have no leading zero
yy	Year of century. Single-digit years have a leading zero
yyyy	Full year including century
gg	Era. Ignored if not appropriate
h	Hour in 12-hr clock. Single-digit hours have no leading zero
hh, hh*	Hour in a 12-hr clock. Single-digit hours have a leading zero
H	Hour in 24-hr clock. Single digit hours have no leading zero
HH, HH*	Hour in 24-hr clock with leading zero if necessary
m	Minute with no leading zero
mm, mm*	Minute with leading zero if necessary
s	Second with no leading zero
ss, ss*	Second with leading zero if necessary
t	First character in AP/PM designator
tt, tt*	Complete AM/PM designator
z	Time zone offset with no leading zero
zz	Time zone offset with leading zero
zzz, zzz*	Full time zone offset with minutes
:	Default Time separator
/	Default date separator
%c	Substitute a custom format pattern for "c"
\c	Displays any character <c> literally

There are quite a few other methods to this class including methods to get names of the current day, month, and era. An era in the Gregorian calendar is either "BC" or "AD." I encourage you to look at the documentation for the complete list. What I have shown you here is mostly all you will need from this class.

NumberFormatInfo Class

What if I told you ditto for the DateFormatInfo class? Seriously this class is much the same and has the same functionality. It is used to set and get formatting parameters for numbers. Perhaps I should say values instead of numbers. It also encompasses how currency is formatted. Table 4-7 in the NumberFormat section of this chapter shows the standard formatting characters for this class.

As you can see from Table 4-7 there are no custom pattern specifiers as in the DateTimeFormat. Instead you must create custom templates and use the existing formatting characters. You can create custom templates for the currency format and the number format. The currency format properties you can change to create a custom template follow:

- CurrencyNegativePattern

- CurrencyPositivePattern

- CurrencySymbol

- CurrencyGroupSizes

- CurrencyGroupSeparator

- CurrencyDecimalDigits

- CurrencyDecimalSeparator

Here is the list of the number format properties you can change.

- NumberNegativePattern

- NumberGroupSizes

- NumberGroupSeparator

- NumberDecimalDigits

- NumberDecimalSeparator

Let's say your current culture is U.S. English. You want to make a visiting accountant from France feel at home when viewing and inputting numbers. This accountant is fluent in English. You would keep the same culture so you can read what he is reading, but you change the number and currency formats to those he is accustomed to. If he had to constantly remember to press the period instead of the comma as a decimal separator his productivity would go way down. Typing in a period where a comma should be can turn your profits from thousands of dollars to tens of dollars. Try this code in Listing 4-3.

Listing 4-3. Changing numeric format for current culture

VB .NET

```
Dim MyCulture As New CultureInfo(Thread. _
                                    CurrentThread. _
                                    CurrentUICulture. _
                                    LCID)
Dim Vnf As NumberFormatInfo

Console.WriteLine(123456.ToString("c", MyCulture))

Vnf = MyCulture.NumberFormat
Vnf.CurrencyDecimalSeparator = ","
Vnf.CurrencyGroupSeparator = "."
Vnf.NumberDecimalSeparator = ","
Vnf.NumberGroupSeparator = "."
MyCulture.NumberFormat = Vnf

Console.WriteLine(123456.ToString("C", MyCulture))
```

C#

```
CultureInfo MyCulture = new CultureInfo(Thread.
                                    CurrentThread.
                                    CurrentUICulture.
                                    LCID);
NumberFormatInfo Vnf = new NumberFormatInfo();

Console.WriteLine(123456.ToString("c", MyCulture));

Vnf = MyCulture.NumberFormat;
Vnf.CurrencyDecimalSeparator = ",";
Vnf.CurrencyGroupSeparator = ".";
```

```
Vnf.NumberDecimalSeparator = ",";
Vnf.NumberGroupSeparator = ".";
MyCulture.NumberFormat = Vnf;

Console.WriteLine(123456.ToString("C", MyCulture));
```

As you can see I am changing the cultures separators. The output would be:

```
$123,456.00
$123.456,00
```

Here you have American dollars formatted to look like something European. Very simple. But why not just get the NumberFormat from the French culture and install it in MyCulture? Let's see what happens.

```
Dim FRCulture As New CultureInfo("fr-FR")
MyCulture.NumberFormat = FRCulture.NumberFormat
Console.WriteLine(123456.ToString("c", MyCulture))
```

Seems much simpler. However, look at the output:

```
123.456,00 ?
```

The format is correct but the currency is in French francs. At least it would be if you had a franc symbol. When you do something like this make sure you change only those attributes that you are concerned with. A wholesale change such as this can give undesired results.

RegionInfo Class

Ah, I've been waiting for this one to show up. As you can see almost all the examples have been related to the complete culture. That is the language + region/country. You have also done a little on the language aspect and now you learn about the region.

RegionInfo is much like CultureInfo in what it is used for and what it can do for you. The following table lists all the regions known to .NET.

Table 4-7. ISO Codes and LCID Codes

ISO 3166 2-LETTER CODE	COUNTRY/REGION	LCID
AE	U.A.E.	14337
AL	Albania	1052
AM	Armenia	1067
AR	Argentina	11274
AT	Austria	3079
AU	Australia	3081
AZ	Azerbaijan	1068
AZ	Azerbaijan	2092
BE	Belgium	2060
BE	Belgium	2067
BG	Bulgaria	1026
BH	Bahrain	15361
BN	Brunei Darussalam	2110
BO	Bolivia	16394
BR	Brazil	1046
BY	Belarus	1059
BZ	Belize	10249
CA	Canada	4105
CA	Canada	3084
CB	Caribbean	9225
CH	Switzerland	2055
CH	Switzerland	4108
CH	Switzerland	2064
CL	Chile	13322
CN	People's Republic of China	2052
CO	Colombia	9226
CR	Costa Rica	5130
CZ	Czech Republic	1029
DE	Germany	1031
DK	Denmark	1030
DO	Dominican Republic	7178
DZ	Algeria	5121

Table 4-7. ISO Codes and LCID Codes (continued)

ISO 3166 2-LETTER CODE	COUNTRY/REGION	LCID
EC	Ecuador	12298
EE	Estonia	1061
EG	Egypt	3073
ES	Spain	1027
ES	Spain	3082
ES	Spain	1069
ES	Spain	1110
FI	Finland	1035
FI	Finland	2077
FO	Faeroe Islands	1080
FR	France	1036
GB	United Kingdom	2057
GE	Georgia	1079
GR	Greece	1032
GT	Guatemala	4106
HK	Hong Kong S.A.R.	3076
HN	Honduras	18442
HR	Croatia	1050
HU	Hungary	1038
ID	Indonesia	1057
IE	Ireland	6153
IL	Israel	1037
IN	India	1081
IN	India	1094
IN	India	1095
IN	India	1097
IN	India	1098
IN	India	1099
IN	India	1102
IN	India	1103
IN	India	1111
IQ	Iraq	2049

Table 4-7. ISO Codes and LCID Codes (continued)

ISO 3166 2-LETTER CODE	COUNTRY/REGION	LCID
IR	Iran	1065
IS	Iceland	1039
IT	Italy	1040
JM	Jamaica	8201
JO	Jordan	11265
JP	Japan	1041
KE	Kenya	1089
KG	Kyrgyzstan	1088
KR	Korea	1042
KW	Kuwait	13313
KZ	Kazakhstan	1087
LB	Lebanon	12289
LI	Liechtenstein	5127
LT	Lithuania	1063
LU	Luxembourg	4103
LU	Luxembourg	5132
LV	Latvia	1062
LY	Libya	4097
MA	Morocco	6145
MC	Principality of Monaco	6156
MK	Former Yugoslav Republic of Macedonia	1071
MN	Mongolia	1104
MO	Macau S.A.R.	5124
MV	Maldives	1125
MX	Mexico	2058
MY	Malaysia	1086
NI	Nicaragua	19466
NL	Netherlands	1043
NO	Norway	1044
NO	Norway	2068
NZ	New Zealand	5129

Table 4-7. ISO Codes and LCID Codes (continued)

ISO 3166 2-LETTER CODE	COUNTRY/REGION	LCID
OM	Oman	8193
PA	Panama	6154
PE	Peru	10250
PH	Republic of the Philippines	13321
PK	Islamic Republic of Pakistan	1056
PL	Poland	1045
PR	Puerto Rico	20490
PT	Portugal	2070
PY	Paraguay	15370
QA	Qatar	16385
RO	Romania	1048
RU	Russia	1049
SA	Saudi Arabia	1025
SE	Sweden	1053
SG	Singapore	4100
SI	Slovenia	1060
SK	Slovakia	1051
SP	Serbia	2074
SP	Serbia	3098
SV	El Salvador	17418
SY	Syria	10241
SY	Syria	1114
TA	Tatarstan	1092
TH	Thailand	1054
TN	Tunisia	7169
TR	Turkey	1055
TT	Trinidad and Tobago	11273
TW	Taiwan	1028
UA	Ukraine	1058
US	United States	1033
UY	Uruguay	14346
UZ	Uzbekistan	1091

Table 4-7. ISO Codes and LCID Codes (continued)

ISO 3166 2-LETTER CODE	COUNTRY/REGION	LCID
UZ	Uzbekistan	2115
VE	Venezuela	8202
VN	Viet Nam	1066
YE	Yemen	9217
ZA	South Africa	7177
ZA	South Africa	1078
ZW	Zimbabwe	12297

Seeing double entries? How about nine. India has nine cultures associated with it. Therefore there are nine LCIDs you can use to get the region.

RegionInfo Members

The following section details some of the members of the RegionInfo class. The methods and properties in the RegionInfo class allow you to control and see aspects of the current region. Such aspects include how currency is treated and whether the region is metric. For the most part you can think of the region as the country.

RegionInfo Constructor

There are two overloaded constructors for this class. One takes a string argument in the form of the two-letter ISO 3166 code. The other constructor takes an integer that corresponds to the LCID of the culture that is associated with the region.

In the case of Switzerland you can use the following LCIDs to get the same region.

- 0x100C, which is French – Switzerland

- 0x0807, which is German – Switzerland

- 0x0810, which is Italian – Switzerland

Quite a few cultures have multiple languages within the same region. Here are some lines of code that make an instance of a region for South Africa.

C#

```
RegionInfo Rg = new RegionInfo ( "za" );
RegionInfo Rg = new RegionInfo ( 7177);
RegionInfo Rg = new RegionInfo ( 1078 );
```

VB

```
Dim Rg as RegionInfo = new RegionInfo ("za")
Dim Rg as RegionInfo = new RegionInfo (7177)
Dim Rg as RegionInfo = new RegionInfo (1078)
```

By the way, how did I build this table of regions? You know enough about CultureInfo, RegionInfo, and ToString() to do this. You should also know enough .NET code to perform a FOR. . .EACH loop. Listing 4-4 contains the code necessary to do this. It is included later in this chapter.

RegionInfo.CurrentRegion

The RegionInfo.CurrentRegion property returns an instance of the region that is used by the current thread. It is actually the region used by the default culture of the system. If you change the current threads culture to something totally different than your default culture, the CurrentRegion is still the default region of your computer.

RegionInfo.CurrencySymbol

The RegionInfo.CurrencySymbol read only property gets the currency symbol of the region in question. For the United States it would be "$."For Hong Kong it is "HK$." Since it is read-only it cannot be changed using this property. How do you change the currency symbol for a region? Override it in a derived class.

RegionInfo.ISOCurrencySymbol

The RegionInfo.ISOCurrencySymbol read-only property returns the ISO 4217 3-letter currency symbol for the country/region. The US ISO currency symbol is "USD." For Bolivia it is "BOB."

RegionInfo.DisplayName, RegionInfo.EnglishName, Name

These properties are the same as the analogs in the CultureInfo.

- DisplayName returns the full name of the region in the language of the installed .NET Framework.

- EnglishName returns the DisplayName but in English no matter what version of .NET you installed.

- Name returns the two-letter code for the region.

RegionInfo.IsMetric

The RegionInfo.IsMetric property returns true or false depending on if the country is using the metric system or not. What about the USA? Care to guess? Over here we went halfway then stopped. We measure fat grams to control our weight measured in pounds. As you probably guessed, the answer is false. If ever there was a need for a half-truth this is it. Perhaps we should invent a fuzzy Boolean.

RegionInfo.ThreeLetterISORegionName, RegionInfo.TwoLetterISORegionName, RegionInfo.ThreeLetterWindowsRegionName

Table 4-7 showed all the regions that had a two-letter code identifier. You can get this ID code from the TwoLetterISORegionName property. There is also a three-letter code and a three-letter Windows code for each region. The three-letter codes are not really used for anything in .NET. Only the two-letter codes are needed for constructors and to identify a region.

Listing 4-4. RegionInfo table generator program

VB

```
Imports System
Imports System.Globalization

Module Module1
```

```
    Sub Main()

        Dim AllCultures() As CultureInfo
        Dim ACulture As CultureInfo
        Dim Rg As RegionInfo
        Dim k As Integer

        AllCultures = CultureInfo. _
GetCultures(CultureTypes. _
SpecificCultures)
        For Each ACulture In AllCultures
            Rg = New RegionInfo(ACulture.LCID)
            Console.WriteLine _
(Rg.TwoLetterISORegionName.ToString(). _
PadRight(5, " ") + _
                        "," + Rg.EnglishName.PadRight(40, " ") + _
                        "," + ACulture.LCID.ToString())
        Next

        Console.ReadLine()
    End Sub

End Module
```

C#

```
using System;
using System.Globalization;

namespace Ch7RegionInfoTable_C
{
    /// <summary>
    /// Summary description for Class1.
    /// </summary>
    class Class1
    {
        static void Main(string[] args)
        {

          CultureInfo[] AllCultures;
            RegionInfo Rg;

          AllCultures = CultureInfo.GetCultures
              (CultureTypes.SpecificCultures);
          foreach (CultureInfo ACulture in AllCultures)
```

```
            {
              Rg = new RegionInfo(ACulture.LCID);
              Console.WriteLine
                  (Rg.TwoLetterISORegionName.ToString()
                   .PadRight(5, ' ') +
                    "," + Rg.EnglishName.PadRight(40, ' ') +
                    "," + ACulture.LCID.ToString());
            }
          Console.ReadLine();
        }
    }
}
```

StringInfo Class

This class allows you to iterate over a string. The string can be Unicode, and each printable character can consist of up to 4 bytes. The ability to iterate over a string also implies that you can split a string into its constituent characters.

Okay, so why would you want to do this? Well, how about for parsing a string? You could have a program that took in characters from a stream such as RS-232 or a text file. This stream of characters could be parsed according to a protocol you have defined. A parsing class that uses this StringInfo class would be handy indeed.

Some of you are VB programmers and are wondering why not use the MID$, LEFT$, and RIGHT$ functions I am used to? Why did Microsoft even include this? .NET is has a common language specification. It is not just the next generation of VB. There are other languages that do not have the VB functions but still need powerful string functions. You can call MID$ from C# by including the Microsoft.VisualBasic namespace.

The StringInfo class is fairly simple and straightforward. I go over the more important members first and then provide an example on how to use this class.

Constructor

The StringInfo constructor takes no arguments. Therefore, you always get a default instance. The StringInfo class works on Unicode strings and is therefore language blind.

StringInfo.GetNextTextElement

This property has two overloaded forms. The first one gets the first character in a Unicode string. The second version takes as an argument an integer indicating which character you want returned.

StringInfo.GetTextElementEnumerator

This function returns the TextElementEnumerator for the string in question. A TextElementEnumerator is only able to get a read-only element from the string. Also when the enumerator is obtained, a copy of the string is made. It is this copy that the enumerator iterates over. See a potential problem here? The enumerator assumes that the string is immutable. That is it assumes that characters will not be added or deleted from the original string. If the original and copy are (and this is entirely possible) out of synch then the enumerator throws an exception.

It is entirely plausible that a program can get two enumerators for the same string at the same time. Since each enumerator gets its own copy of the string, the enumerators are different. Watch out for this scenario. A table of operations for the TextElementEnumerator is shown in Table 4-8.

Table 4-8. TextElementEnumerator Functionality

PROPERTY/METHOD	DESCRIPTION
Current	Returns character at the current position in the string
GetTextElement	Same as Current
ElementIndex	Returns the position of the index within the string
MoveNext	Increments the element index to the next character
Reset	Repositions the index to the start of the string -1
Equals	Returns true if two strings are equal. False if not.

StringInfo.ParseCombiningCharacters

This function returns an array of integers whose elements define the start of each character in a Unicode string. Hmm, Unicode is 2 bytes per character so this array would contain integers for every other byte in the string right? Wrong. As I pointed out in Chapter 3 there are only 64k unique characters in the Unicode set. Each Unicode character is 16 bits so $2^{16} = 65536$ or 64k. I also stated that you could have over a million characters by using surrogate pairs. This means that there are two Unicode code points per character for some of the languages.

The length in bytes of a character in a particular string can be determined by getting the difference between successive elements in this array of indexes. Listing 4-5 shows how to do this.

Listing 4-5. Parsing strings

C#

```csharp
using System;
using System.Globalization;
using Microsoft.VisualBasic;

namespace CH7StringInfo_C
{
    /// <summary>
    /// StringInfo demonstration
    /// </summary>
    class Class1
    {
    static void Main(string[] args)
        {
            TextElementEnumerator Iter;
            String MyStr, OutBuf;

            MyStr = "The Quick programmer ran rings around the lazy manager";

            //Let's do the iterator thing
            Iter = StringInfo.GetTextElementEnumerator(MyStr)
            while (Iter.MoveNext())
              {
                OutBuf = "Character at position " +
                            Iter.ElementIndex.ToString() +
                            " = " + Iter.Current;
                Console.WriteLine(OutBuf);
              }

            //Let's do the manual loop thing
            for (int k=0; k<MyStr.Length; k++)
              {
                OutBuf = "Character at position " +
                            k.ToString() + " = " +
                            StringInfo.GetNextTextElement(MyStr, k);
                Console.WriteLine(OutBuf);
              }
```

```csharp
        //Let's do the Visual Basic MID$ thing.
        for (int j=1; j<MyStr.Length; j++)
          {
            OutBuf = "Character at position " + j.ToString() +
                     " = " + Strings.Mid(MyStr, j, 1);
            Console.WriteLine(OutBuf);
          }

          Console.ReadLine();
        }
    }
}
```

VB

```vb
Imports System.Globalization
Module Module1

    Sub Main()

        Dim MyStr, OutBuf As String
        Dim Iter As TextElementEnumerator

        MyStr = "The quick programmer ran rings around the lazy manager"

        'Let's go the iteration route
        Iter = StringInfo.GetTextElementEnumerator(MyStr)
        Do While (Iter.MoveNext)
            OutBuf = "Character at position " + _
                    Iter.ElementIndex.ToString() + _
                    " = " + Iter.Current
            Console.WriteLine(OutBuf)
        Loop

        'Let's do the manual loop route
        Dim k As Int16
        For k = 0 To Len(MyStr) - 1
            OutBuf = "Character at position " + _
                    k.ToString + " = " + _
                    StringInfo.GetNextTextElement(MyStr, k)
            Console.WriteLine(OutBuf)
        Next
```

```
        'Let's do the mid$ thing
        Dim j As Int16
        For j = 1 To Len(MyStr)
            OutBuf = "Character at position " + _
                    j.ToString + " = " + _
                    Mid(MyStr, j, 1)
            Console.WriteLine(OutBuf)
        Next

        Console.ReadLine()
    End Sub

End Module
```

Before you leave here let's go over one thing in the C# program. I am using a function from VB within the C# program. It is the MID function. Importing the Microsoft.VisualBasic namespace allows me to use any of the VB commands. The string commands such as MID, LEFT, RIGHT, TRIM, and so on are all in the Strings class.

In addition to using the namespace you must also add a reference to the Microsoft.VisualBasic.NET runtime. Use the Add references command in the Project window.

Summary

This chapter went over in depth the classes and methods included in the System.Globalization namespace. There were quite a few concepts introduced here, and you got to see first hand how .NET works by typing in some of the examples.

While the examples were not long, I tried to include at least one example for every class and/or method I examined. You found out that the System.Globalization namespace is very comprehensive indeed. However, these examples and this namespace only relate to setting up your program for running in a localized setting. They do not explain how to use resources or even what resources really are in the .NET world.

Chapter 5 delves into another namespace related to localization. That namespace is System.Resources. As you can probably guess this is where you handle everything having to do with resource files.

System.Resources and System.Threading Namespaces

THIS CHAPTER INTRODUCES YOU to the System.Resources namespace. Here I go over the important classes and methods involved in handling resource files. I also go over miscellaneous classes from the System.Threading namespace having to do with localization.

System.Resources Namespace

Where the System.Globalization namespace is used to describe various aspects of a culture; the System.Resources namespace is used to manipulate resources within a program.

I have spent quite a bit of space going over defining cultures and how resources should be defined for those cultures. In this section I move to the all-important aspect of getting and manipulating those resources.

ResourceManager Class

The ResourceManager class provides the functionality necessary to read in resources in a controlled manner. What do I mean by controlled manner? I touched on this in previous chapters but I go into a full explanation here.

Resources, whether they are strings or binary elements such as pictures or fonts, and so forth, should be installed in what are called satellite assemblies. .NET provides a scheme of naming and saving resource files in certain directories. Part of this scheme also involves saving a last ditch resource file as part of the program assembly.

BaseName.CultureName.Resources is the naming convention for a resource file. The BaseName is the name of your program. The CultureName is the two- or five-letter name for your culture. The two-letter name is the language identifier with no country-specific aspects. The five-letter name is the two-letter language identifier followed by the two-letter country/region identifier separated by a dash.

The storage convention for a resource file is based on the CultureName of the resource file. Each resource file gets stored in a subdirectory of the main assembly. Table 5-1 lists some resource file names and locations.

Table 5-1. Resource Files for Myprog.exe

RESOURCE FILE NAME	LOCATION	DESCRIPTION
Myprog.de-CH.resources	\de-CH	German for Switzerland
Myprog.de.resources	\de	German for general use
Myprog.en-US.resources	\en-US	English for USA
Myprog.es-ES.resources	\es-ES	Spanish for Spain
Myprog.es-MX.resources	\es-MX	Spanish for Mexico
Myprog.es.resources	\es	Spanish for general use
Myprog.resources	NA	Invariant. Embedded in executable

If a resource file name has no language/culture name associated with it then this is the invariant culture. You went over the invariant culture in the CultureInfo section of Chapter 4. To reiterate, the invariant culture is usually based on English and the invariant resource file contains resources that the resource manager cannot find anywhere else.

How does the resource manager know where to find resources? Look at Table 5-1. It lists resource file names and locations. Suppose your program changed to the culture "es-MX." You also wanted to get a string for the key "MexicanLanguage." Here is what would happen.

1. The resource manager would look in the directory "\es-MX" for a satellite resource file called "es-MX.dll."

2. If the file is not found or the resource within that file is not found, the resource manager looks in the directory "\es" for a satellite resource file called "es.dll."

3. If the file is not found, or the resource does not exist in that file, the resource manager looks in the resource file that was linked in with the assembly.

4. If there is no linked-in invariant resource file, or the resource does not exist, the resource manager throws an exception.

What is happening in this scenario is the fallback scheme that .NET uses to get a resource. As you can see, the fallback scheme consists of the following steps.

- Look in the <language>-<country/region> subdirectory.

- Look in the <language> subdirectory.

- Look in the assembly itself.

- Throw an error.

The fallback scheme exhausts all options first before giving up.

Recall the VB 6 program from Chapter 3. It involved all kinds of code to enable a similar fallback scheme for a VB 6 program. As you can see, .NET gives you this mechanism for free. Do you have to follow this scheme? In a word, no. There is a method you can use to create a file-based resource manager that looks in a specific directory for resources. If the resource is not found there is no fallback mechanism involved. You get an error right away. Should you follow this scheme? In another word, yes. The resource file naming convention and fallback scheme give your program the best chance at always getting whatever resource it needs. It also allows you, the programmer, to better organize your resources.

Here are some ways to take advantage of the fallback scheme:

- Put all strings you do not want translated in the invariant resource file.

- Put all generic language strings in a language-only resource file. An example would be the Spanish string for "yes" which is "si." This string will not change from culture to culture.

- Put all culture specific strings in the language-country resource file.

If you want to get a string that was invariant, you can rely on the fallback mechanism of .NET to eventually get it for you. You could also know this ahead of time and tell .NET to go directly to the invariant culture and get it. Each of the following lines of code get a string from the invariant resource file.

```
GetString("yes");
GetString("yes", MyCulture.InvariantCulture);
```

The second line of code "knows" where the string is and gets it directly. The first line relies on the fallback mechanism to get the string. The second approach is faster.

ResourceReader Class

The ResourceReader class is used to open a resource file and iterate over all the resource keys in that file. There are two uses for this class. The first is to dump the contents of a resource file and the second is to parse the contents of a resource stream. Why a stream? Well you could be getting a transmission of a resource file over an RS-232 link. A stream could also be the result of parsing an XML text file using the .NET XML parser. It is an easy task to make a class that implements a ResourceReader to parse the data as it comes in.

It is worth mentioning that this class uses a default implementation of the IResourceReader interface. If you want to read a resource file or resource stream that was generated in a different format then you would make a different implementation of this interface. The examples in this book use the default implementation.

There are three members of this class that are interesting. They are:

- ResourceReader Constructor. Provides an argument of a resource file or a stream.

- GetEnumerator. This method returns an enumerator of the type IDictionaryEnumerator.

- Close. This function releases all memory and closes all files or streams associated with this instance of the ResourceReader.

Listing 5-1 is a simple resource dump program.

Listing 5-1. Resource dumper

VB

```
Imports System.Resources
Imports System.Collections

Module Module1

    Sub Main()

        'Open a resource reader and get an enumerator from it
        Dim reader = New ResourceReader("ch5RR.resources")
        Dim en As IDictionaryEnumerator = reader.GetEnumerator()
```

```
        Do While (en.MoveNext)
            Console.WriteLine("Name: {0} - Value: {1}", _
                        en.Key.ToString().PadRight(10, " "), _
                        en.Value)
        Loop
        reader.Close()

        Console.ReadLine()

    End Sub

End Module
```

C#

```
using System;
using System.Resources;
using System.Collections;

namespace CH5ResourceReader_C
{
    /// <summary>
    /// Simple resource dump program
    /// </summary>
    class Class1
    {       static void Main(string[] args)
        {
            //Open a resource reader and get an enumerator from it
            IResourceReader reader = new ResourceReader("ch5RR.resources");
            IDictionaryEnumerator en = reader.GetEnumerator();

            while (en.MoveNext())
            {
                Console.WriteLine("Name: {0} - Value: {1}",
                        en.Key.ToString().PadRight(10, ' '),
                        en.Value);
            }
            reader.Close();

            Console.ReadLine();
        }
    }
}
```

ResourceSet Class

A ResourceSet is a mechanism that lets you load all the resources for a particular culture all at once. Since you are not calling resources at runtime there is no way to know if the resource you need is in a particular resource file or not. Because of this, a ResourceSet ignores all fallback rules.

So how does the ResourceSet get filled? It fills by iterating through a resource file using the ResourceReader class. It uses the IResourceReader enumerator and stores each value in a hash table. The hash table makes for speedy look up later.

There are four constructors for this class. Table 5-2 summarizes them.

Table 5-2. ResourceSet Constructor Descriptions

CONSTRUCTOR	DESCRIPTION
ResourceSet ()	Default properties
ResourceSet (IResourceReader)	Uses specified IResourceReader (roll your own)
ResourceSet (String)	Default reader for a specified resource file
ResourceSet (Stream)	Default reader for a specified resource stream

The important members of this class are enumerated in the list that follows:

- GetString(String). This returns a string that matches the key value given as the argument. The overloaded version is GetString(String, Bool). If the Boolean argument is true then the key is searched without regard to case.

- GetObject(String), GetObject(String, Bool). This method returns an object according to the key. An object could be a font or a picture, etc. If the second version is used and the Bool is true then the key is considered case-insensitive.

- GetDefaultReader(). This method returns the default type of the ResourceReader used in this class.

- GetDefaultWriter(). This method returns the default type of the ResourceWriter used with this class.

- Close(). This method closes all resources and frees all memory associated with an instance of this class. Close calls the Dispose() method.

- Dispose(). Close calls this method. It releases all resources associated with an instance of this class.

What happens if the resource is not found? Nothing. That is, suppose you wanted a string that did not exist? The GetString() method returns a null string. No error is thrown.

Why use the GetDefaultReader() and GetDefaultWriter() methods? You use these for reflection. Remember that by using reflection it is possible to walk a .NET assembly and get all information on all classes. This information includes the types of objects. Listing 5-2 shows how to use a resource set.

Listing 5-2. Simple resource set

VB

```
Imports System
Imports System.Resources

Module Module1

    Sub Main()

        Dim Rs As New ResourceSet("ch5rr.resources")

        Console.WriteLine(Rs.GetString("first", True))
        Console.WriteLine(Rs.GetString("second", True))
        Console.WriteLine(Rs.GetString("third", True))
        Console.WriteLine(Rs.GetString("fourth", True))
        Console.WriteLine(Rs.GetString("not here", True))
        Console.WriteLine(Rs.GetDefaultReader.ToString())

        Rs.Close()
        Console.ReadLine()
    End Sub

End Module
```

C#

```
using System;
using System.Resources;

namespace CH5ResourceSet_C
{
```

```csharp
/// <summary>
/// Resource set C# example
/// </summary>
class Class1
{
    static void Main(string[] args)
    {
        ResourceSet Rs = new ResourceSet("ch5rr.resources");

        Console.WriteLine(Rs.GetString("first", true));
        Console.WriteLine(Rs.GetString("second", true));
        Console.WriteLine(Rs.GetString("third", true));
        Console.WriteLine(Rs.GetString("fourth", true));
        Console.WriteLine(Rs.GetString("not here", true));
        Console.WriteLine(Rs.GetDefaultReader().ToString());

        Rs.Close();
        Console.ReadLine();
    }
}
```

The result of this code is:

```
first resource
second resource
third resource
fourth resource
System.Resources.ResourceReader
```

Notice the blank line between the last two outputs? This is the string that was not found. Notice also that I used the overloaded version of the GetString() method. I made sure that the key I used was case-insensitive. When you think of case sensitivity as a programmer, you think that there can be two words spelled the same but with different case. For reading resources this is true. However when you read a resource file that was made using the ResourceWriter class this is not true. The ResourceWriter does not allow you to have multiple keys of the same spelling with different case in the same resource file. Why? How many of you are from the VB world? You are used to the Intellisense capability of VB automatically converting case for you. If you are like me you are careful with case on the variable name declaration but careless with the variable because VB corrects case for you. If you have been typing in the examples you have already found out this is not true for C#. It is possible in C# to have multiple variables of the same name but different case. This is a major source of bugs.

In an effort to reduce bug count, the ResourceWriter class prevents you from having keys of the same spelling but different case.

ResourceWriter Class

The ResourceWriter class is used to create a resource file. The resource file created is a binary resource file like the one output by the ResGen.exe program. You can send the resources to a stream or to a resource file depending on the constructor used. The constructor has only two overloaded forms. The argument is either a stream or a string. The following list describes the important members of this class:

- Constructor. Instantiates the class and makes the file if necessary.

- AddResource(String, Byte). This overloaded method adds a resource to the stream as a key, value pair. The byte is an 8-bit unsigned integer array of any length.

- AddResource(String, Object). This overloaded method adds a resource to the stream as a key, value pair. The object can represent a font or a picture, and so on.

- AddResource(String, String). This overloaded method adds a resource to the stream as a key, value pair. The second argument is the string resource.

- Generate(). This method is called after you have added all the resources to your stream. This method writes the resources to the resource file or the stream.

- Close(). This method closes all resources and releases all memory associated with the current ResourceWriter instance. This method calls Dispose().

Listing 5-3 writes out a resource file using the ResourceWriter and then reads it back and enumerates it using the ResourceReader.

Listing 5-3. Simple resource reader + writer

VB

```
Imports System
Imports System.Resources
Module Module1
```

```vbnet
    Sub Main()
        Dim Rw As New ResourceWriter("CH5Rrw.resources")
        Dim Rr As ResourceReader
        Dim RrEn As IDictionaryEnumerator

        Rw.AddResource("key 1", "First value")
        Rw.AddResource("key 2", "Second value")
        Rw.AddResource("key 3", "Third value")
        Rw.Generate()
        Rw.Close()

        Rr = New ResourceReader("CH5Rw.resources")
        RrEn = Rr.GetEnumerator
        Do While (RrEn.MoveNext)
            Console.WriteLine("Name: {0} - Value: {1}", _
                        RrEn.Key.ToString().PadRight(10, " "), _
                        RrEn.Value)
        Loop
        Rr.Close()

        Console.ReadLine()
    End Sub

End Module
```

C#

```csharp
using System;
using System.Resources;
using System.Collections;

namespace CH5ResourceWriter_C
{
    /// <summary>
    /// ResourceWriter and reader example
    /// </summary>
    class Class1
    {
        static void Main(string[] args)
        {
            ResourceWriter Rw = new ResourceWriter("CH5Rw.resources");
```

```
Rw.AddResource("key 1", "First value");
Rw.AddResource("key 2", "Second value");
Rw.AddResource("key 3", "Third value");
Rw.Generate();
Rw.Close();

ResourceReader Rr = new ResourceReader("CH5Rrw.resources");
IDictionaryEnumerator RrEn = Rr.GetEnumerator();
while (RrEn.MoveNext())
  {
    Console.WriteLine("Name: {0} - Value: {1}",
    RrEn.Key.ToString().PadRight(10, ' '),
    RrEn.Value);
  }
Rr.Close();

Console.ReadLine();
    }
  }
}
```

You should have gotten the same values written to the screen as you put into the resource file.

ResXResourceReader Class, ResXResourceSet Class, ResXResourceWriter Class

These classes are almost identical to the ResourceReader, ResourceSet, ResourceWriter classes. The ResXResourceReader class opens a resource file and allows you to iterate over the file. The ResXResourceSet class loads all the resources from a resource file at once. It allows you to work with resources as a set rather than loading them dynamically. The ResXResourceWriter class allows you to create a resource file and to output resources to this file.

So, what's the difference? Why the "X?" The difference is in the type of file it works with. There are two types of text-based resources files. The first you have already seen. It is just a plain, easily readable text file that contains only string resources. The ResX classes work with an XML-based resource file. An XML resource file can contain any strings resources but can also contain BLOB data. You can store a picture in an XML resource file if you like. The extension for an XML resource file is, you guessed it, .resx.

Remember the ResourceWriter class? It also could save BLOB data to a resource file. The difference between the ResourceWriter and

ResXResourceWriter classes is that the ResourceWriter class saves resources straight to a binary file. It does not create a human readable text file. The ResXResourceWriter saves data to a human readable XML file. This XML file is an intermediate file in that it still needs to be compiled into a binary.resources file before it can be used.

By the way, being an object-oriented programmer you have probably wondered if ResourceReader and ResXResourceReader are the same base classes. How about ResourceWriter and ResXResourceWriter? Well yes, they are the same. The difference comes from the implementation of the IResourceReader and IResourceWriter interfaces. The ResourceReader uses the default implementation of the IResourceReader and the ResXResourceReader uses a specialized implementation of the IResourceReader. The same goes for the different resource writers. Code reuse and polymorphism at work.

Listing 5-4 is an example of the ResX reader and writer.

Listing 5-4. ResXReader and writer

VB

```
Imports System.Resources

Module Module1

    Sub Main()
        Dim RwX As New ResXResourceWriter("CH5Rwx.resx")
        Dim RrX As ResXResourceReader
        Dim RrXEn As IDictionaryEnumerator

        RwX.AddResource("key 1", "First value")
        RwX.AddResource("key 2", "Second value")
        RwX.AddResource("key 3", "Third value")
        RwX.Generate()
        RwX.Close()

        RrX = New ResXResourceReader("CH5Rwx.resx")
        RrXEn = RrX.GetEnumerator
        Do While (RrXEn.MoveNext)
            Console.WriteLine("Name: {0} - Value: {1}", _
                        RrXEn.Key.ToString().PadRight(10, " "), _
                        RrXEn.Value)
        Loop
        RrX.Close()
```

```
        Console.ReadLine()
    End Sub


End Module
```

C#

```csharp
using System;
using System.Resources;
using System.Collections;

namespace CH5ResourceWriter_C
{
    /// <summary>
    /// ResXResourceWriter and reader example
    /// </summary>
    class Class1
    {
        static void Main(string[] args)
        {
            ResXResourceWriter RwX = new
            ResXResourceWriter("CH5RwX.resx");

            RwX.AddResource("key 1", "First value");
            RwX.AddResource("key 2", "Second value");
            RwX.AddResource("key 3", "Third value");
            RwX.Generate();
            RwX.Close();

            ResXResourceReader RrX = new ResXResourceReader("CH5RwX.resx");
            IDictionaryEnumerator RrEn = RrX.GetEnumerator();
            while (RrEn.MoveNext())
            {
                Console.WriteLine("Name: {0} - Value: {1}",
                    RrEn.Key.ToString().PadRight(10, ' '),
                    RrEn.Value);
            }
            RrX.Close();

            Console.ReadLine();
        }
    }
}
```

Start a new console application in VB. Try typing this program in. It is not too long. Found the problem yet? You are not able to get past the first line in Main. The Intellisense drops down and you can find ResourceWriter but where is ResXResourceWriter? For that matter, where is ResX anything? Do this: Add a reference to System.Windows.Forms.DLL. You can do this from the project window or from the menu system.

Now try the first line again. All of a sudden you can see the ResX stuff.

Using Reflection to Find Missing Classes

Let's take a small side trip. When I first tried using the ResX classes I had the annoying problem of not being able to find the ResXResourceReader/Writer classes. I imported the System.Resources Namespace. Where was all my ResX stuff? The MSDN documentation was very scant on this particular topic but I was led to believe it was in .NET somewhere. The .NET documentation actually does say where to find this and I could tell you as well but then I wouldn't have this little diversion would I?

I had a couple of choices here. I could skip this subject altogether, whine to my editor that I could not find the classes, or tell Microsoft it had a big bug in its software. While it is entirely possible that Microsoft left this out I seriously doubted it.[1] I am not the whiny type and this subject is way too important to skip. What to do? I knew this ResX stuff had to be in here somewhere.

Well I have talked about reflection a little in the context of various class members. If you remember, I said it was a way to expose metadata for an assembly. It is possible to find out anything about any program written using .NET. Here is what I did to find the ResX classes.

I looked for all the DLLs that I thought would contain the System.Resources namespace. I found them in C:\WINNT\Microsoft.NET\Framework\v1.0.3328. There are quite a few .NET DLLs in this directory. Perhaps it was in here somewhere.

Next I wrote a small VB program that loaded in all the DLLs and used reflection to search through them to find any class in either the System.Resources or System.Globalization namespaces. Although I had not found this to be the case, perhaps something was missing from the Globalization namespace that I had not come across yet. If so let's find that too. Listing 5-5 shows the code I used to find the missing resources classes.

Listing 5-5. Simple reflection program to find resources namespace

```
Imports System.Reflection
Module Module1
    Sub Main()
```

```
        Dim Index As Integer
        Dim ReflA As System.Reflection.Assembly
        Dim ReflA_Types() As Type
        Dim fname As String
        ' MSCORLIB.DLL may reside In a different directory depending on
        '   the .NET release version you have
        fname = "C:\WINNT\Microsoft.NET\Framework\v1.0.3328\mscorlib.dll"
        ReflA = ReflA.LoadFrom(fname)
        ReflA_Types = ReflA.GetTypes()
        Console.WriteLine(fname)
        For Index = 0 To UBound(ReflA_Types)
            If ReflA_Types(Index).Namespace = "System.Resources" Or _
               ReflA_Types(Index).Namespace = "System.Globalization" Then
               Console.WriteLine("  Found -> " +
                        ReflA_Types(Index).FullName)
               System.Threading.Thread.Sleep(100)
            End If

        Next
        Console.WriteLine("End")
        Console.ReadLine()
    End Sub


End Module
```

The program that I used enumerated all DLL files in the directory automatically. I left this part out for clarity. I added a sleep function so I could see the classes as they came up on the screen. If you're a speed demon leave this line out.

Anyway, here is what I found.

```
C:\WINNT\Microsoft.NET\Framework\v1.0.2914\System.Windows.Forms.dll
      Found -> System.Resources.ResXResourceReader
      Found -> System.Resources.ResXResourceReader+ResXResourceEnumerator
      Found -> System.Resources.ResXResourceWriter
      Found -> System.Resources.ResXResourceSet
      Found -> System.Resources.ResXFileRef
      Found -> System.Resources.ResXFileRef+Converter
      Found -> System.Resources.ResXNullRef

C:\WINNT\Microsoft.NET\Framework\v1.0.3328\mscorlib.dll
      Found -> System.Resources.NeutralResourcesLanguageAttribute
      Found -> System.Resources.ResourceSet
      Found -> System.Resources.ResourceManager
      Found -> System.Resources.RuntimeResourceSet
```

```
Found -> System.Resources.FastResourceComparer
Found -> System.Resources.IResourceWriter
Found -> System.Resources.ResourceWriter
Found -> System.Resources.IResourceReader
Found -> System.Resources.ResourceReader
Found -> System.Resources.ResourceReader+ResourceEnumerator
Found -> System.Resources.SatelliteContractVersionAttribute
Found -> System.Resources.MissingManifestResourceException

Found -> System.Globalization.RegionInfo
Found -> System.Globalization.NameLCIDInfo
Found -> System.Globalization.Calendar
Found -> System.Globalization.HebrewCalendar
Found -> System.Globalization.HebrewCalendar+__DateBuffer
Found -> System.Globalization.CultureTypes
Found -> System.Globalization.CharacterInfo
Found -> System.Globalization.JulianCalendar
Found -> System.Globalization.DateTimeStyles
Found -> System.Globalization.SortKey
Found -> System.Globalization.GlobalizationAssembly
Found -> System.Globalization.GregorianCalendarTypes
Found -> System.Globalization.GregorianCalendar
Found -> System.Globalization.EncodingTable
Found -> System.Globalization.InternalEncodingDataItem
Found -> System.Globalization.InternalCodePageDataItem
Found -> System.Globalization.CalendarTable
Found -> System.Globalization.TextElementEnumerator
Found -> System.Globalization.RegionTable
Found -> System.Globalization.DefaultLCIDMap
Found -> System.Globalization.NumberFormatInfo
Found -> System.Globalization.UnicodeCategory
Found -> System.Globalization.KoreanCalendar
Found -> System.Globalization.EraInfo
Found -> System.Globalization.GregorianCalendarHelper
Found -> System.Globalization.TaiwanCalendar
Found -> System.Globalization.NumberStyles
Found -> System.Globalization.DaylightTime
Found -> System.Globalization.JapaneseCalendar
Found -> System.Globalization.CultureInfo
Found -> System.Globalization.CultureTable
Found -> System.Globalization.IDOffset
Found -> System.Globalization.NameOffsetItem
Found -> System.Globalization.CultureInfoHeader
```

```
   Found -> System.Globalization.TextInfo
   Found -> System.Globalization.CalendarWeekRule
   Found -> System.Globalization.ThaiBuddhistCalendar
   Found -> System.Globalization.CodePageDataItem
   Found -> System.Globalization.DateTimeFormatInfo
   Found -> System.Globalization.StringInfo
   Found -> System.Globalization.CompareOptions
   Found -> System.Globalization.CompareInfo
   Found -> System.Globalization.HijriCalendar
End
```

All of the System.Globalization and most of the System.Resources classes are in the mscorlib.dll file. This file is referenced as a matter of course in any .NET project. However I also found that all the ResX stuff was in the System.Windows.Forms.dll file. Interesting. All I needed to do to get access to these classes was to add a reference to this file in my project. Sure enough it worked.

Why was the ResX stuff in a different DLL than the rest of the System.Resources namespace? Why this particular file? This is pure speculation on my part but here is an explanation. XML file resources are used by the built in resource editor. Most of the time you would have a resource file when building a forms application. Why put it in the basic DLL if in most cases you will never use it? This makes some sense to me. By the same token, if you were building a windows forms program you would most likely use the built-in resource editor.

Be tenacious. If you cannot find something or want to know something in depth, start digging. You have all the tools necessary to find what you want. You want to be known as the house guru right? .NET puts everyone back on the same starting block. Do not count on getting to be the guru by long-term experience. You have too much competition. Now is your chance to dig in and discover!

System.Threading Namespace

Most of the classes in this namespace are out of the scope of this book. Explaining threading is a book in itself. Look for one coming to a bookstore near you!

True threading, as in free threading, has long been the Holy Grail of VB programmers. As someone who has written multithreaded code in C++, let me tell you it is definitely a two-edged sword. This is a case of "be careful what you wish for" because now you've got it. But I digress.

This section deals only with the threading classes that have to do with localization. These classes are:

- Thread.CurrentThread.CurrentCulture

- Thread.CurrentThread.CurrentUICulture

You will find that the documentation alludes to being able to get at the culture for the Thread class. However, you need to go down a level to the current thread before you can get a culture reference.

I have been using, setting, and displaying the current threads culture in quite a few of the examples I have written. Just to reiterate, I will go over what it means to get the culture from the thread.

Thread.CurrentThread.CurrentCulture

Thread.CurrentThread.CurrentCulture is an instance of the current threads culture. Duh! What this means is that in a multithreaded program you can have many cultures that are enabled, one for each thread. The CurrentCulture refers to the culture in which the thread performs.

Thread.CurrentThread.CurrentUICulture

Thread.CurrentThread.CurrentUICulture is an instance of the current threads UI culture. Duh! Again! This means essentially the same as the CurrentCulture. The CurrentUICulture, however, is the culture used by the resource manager to get resources.

These two classes imply that you can have a culture for the resource manager that is different from the culture that the thread is working under. In fact, this is true. Consider the following piece of code.

```
. . .
Thread.CurrentThread.CurrentCulture = New CultureInfo("es-ES")
Console.WriteLine(Thread.CurrentThread.CurrentCulture.DisplayName)
Console.WriteLine(Thread.CurrentThread.CurrentUICulture.DisplayName)
. . .
```

The resulting display would be:

```
Spanish (Spain)
English (United States)
```

Try this piece of code:

```
Console.WriteLine(Thread.
    CurrentThread.
    CurrentThread.
    CurrentThread.
    CurrentThread.
    CurrentThread.
    CurrentThread.
    CurrentUICulture.DisplayName());
```

Why do they allow this? It comes under the heading of Stupid Code Tricks.

Resource File Types

I have been dealing so far with resource files that are text-based and contain only strings. There are, however, other kinds of resource files and other ways to make them.

Basic Text Resource File

The basic Text resource file is your plain vanilla resource file. It is also your workhorse. Its only use is to hold localized strings.

The naming convention for a text resource file is <program name>.txt. Table 5-3 shows what can be included in a text resource file.

Table 5-3. Text Resource File Format

TEXT	DESCRIPTION
[header]	This is optional and must be the same as the name of the resource file.
Comment	Comment. This is filtered out when you compile this file to a .resources file.
Key = value	The actual string resource. The key and value strings do not need to be quoted. They do need to be separated by an = sign.

If you read the table carefully perhaps a question came to mind. It was the first thing I thought of when I came across this. Why not make the value a quoted string? And what happens if you do quote it? Well if you have been doing string-based localization for any amount of time you soon find out that it is near impossible to put quote marks in a resource file. Microsoft has eliminated the necessity for a quoted string just so you can put quotes in if you need them.

Suppose you had a resource file with the following strings:

```
. . .
key1 = Non Quoted String
key2 = "Quoted String"
. . .
```

Now you have a piece of code like this:

```
. . .
Console.WriteLine(ResReader.GetString("Key1");
Console.WriteLine(ResReader.GetString("Key2");
. . .
```

You would see the following on the screen:

```
Non Quoted String
 "Quoted String"
```

Pretty cool, huh?

ResX Resource File

We went over this a little in the ResXResourceWriter class. A .resX file is an XML version of a resource file. Where the text-based file was used to handle only strings, this file can handle strings and objects. The nice thing about this file format, of course, is that it is human readable.

If you want, you can type in a .resX file. I encourage you to try. It is a great learning experience. However, I have better things to do. Instead .NET has a host of tools to make the .resX file for you.

For those of you unfamiliar with XML I explain it in the Enter XML section of this chapter.

.Resources File

The .resources file is the intermediate binary form of a resource file. There are three stages to a resource file to be included in a satellite assembly.

1. Text-based resource file in basic text format or in XML format

2. Compiled resource file in .resources format

3. A dll containing the .resources binary resource file

The .resources file can be created by using the resgen.exe utility or by writing it directly using the ResourceWriter classes. Also the .resources file is the final stage before being embedded in an assembly.

Remember the fallback scheme? First, the program looks for a satellite resource file in the <language>-<country> resource file. Failing that, it looks in the <language> resource file. Failing *that*, it looks in the assembly itself for the resource. The resource file that you embed in the assembly is a .resources file.

A .resources file can also be considered a loose resource. A loose resource file is one that does not necessarily live in a directory that is searched by the resource manager. Instead, it can be a resource file that you can load explicitly without any fallback scheme involved. You can retrieve loose resources by using the CreateFileBasedResourceManager() method in the resource manager.

Listing 5-6 shows a small program that uses loose resources. It is actually an expansion of the resource dump program.

Listing 5-6. Loose resources

VB

```vb
Imports System.Resources
Imports System.Collections

Module Module1

    Sub Main()

        'Open a resource reader and get an enumerator from it
        Dim reader = New ResourceReader("ch5RR.resources")
        Dim en As IDictionaryEnumerator = reader.GetEnumerator()

        Do While (en.MoveNext)
           Console.WriteLine("Name: {0} - Value: {1}", _
                      en.Key.ToString().PadRight(10, " "), _
                      en.Value)
        Loop
        reader.Close()

        'Loose resource example
        Dim rm as ResourceManager.CreateFileBasedResourceManager _
                ("ch5rr", ".", Nothing)
        Console.WriteLine(rm.GetSting("first"))
```

```
        Console.ReadLine()

    End Sub

End Module
```

C#

```csharp
using System;
using System.Resources;
using System.Collections;

namespace CH5ResourceReader_C
{
    /// <summary>
    /// Simple resource dump program
    /// </summary>
    class Class1
    {
        static void Main(string[] args)
        {
            //Open a resource reader and get an enumerator from it
            IResourceReader reader = new ResourceReader("ch5RR.resources");
            IDictionaryEnumerator en = reader.GetEnumerator();

            while (en.MoveNext())
            {
                Console.WriteLine("Name: {0} - Value: {1}",
                        en.Key.ToString().PadRight(10, ' '),
                        en.Value);
            }
            reader.Close();

            //Loose resource example
            ResourceManager rm as ResourceManager.CreateFileBasedResourceManager
                    ("ch5rr", ".", Nothing);
            Console.WriteLine(rm.GetSting("first"));

            Console.ReadLine();
        }
    }
}
```

I have created a resource manager that looks in the current directory for the resource file. I then get a string from this resource file.

Enter XML

I have this really huge book at home on XML. It is over 1000 pages long. How can I possibly boil down XML to a few paragraphs? XML is so important to .NET. Well this book is about internationalization using .NET so I will try to keep the explanation focused and short.

In the beginning there was SGML, the Standard General Markup Language. SGML begat HTML and XML. When the web was young people started using HTML to design web pages. HTML, however, suffers from chronic over use and violation of the original meaning of the tags.

The definition list for HTML tags show that they are supposed to be used only for crude page layout and presentation of text. Over the years, artistic programmers subverted the use of the HTML tags in order to paint nice and captivating pages for the surfing masses. Both Microsoft and Netscape saw this and with every new version of browser they added new features to handle these rogue uses of HTML. In the effort to provide newer and better presentation features, the original intent of HTML got lost in the shuffle.

HTML also suffers from the inherent flaw that it does not describe data in any way. The HTML tags are defined. There is really no way to extend them by adding new tags to describe what you want. Instead, different uses are found for all the existing tags.

Well, enough HTML bashing. What can be done to fix this problem? XML that's what. XML, like HTML is a subset of SGML. Unlike HTML though, XML can be used to describe almost anything.

It is possible to make any kind of tags you want. These tags could represent data peculiar to your situation. Suppose you had a Windows Form that you wanted to describe using XML. You could invent some tags that were meant just for describing a Form.

```
<Vbform>
    <content>
        <button>
            <Button-Name>
                cmdQuit
            </Button-Name>
            <Button-label>
                Quit
            </Button-label>
        </button>

    </content>
</Vbform>
```

This is a legal XML form. It is very easy to understand and very easy to parse as well. Keep in mind that all tags must be nested. HTML does not make this restriction. The tags shown here are made up, but they do not have to be. Tag definitions can be kept in a DTD file. This Document Type Definition file lets you share information about your tags with anyone who needs to know. There are many industry-specific DTDs that describe XML tags. There may already be a DTD that you can use or extend. An in-depth discussion of DTDs is out of the scope of this book but if you want I will lend you my 6 lb XML book to read, although it is currently holding up one corner of my house.

Know what else is nice about XML? If you have a firewall that lets through HTML, then XML will fly right through as well. Try that with COM.

XML is used in .NET resource files. You saw this with the .resX files and the ResXResourceReader/Writer classes. Listing 5-7 shows the XML output for the previous ResXResourceWriter example. Remember there are only three string resources in this file.

Listing 5-7. XML resource file

```
<?xml version="1.0" encoding="utf-8"?>
<root>
  <xsd:schema id="root" targetNamespace="" xmlns=""
 xmlns:xsd="http://www.w3.org/2001/XMLSchema" xmlns:msdata=
 "urn:schemas-microsoft-com:xml-msdata">
    <xsd:element name="root" msdata:IsDataSet="true">
      <xsd:complexType>
        <xsd:choice maxOccurs="unbounded">
          <xsd:element name="data">
            <xsd:complexType>
              <xsd:sequence>
                <xsd:element name="value" type="xsd:string" minOccurs="0"
                                          msdata:Ordinal="1" />
                <xsd:element name="comment" type="xsd:string" minOccurs="0"
                                          msdata:Ordinal="2" />
              </xsd:sequence>
              <xsd:attribute name="name" type="xsd:string" />
              <xsd:attribute name="type" type="xsd:string" />
              <xsd:attribute name="mimetype" type="xsd:string" />
            </xsd:complexType>
          </xsd:element>
          <xsd:element name="resheader">
```

```xml
          <xsd:complexType>
            <xsd:sequence>
              <xsd:element name="value" type="xsd:string" minOccurs="0"
                                            msdata:Ordinal="1" />
            </xsd:sequence>
            <xsd:attribute name="name" type="xsd:string" use="required" />
          </xsd:complexType>
        </xsd:element>
      </xsd:choice>
    </xsd:complexType>
  </xsd:element>
</xsd:schema>
<data name="key 1">
  <value>First value</value>
</data>
<data name="key 2">
  <value>Second value</value>
</data>
<data name="key 3">
  <value>Third value</value>
</data>
<resheader name="ResMimeType">
  <value>text/microsoft-resx</value>
</resheader>
<resheader name="Version">
  <value>1.0.0.0</value>
</resheader>
<resheader name="Reader">
  <value>System.Resources.ResXResourceReader</value>
</resheader>
<resheader name="Writer">
  <value>System.Resources.ResXResourceWriter</value>
</resheader>
</root>
```

The actual XML resource data is at the end of the file. All the XSD tags refer to the XML schema data. The XSD schema is the validating code necessary to make sure that the XML data is proper. This file is heavy on the XSD code but in a resource file with thousands of strings, the XSD header code would soon get lost in XML data. XSD is an analog to the XML DTD.

I have said quite a few times that .resx files can contain pictures. Listing 5-8 shows the altered ResXResourceWriter code to reflect adding a JPG file. Be sure to include a reference to the System.Drawing dll.

Listing 5-8. Save a picture to a resource file

VB

```vb
Imports System
Imports System.Resources
Imports System.Drawing

Module Module1

    Sub Main()
        Dim RwX As New ResXResourceWriter("CH5Rwx.resx")
        Dim RrX As ResXResourceReader
        Dim RrXEn As IDictionaryEnumerator

        RwX.AddResource("key 1", "First value")
        RwX.AddResource("key 2", "Second value")
        RwX.AddResource("key 3", "Third value")

        'Add a picture to the file
        Dim img = Image.FromFile("crane.jpg")
        RwX.AddResource("crane", img)

        RwX.Generate()
        RwX.Close()

        RrX = New ResXResourceReader("CH5Rwx.resx")
        RrXEn = RrX.GetEnumerator
        Do While (RrXEn.MoveNext)
           Console.WriteLine("Name: {0} - Value: {1}", _
                    RrXEn.Key.ToString().PadRight(10, " "), _
                    RrXEn.Value)
        Loop
        RrX.Close()

        Console.ReadLine()
    End Sub

End Module
```

C#

```csharp
using System;
using System.Resources;
using System.Drawing;
using System.Collections;

namespace CH7ResourceWriter_C
{
    /// <summary>
    /// ResXResourceWriter and reader example
    /// </summary>
    class Class1
    {
        static void Main(string[] args)
        {
            ResXResourceWriter RwX = new ResXResourceWriter("CH7RwX.resx");

            RwX.AddResource("key 1", "First value");
            RwX.AddResource("key 2", "Second value");
            RwX.AddResource("key 3", "Third value");

            // add an image to the resource file
            Image img = Image.FromFile("crane.jpg");
            RwX.AddResource("crane.jpg", img);

            RwX.Generate();
            RwX.Close();

            ResXResourceReader RrX = new ResXResourceReader("CH7RwX.resx");
            IDictionaryEnumerator RrEn = RrX.GetEnumerator();
            while (RrEn.MoveNext())
            {
                Console.WriteLine("Name: {0} - Value: {1}",
                    RrEn.Key.ToString().PadRight(10, ' '),
                    RrEn.Value);
            }
            RrX.Close();

            Console.ReadLine();
        }
    }
}
```

I have imported the System.Drawing namespace and instantiated an internal image of a lock. I then added the lock to the resource file using the AddResource method. The Screen output is as follows:

```
Name: key 1 - Value: First value
Name: key 2 - Value: Second value
Name: key 3 - Value: Third value
Name: lock.bmp - Value: System.Drawing.Bitmap
```

The fourth resource is a bitmap. The actual .resX file is shown in Listing 5-9.

Listing 5-9. XML resource file with bitmap image

```xml
<?xml version="1.0" encoding="utf-8"?>
<root>
  <xsd:schema id="root" targetNamespace="" xmlns=""
 xmlns:xsd="http://www.w3.org/2001/XMLSchema" xmlns:msdata="urn:schemas-
                                         microsoft-com:xml-msdata">
    <xsd:element name="root" msdata:IsDataSet="true">
      <xsd:complexType>
        <xsd:choice maxOccurs="unbounded">
          <xsd:element name="data">
            <xsd:complexType>
              <xsd:sequence>
                <xsd:element name="value" type="xsd:string" minOccurs="0"
                          msdata:Ordinal="1" />
                <xsd:element name="comment" type="xsd:string" minOccurs="0"
                          msdata:Ordinal="2" />
              </xsd:sequence>
              <xsd:attribute name="name" type="xsd:string" />
              <xsd:attribute name="type" type="xsd:string" />
              <xsd:attribute name="mimetype" type="xsd:string" />
            </xsd:complexType>
          </xsd:element>
          <xsd:element name="resheader">
            <xsd:complexType>
              <xsd:sequence>
                <xsd:element name="value" type="xsd:string" minOccurs="0"
                                          msdata:Ordinal="1" />
              </xsd:sequence>
              <xsd:attribute name="name" type="xsd:string" use="required" />
            </xsd:complexType>
```

```
      </xsd:element>
    </xsd:choice>
  </xsd:complexType>
</xsd:element>
</xsd:schema>
<data name="key 1">
  <value>First value</value>
</data>
<data name="key 2">
  <value>Second value</value>
</data>
<data name="key 3">
  <value>Third value</value>
</data>
<data name="crane.jpg" mimetype="text/microsoft-urt/binary-serialized/base64">
  <value>
```
```
        AAEAAAD/////AQAAAAAAAAMAgAAAFRTeXN0ZWOuRHJhd2luZywgVmVyc2lvbjOxLjA
uMjQxMS4wLCBD
        dWx0dXJlPW5ldXRyYWwsIFB1YmxpYY0tleVRva2VuPWIwM2Y1ZjdmMTFkNTBhM2EFA
QAAABVTeXN0ZWOu
        RHJhd2luZy5CaXRtYYXABAAAABERhdGEHAgIAAAAJAwAAAA8DAAAANgMAAAJCTTYDA
AAAAAANgAAACgA
        AAAQAAAAEAAAAEAGAAAAAAAAAAAMQOAADEDgAAAAAAAAAAAAD///8AAP8AAP8AAP8
AAP8AAP8AAP8AAP8A
        AP8AAP8AAP8AAP8AAP////////////8AAP/AwMDAwMDAwMDAwMD
AwMDAwMDAwMDA
        wMAAAP////////////8AAP/AwMDAwMDAwMAAAP/AwMDAwMDAw
MDAwMAAAP/////////
        //////8AAP/AwMDAwMDAwMAAAP/AwMDAwMDAwMDAwMAAAP//////
//////////8AAP/AwMDA
        wMDAwMAAAP////8AAP/AwMDAwMDAwMAAAP////////////8AAP/AwMD
AwMDAwMAAAP8AAP8A
        AP/AwMDAwMDAwMAAAP////////////8AAP/AwMDAwMDAw
MDAwMDAwMDAwMDA
        wMAAAP////////////8AAP8AAP/AwMDAwMDAwMDAwMDAwMDAw
MAAAP8AAP/////////
        /////////8AAP8AAP8AAP8AAP8AAP8AAP8AAP8AAP8AAP////////////////
/////////8A
        AP8AAP/////////////8AAP8AAP///////////////////////////8AAP8AAP//
////////
        //////8AAP8AAP///////////////////////8AAP8AAP////////////////8A
AP8AAP//
        ///////////////////////////8AAP8AAP////////////8AAP8AAP////////////
///////
```

```
                ///////////////8AAP8AAP/////////8AAP8AAP//////////////////////////////
///////
                //////8AAP8AAP8AAP8AAP//////////////////////////////////////////////
/8AAP8A
                AP/////////////////////////////8L
</value>
   </data>
   <resheader name="ResMimeType">
     <value>text/microsoft-resx</value>
   </resheader>
   <resheader name="Version">
     <value>1.0.0.0</value>
   </resheader>
   <resheader name="Reader">
     <value>System.Resources.ResXResourceReader</value>
   </resheader>
   <resheader name="Writer">
     <value>System.Resources.ResXResourceWriter</value>
   </resheader>
</root>
```

You cannot only see the resource strings but you can now see the binary representation of a bitmap image. Pretty neat huh?

Summary

In this chapter I went over all the important classes and methods having to do with the System.Resources namespace. I included quite a bit of code here in the form of small examples for each class.

Next I went off the track a little and showed you how .NET arranges its namespaces. I used a reflection example to find some missing classes that should have appeared when I included the System.Resources namespace. We found out that .NET puts some classes in one assembly and some in another. This is an important point to think about. It means that in your designs you can also spread out classes belonging to a namespace among several assemblies to improve efficiency.

I also touched on the Threading namespace and looked at an XML resource file.

The next chapter goes over XML resource files in depth. It also goes over the different tools .NET provides to edit and manipulate resource files without using code.

CHAPTER 6

Resource File Tools

THIS CHAPTER IS DEVOTED to those tools that .NET provides to help edit and manipulate resource files without using code. Many of these tools are external to the IDE. They either require you to dig up old "DOS days" memories or to acquire new ones. It all depends on how old you are!

I also go into quite a bit of depth concerning XML resources. While this is not a book on XML, it is necessary that you understand the XML files that are generated by .NET and why they are necessary.

Resource Tools

There are a few tools that .NET provides to aid in handling resource files.

XML Designer in Visual Studio

Here is where I think most people will externalize their resource files. It's easy and the casual programmer never need know the files he or she creates are XML files.

To invoke this tool you need to be editing a resource file from within the VS IDE. Bring up a new project; either form-based or console-based. Go to the project window and add a new a new item of type "Assembly Resource File." Alternately, you can do this from the File/Add new menu selection. You are immediately taken into the XML designer in data view. Anytime you want to edit this file just double-click it and the XML designer will appear.

* "resource file"
* Project... Add, new

There are two views for this designer. One is the XML view and the other is the data view. The XML view includes color-coding, IntelliSense, word completion, and member lists. The data view is simple. Just type in the key, comment (if any), and value. There you go. Easy as pie.

OK, so there you are, happy as a clam inputting hundreds of strings into this resource file. It is time to translate the strings. What now? Try sending the .resX file to a translation service. It is not the best format for translating strings. Not only that, but what about pictures and sounds, and so on? The XML designer does not even allow you to input objects.

The XML designer is okay for simple programs but becomes woefully inadequate for large ones. You are better off making your own resource file editor. You do just that in the next chapter.

The XML designer is not just there for resource files. It is there as an aid in developing XSD schemas and XML documents. It has a great design and layout facility for creating schemas and editing data sets. This is where it really shines. I could go much further into this aspect of XML in .NET but I promised I would focus on the resource file aspects.

ResGen.exe

ResGen is a great utility. It allows you to take a resource file in any of its three forms and translate it to any of the other three forms. You can do the following:

- Convert a .txt resource file into a .resources file

- Convert a .txt file into a .resx file

- Convert a .resx file into a .resources file

- Convert a .resx file into a .txt file

- Convert a .resources file into a .resx file

- Convert a .resources file into a .txt file

ResGen is a must-use utility. To embed a resource file into an assembly or into a satellite resource file you must first convert it from one of the text forms to the binary .resources form.

ResGen also takes as a command line argument, the /Compile switch. This allows ResGen to do batch processing. You can put in any number of *.txt or *.resx files and it processes each in turn. Table 6-1 shows a matrix of ResGen uses.

Table 6-1. ResGen Uses

COMMAND LINE	DESCRIPTION
Resgen myres.txt	Compiles myres.txt into myres.resources
Resgen myres.txt mybinaryres.resources	Compiles myres.txt into mybinaryres.resources
Resgen myres.txt myresx.resx	Converts myres.txt into myresx.resx XML file
Resgen myxres.resx	Compiles myxres.resx into myxres.resources
Resgen myxres.resx mybinaryres.resources	Compiles myxres.txt into mybinaryres.resources
Resgen myxres.resx myres.txt	Converts myxres.resx into myres.txt text file
Resgen mybinaryres.resources myres.txt	Converts mybinaryres.resources into myres.txt text file
Resgen mybinaryres.resources myxres.resx	Converts mybinaryres.resources into myxres.resx
Resgen /compile res1.txt res2.txt res3.txt	Compiles all res files into separate .resources files

ResGen Caveats

- Compiling from a text file to .resources file loses all your comments. This means that converting from a .resources file to a text file leaves you with your data only.

- Converting a text resource file to an XML resource file also loses the comments.

- Place a comment on its own line. Comments tacked on the end of a resource line make the ResGen compiler think it is part of the string text.

- Converting a .resources file to a text file gives a text representation of any objects such as pictures, and so on. This means that you cannot reverse this process and reconvert to a .resources file. The text file output will have an entry stating what the picture and its type was. The data will not be converted.

The following entries illustrate how to write a text-based resource file.

```
STR_ONE = one
STR_two = two
Str_three = three
;This is a legal comment line
str_4 = four;This comment is taken to be part of the string value
str5 = "String five"
```

The ResGen compiler happily compiles this file to a .resources file. The only problem is that it believes everything after the = sign on the str_4 line is the actual string.

Al.exe

This is the assembly generation tool. It has only one use as far as resource files go.

- Generate a satellite assembly out of a resource file.

Remember the satellite assembly? This is the binary .resources file compiled into a separate DLL. The binary resource file should have the following name convention: <basename>.<culture>.resources. These satellite DLLs should be put in their proper directories for the resource fallback mechanism to work.

There are quite a few options for the Al tool. I'll go over how to use this tool to embed resource files into satellite resource files.

The following is a way to make a satellite resource file that can be used in a resource fallback scheme.

```
Al /out:Myprog.Resources.DLL /v:1.2.3.4 /c:es-ES /embed:MyStrings.es-
ES.resources,MyStrings.es-ES.resources,private
```

- /out: Specifies the output satellite file

- /v: Specifies the version of this assembly

- /c: This is the internal culture identifier

- /embed: <file>,<name><file> is the name of the file that is getting embedded. <name> is the internal identifier for the resource

- private This specifies that the resource is not visible to other assemblies.

The following use is also legal. The missing options are all defaulted.

```
Al /out:MyprogRes.dll /embed:MyprogRes.resources
```

Note that the Al tool only takes a binary resource file as an argument. It cannot make a DLL out of a text file or an XML file.

Embedding

What about embedding a resource file directly into the executable? Why should you use embedding again? It is best practice to embed a culture-invariant resource file in the program executable. This allows for resource fallback. If you have a small program that you are not translating, the embedded resource file could also serve as the only resource file. This makes for a simpler installation. You can embed a resource file into an executable using the command line compiler.

Here is a sample used to generate a C# program with an embedded resource file:

```
csc /target:winexe /out:Myprog.exe /res:MyStrings.resources Myprog.cs
```

The csc compiler can also be used to generate a VB program with an embedded resource file.

```
csc /target:winexe /out:Myprog.exe /res:MyStrings.resources Myprog.vb
```

Here is a scenario. You have a large program written in VB that also has a large string resource file. Perhaps it has a few hundred strings. Your boss has just told you to convert the program to VB.NET. What do you do about the resource file? Do you chuck it? Do it over? Well it just so happens that the Al.exe tool will also build a satellite assembly out of a Win32 resource file. This is the file you create using Visual Studio V 5 or V 6. The Win32 resource text file has the extension of .rc and the compiled resource file has the extension of .res. Here is the command to compile a .res file into a .NET satellite DLL.

```
Al /embed:MyStrings.res /win32res:MyStrings.res
```

Keep in mind what I went through in Chapter 5. To reference these resources in this file you need to use numbers.

The intricacies of the Al.exe tool and the csc.exe tool are beyond the scope of this book. What I have explained here is the most basic use. But I want to remind you of something about compiling .NET code. Perhaps you did not know this.

The Visual Studio .NET IDE compiles only single-file assemblies. In order to create multifile assemblies you need to resort to DOS and use the command line Al.exe or csc.exe compilers. The command line csc.exe compiler can be used to create the individual assemblies and the Al.exe tool can be used to create a manifest that contains all references to external modules.

I strongly encourage you to read and understand the documentation concerning the command line compilers. If you want to do any kind of sophisticated compiling and linking you will need to use them.

NOTE   *It seems to me that we have come full circle here. I have been programming long enough to remember using command line compilers and linkers with long lists of .obj files to be linked in. The past several years have been spent inside the IDE. It is now necessary to go outside the IDE to the command line to do any sophisticated compiling and linking. This after Microsoft has been trying to hide the DOS box from the casual user.*

IDE Forms Designer

Here is an interesting way to design a localized program. It is possible using the IDE in either C# or in VB to create a form for each language you want your program to run in. The IDE does all the work for you insofar as making resource files and satellite assemblies and putting them in all in their correct directories.

This process involves changing some of the forms' properties at design time and typing in your translations. In a complex form with many controls, this can be quite the time-consuming and error-prone task.

I will say this, however, for the IDE designer approach. It may be the best way to achieve a form that looks like it was written in the target language. This is because for each language you are able to move and resize the controls on the form. No longer do your controls have to be much larger than necessary to accommodate possibly longer translated strings. They can all be just the right size for the particular languages needs. This is pretty neat if you ask me.

Start up a Windows Forms project in either C# or VB. and click the form itself. Look at the properties box. You should see something like what you see in Figure 6-1.

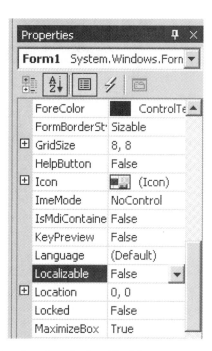

Figure 6-1. Form properties showing the localizable property

The two properties we are interested in are the localizable and the language properties.

If we want to start this process we need to change the localizable property from false to true. The language property is by default; default. What this means is that the resource file that gets generated is the culture-invariant resource file for this project. This form resource file is created if you use localization or not.

You may wonder if you can see this resource file. Yes, you can. Go into the Solution Explorer pane and turn on "Show all files." You should now see what is shown in Figure 6-2.

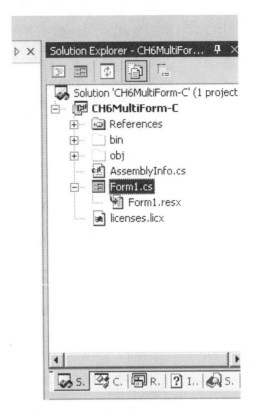

Figure 6-2. Click "Show All Files" to see the localized form resource

As you can see, the file generated is Form1.resx. This an XML-based resource file. You see what is inside in a little while. First, expand the references node in this pane. See anything interesting? I am talking about the reference to the System.Windows.Forms dll. Of course you cannot get a form on the screen without this dll but remember also that it contains the ResXResourceWriter, ResXResourceReader, and other ResXnnn classes. These are the classes in the System.Resources namespace that are necessary to write XML based resource files.

Are you starting to understand a little of how .NET was put together?

Back at the ranch . . . Drag a control; let's say a label onto the form. Drag a few more controls on the form. Enter text values for all these controls. Here is what I placed on my form shown in Figure 6-3.

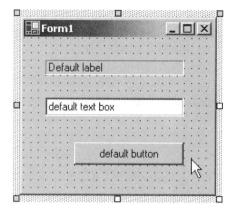

Figure 6-3. Basic form with some controls to show localization

Not much here but there is enough to continue. Click the form again and change the language property to Azeri (Cyrillic)(Azerbaijan). Look in the Solution Explorer and you should see two more resource files. They are shown in Figure 6-4.

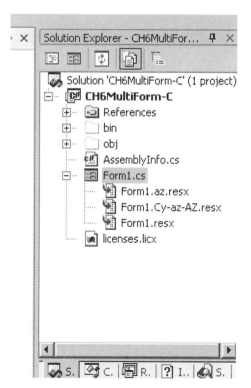

Figure 6-4. All localized forms shown for this example

See how they are named? They are named according to the culture and region. Now go ahead and change the text in the controls to some thing else that identifies the form. Here is what I have in Figure 6-5.

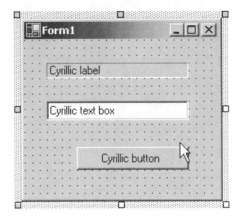

Figure 6-5. Cyrillic form with text to identify it as such

Now is a good time to save and compile your program. This is so cookie cutter that you should have no errors. You have yet to type any code! Okay so now is the time to go answer that question that has been burning in your mind. Why were two resources files generated when I changed languages in the form, and what is in them?

A Look at IDE-Generated Resource Files

Go into the Windows Explorer and find the resource file named Form1.az-AZ-Cyrl.resx. Open this file with notepad or a similar text editor. Listing 6-1 is what you should see.

Listing 6-1. Incremental form resource file

```
<?xml version="1.0" encoding="utf-8"?>
<root>
  <xsd:schema id="root" targetNamespace="" xmlns=""
  xmlns:xsd="http://www.w3.org/2001/XMLSchema" xmlns:msdata=
  "urn:schemas-microsoft-com:xml-msdata">
    <xsd:element name="root" msdata:IsDataSet="true">
      <xsd:complexType>
        <xsd:choice maxOccurs="unbounded">
```

```
        <xsd:element name="data">
          <xsd:complexType>
            <xsd:sequence>
              <xsd:element name="value" type="xsd:string" minOccurs="0"
                msdata:Ordinal="1" />
              <xsd:element name="comment" type="xsd:string" minOccurs="0"
                msdata:Ordinal="2" />
            </xsd:sequence>
            <xsd:attribute name="name" type="xsd:string" />
            <xsd:attribute name="type" type="xsd:string" />
            <xsd:attribute name="mimetype" type="xsd:string" />
          </xsd:complexType>
        </xsd:element>
        <xsd:element name="resheader">
          <xsd:complexType>
            <xsd:sequence>
              <xsd:element name="value" type="xsd:string" minOccurs="0"
                msdata:Ordinal="1" />
            </xsd:sequence>
            <xsd:attribute name="name" type="xsd:string" use="required" />
          </xsd:complexType>
        </xsd:element>
      </xsd:choice>
    </xsd:complexType>
  </xsd:element>
</xsd:schema>
<data name="label1.ImeMode" type="System.Windows.Forms.ImeMode,
      System.Windows.Forms">
  <value>NoControl</value>
</data>
<data name="label1.Text">
  <value>Cyrillic label</value>
</data>
<data name="textBox1.Text">
  <value>Cyrillic text box</value>
</data>
<data name="button1.ImeMode" type="System.Windows.Forms.ImeMode,
 System.Windows.Forms">
  <value>NoControl</value>
</data>
<data name="button1.Text">
  <value>Cyrillic button</value>
</data>
```

```
<resheader name="ResMimeType">
  <value>text/microsoft-resx</value>
</resheader>
<resheader name="Version">
  <value>1.0.0.0</value>
</resheader>
<resheader name="Reader">
  <value>System.Resources.ResXResourceReader</value>
</resheader>
<resheader name="Writer">
  <value>System.Resources.ResXResourceWriter</value>
</resheader>
</root>
```

First, notice that it starts out with XSD schema commands that define the data that follows. Next notice that some of the properties of all the forms' constituent controls are in here. These properties relate to what you have done to localize this form. So far you see just the text changes you made. Later you will make some other positional changes and revisit this file.

One important thing to note here is that this resource file is an incremental change file from the base form. Open up the form1.resx file in another instance of notepad. See that it is much larger. It contains everything having to do with the form including a binary representation of the form's icon. Including it here would add too much weight to the book. And this is a small resource file! The size of this file and what is—or is not—in it will be important to remember when you get to the WinRes.exe tool. Stay tuned!

Go back to the project and make the button the same size as the other controls on the form. You should still be in the Cyrillic form. Here is what you should see in Figure 6-6.

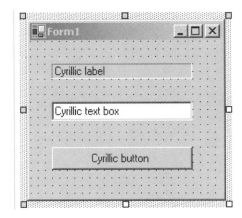

Figure 6-6. Cyrillic form showing different button size

Save and recompile your code. Here is the cool part. Open up the Form1.az-AZ-Cyrl.resx file again. Notice any differences? Listing 6-2 is mine.

Listing 6-2. Incremental form resource file with changes

```
<?xml version="1.0" encoding="utf-8"?>
<root>
  <xsd:schema id="root" targetNamespace="" xmlns=""
  xmlns:xsd="http://www.w3.org/2001/XMLSchema" xmlns:msdata=
   "urn:schemas-microsoft.com:xml-msdata">
    <xsd:element name="root" msdata:IsDataSet="true">
      <xsd:complexType>
        <xsd:choice maxOccurs="unbounded">
          <xsd:element name="data">
            <xsd:complexType>
              <xsd:sequence>
                <xsd:element name="value" type="xsd:string" minOccurs="0"
                                         msdata:Ordinal="1" />
                <xsd:element name="comment" type="xsd:string" minOccurs="0"
                                         msdata:Ordinal="2" />
              </xsd:sequence>
              <xsd:attribute name="name" type="xsd:string" />
              <xsd:attribute name="type" type="xsd:string" />
              <xsd:attribute name="mimetype" type="xsd:string" />
            </xsd:complexType>
          </xsd:element>
          <xsd:element name="resheader">
            <xsd:complexType>
              <xsd:sequence>
                <xsd:element name="value" type="xsd:string" minOccurs="0"
                                          msdata:Ordinal="1" />
              </xsd:sequence>
              <xsd:attribute name="name" type="xsd:string" use="required" />
            </xsd:complexType>
          </xsd:element>
        </xsd:choice>
      </xsd:complexType>
    </xsd:element>
  </xsd:schema>
  <data name="label1.ImeMode" type="System.Windows.Forms.ImeMode,
                                 System.Windows.Forms">
    <value>NoControl</value>
  </data>
```

```
<data name="label1.Text">
  <value>Cyrillic label</value>
</data>
<data name="textBox1.Text">
  <value>Cyrillic text box</value>
</data>
<data name="button1.ImeMode" type="System.Windows.Forms.ImeMode,
                                    System.Windows.Forms">
  <value>NoControl</value>
</data>
<data name="button1.Location" type="System.Drawing.Point, System.Drawing">
  <value>24, 112</value>
</data>
<data name="button1.Size" type="System.Drawing.Size, System.Drawing">
  <value>152, 24</value>
</data>
<data name="button1.Text">
  <value>Cyrillic button</value>
</data>
<resheader name="ResMimeType">
  <value>text/microsoft-resx</value>
</resheader>
<resheader name="Version">
  <value>1.0.0.0</value>
</resheader>
<resheader name="Reader">
  <value>System.Resources.ResXResourceReader</value>
</resheader>
<resheader name="Writer">
  <value>System.Resources.ResXResourceWriter</value>
</resheader>
</root>
```

You see a few more lines this time. Now that you changed the size of the button from that of the original form, you get size and positional information in the resource file. As you can see, these files are only as big as they need to be.

Click the form and change the language back and forth from the Cyrillic to the default. See the form change? You now effectively have two forms.

Second Resource File

I told you I would explain both resource files. The second one was made when you originally changed the form to Cyrillic and is called Form1.az.resx. Open this form with Notepad. What do you see? It is empty. Why? It has the name of a language-only resource file. No region is included in the name of the file. This leads me to believe that it was created as a string resource file for your program. Being empty however is puzzling. It should at least have the necessary XSD information so it can be edited with the XML editor. Well, I am using the Beta2 CD for this book and I can only hope that this file will be properly formed in the release version. By the way, if you try another nonregionalized language such as German you will not get the second resx file.

It is time to see your program at work. Press F5 and start the program. You will see the original default form show up. Close the program and open your code pane.

If you have made this program in C# put the following lines at the top of your code.

```
using System.Threading;
using System.Globalization;
```

Now type the following line of code in the form1 section just before the "InitializeComponent();" line.

```
Thread.CurrentThread.CurrentUICulture=new CultureInfo("az-AZ-Cyrl");
```

If you have made this program in VB put the following lines at the top of your code.

```
Imports System.Threading
Imports System.Globalization
```

Now type the following line of code in the New function just before the "InitializeComponent" line.

```
Thread.CurrentThread.CurrentUICulture=new CultureInfo("az-AZ-Cyrl")
```

Now run your program again. You should see the Cyrillic version of your form appear. Comment out this "Thread" line, run the program again and you should be back to the default form.

Well, this was easy enough. You made a small program that had two different versions of the same form. You saw that the controls on each form could be resized and even moved around. If you took a peek in the forms resource file to see what was going on in there and you saw that .NET makes a base resource file for the form and subsequent incremental form resource files for each language you choose.

Let's take a last peek at the program you just made. Go into the forms code and expand the Windows Form Designer generated code section. Take a look at the code in the InitializeComponent method. This method makes a ResourceManager and goes out to the resource file and gets all the information pertaining to the form. Notice the one thing that does not get saved to the resource file. The name of each control is hard coded. Go back to the form and change the forecolor of one of the controls. Rebuild the project and look at this section of code again. You will see that the color of the control is now also hard coded. There are obviously some things that you are not allowed to externalize in a resource file. Listing 6-3 shows some of this code.

Listing 6-3. Windows generated code to retreive resources

C#

```
#region Windows Form Designer generated code
/// <summary>
/// Required method for Designer support - do not modify
/// the contents of this method with the code editor.
/// </summary>
private void InitializeComponent()
{
System.Resources.ResourceManager resources = new
System.Resources.ResourceManager(typeof(Form1));
this.label1 = new System.Windows.Forms.Label();
this.textBox1 = new System.Windows.Forms.TextBox();
this.button1 = new System.Windows.Forms.Button();
this.SuspendLayout();
//
// label1
//
this.label1.AccessibleDescription =
  ((string)(resources.GetObject("label1.AccessibleDescription")));
this.label1.AccessibleName =
 ((string)(resources.GetObject("label1.AccessibleName")));
this.label1.Anchor =
(System.Windows.Forms.AnchorStyles)(resources.GetObject("label1.Anchor")));
        this.label1.AutoSize = ((bool)(resources.GetObject("label1.AutoSize")));
        this.label1.BorderStyle = System.Windows.Forms.BorderStyle.Fixed3D;
```

```
        this.label1.Cursor =
((System.Windows.Forms.Cursor)(resources.GetObject("label1.Cursor")));
        this.label1.Dock =
((System.Windows.Forms.DockStyle)(resources.GetObject("label1.Dock")));
        this.label1.Enabled = ((bool)(resources.GetObject("label1.Enabled")));
        this.label1.Font =
((System.Drawing.Font)(resources.GetObject("label1.Font")));
        this.label1.ForeColor = System.Drawing.Color.Red;
        this.label1.Image =
((System.Drawing.Image)(resources.GetObject("label1.Image")));
        this.label1.ImageAlign =
((System.Drawing.ContentAlignment)(resources.GetObject("label1.ImageAlign")));
        this.label1.ImageIndex =
((int)(resources.GetObject("label1.ImageIndex")));
        this.label1.ImeMode =
((System.Windows.Forms.ImeMode)(resources.GetObject("label1.ImeMode")));
        this.label1.Location =
((System.Drawing.Point)(resources.GetObject("label1.Location")));
        this.label1.Name = "label1";
        this.label1.RightToLeft =
((System.Windows.Forms.RightToLeft)(resources.GetObject("label1.RightToLeft")));
        this.label1.Size =
((System.Drawing.Size)(resources.GetObject("label1.Size")));
        this.label1.TabIndex = ((int)(resources.GetObject("label1.TabIndex")));
        this.label1.Text = resources.GetString("label1.Text");
        this.label1.TextAlign =
((System.Drawing.ContentAlignment)(resources.GetObject("label1.TextAlign")));
        this.label1.Visible = ((bool)(resources.GetObject("label1.Visible")));
        this.label1.Click += new System.EventHandler(this.label1_Click);
        //
. . .
```

This is a very powerful way to localize your program at the design stage. However, it soon gets unwieldy when you have many forms with many controls running under many languages. It is virtually impossible to manage and localize any kind of large program in this manner. .NET does provide a tool to help localize the forms themselves. This tool is not much better than using the IDE. The tool is called WinRes.exe.

A list of some IDE designer caveats follows:

- The same controls must be on all versions of the form.

- Several properties of the constituent controls are global to all versions of the form.

- All text must be typed by hand into each control on the form

- Incremental form resource files based on language cannot be edited by WinRes.exe.

WinRes.exe

This program is an adjunct to the IDE forms designer. I stated that using the forms designer would be tedious and error prone for the developer to use. This program allows that burden to be put upon the transition service. Is this better? I revisit this question at the end of the section.

WinRes.exe takes as an argument any .NET resource file except for a .txt file. The reason it does not take a text file is that this is a form resource editor. As you recall text-based resource files contain only strings. No objects are allowed. You can either supply a command argument to WinRes or you can open a resource file from within WinRes. Your choice.

NOTE *WinRes is a program that requires certain environment variables to be set if used from the command line. When in DOS you must run the Corvars.bat program located in <drive>:\ProgramFiles\Microsoft.NET\ FrameworkSDK\Bin. You can also use Windows Explorer to go to this directory and double-click directly in WinRes.exe to start it.*

Let's start with the IDE forms example you just finished. I'll do this the easy way.

1. Find WinRes.exe (in <drive>:\Program Files\Microsoft.NET \FrameworkSDK\Bin).

2. Drag a shortcut to this program on your desktop.

3. Open the folder that has your last program—the one for the IDE forms designer.

4. You should now see the forms resource files that pertain to the program. My folder looks like what you see in Figure 6-7.

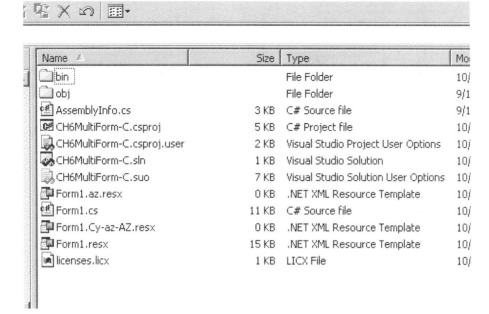

Figure 6-7. Explorer listing showing all resource file forms

Open each of the resx files in turn. First, open the Form1.resx file by dragging it on top of the shortcut to Winres program. The Winres program contains a visual designer and a properties window. Figure 6-8 shows what you should see.

Figure 6-8. WinRes editor screen

What is most noticeable is not what is here but what is missing. Try deleting any of the components on the form. Try right-clicking any of the components. Nothing happening? That is the whole point. The WinRes editor is designed as a tool for the localizer. It is meant as an editing tool only.

The Visual Studio IDE allows you to create any number of forms with any number of controls and abstract them from your code by externalizing the parameters in an XML resource file. The WinRes.exe program allows you to edit these forms by changing certain properties without ever needing access to the original source code. It does not allow the editor to remove or add any controls.

You can think of this tool as a way to externalize what you did in the IDE forms designer example. Inside the IDE you were able to move and resize some of the controls. You were also able to change the displayed text. You are able to do the same thing with this WinRes tool.

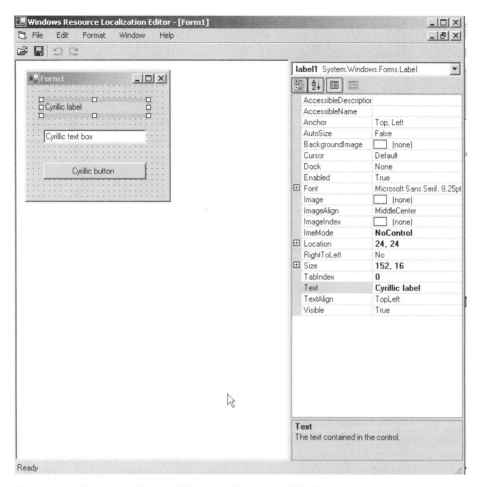

Figure 6-9. Using the WinResEditor to edit the Cyrillic form

Change the size of the button to match that of the text box and label. Now replace the text in these controls with the text we had in the Cyrillic controls from the last example. You should end up with a screen that looks like Figure 6-9.

Now save the file to a different name but in the same directory as Form1.resx. Save it as Form1.az.resx. Open this file with notepad and compare it with the Form1.resx file. You will see that they are identical in content but with some of the properties changed.

Notice that the new resource file is not an incrementally changed resource file like the Cyrillic one that was created by the IDE forms designer. You now have a twin of the original file.

OK, I know you have been dying to do this. Open the incremental form resource file that you created with the IDE forms designer. It is called Form1.az-AZ-Cyrl.resx. How does it look to you? That's right you get an error.

There is not enough information in this file to create the whole form. Remember that this resource file only captures the differences between forms.

Now that we have gone through this WinRes tool you must be wondering what you can really do with it. It is not really a tool for the developer so much as it is a tool for the localization service. It allows you to make a form and have the form itself localized visually without sending out any code. While this is really neat, and it works well, it still suffers from the same problems I mentioned while working in the IDE forms designer. The problem is the tediousness of translation and inputting all the correct strings directly into the form. All you have done is transfer this problem to the translator. It does have the advantage, however, of being able to get a form back from the translation service whose controls are all sized and placed according to the language. You need to weigh the pros and cons of using this tool as opposed to using a straight string file and a resource manager.

Design Issue

Before we begin a working program I need to tell you a pet peeve of mine—a lack of good design. I began my software career writing C code for embedded systems, some that I designed even. (I started out life not as a programmer but as an electrical engineer). Anyway, I gravitated to the DOS world and have been programming in Windows since the start. I have done quite a few projects in C++ and have written several controls in ATL.

When I discovered VB at Version 5 I was amazed at how easy it was to write complex Windows code in such a short time. No longer did I need to write lots of arcane code just to have a window show up. I could concentrate on the code that actually did the work. Visual Basic was a great time saver for me and other programmers. However, like they say, what is good for the goose is good for the gander.

Visual Basic became the great enabler. All of a sudden managers found out that they need not wait for IT to assign a programmer to a task. Visual Basic was so easy to use they could get a nonprogrammer to write something up "real quick." "Honest it's just a demo!" "It will never make it to the public!" How often have we heard that one?

After a while, people who were not trained as programmers found they could do an OK job at it and they became VB programmers. What was missing was the thought process behind many of these programs. Design took a back seat to expediency and therefore maintenance and extendibility suffered.

I have been involved in many language retrofit projects. Some have been easy and some have taken months. It is much harder to go back and internationalize a program that was never designed for that option. Often whole screens have to be changed around. Quite a bit of code must be touched. No matter how careful you are you introduce new bugs. A program that was debugged and working perfectly could go through the localization process and wind up not working as it did before.

Upfront design is the key. As far as multilanguage programs go, do your homework first and design your program with this in mind. These days I never write a production program without designing in multilanguage capability. If Marketing says it will only be sold here it will be back in a year asking how long it will take to make it so it works in Brazil. If you have designed it correctly you can whine and say six weeks and then be the hero and do it in two days. If you have done it right you may not even have to recompile the code!

.NET was designed up front to make localization easy and complete. Make sure your design takes advantage of this work.

Summary

Here you went over the tools provided by .NET to manage resource files internally and externally to the IDE. These tools do not require writing any code. These tools are:

- XML Designer in Visual Studio. This tool allows you to generate and edit a string resource file for your program. The output of this tool is a binary .resources file. Objects such as pictures are not allowed in this tool.

- ResGen.exe. This tool allows you to convert a resource file between any of its three forms. The forms are .txt, .resx, and .resources.

- Al.exe. This tool compiles binary resource files into satellite assemblies.

- CSC.exe. This tool compiles .NET code into executables and also embeds a resource file into that executable.

- IDE forms designer. This tool allows the programmer to edit a program's form of visual localization and generate new forms for new cultures. This is a form of visual localization. He or she can then type in new translated text in the different forms and they will be displayed according to the current culture.

- WinRes.exe. This is a tool for the localizer. A programmer can create a Windows Form and send the resulting XML form resource file to a localizer. The localizer can translate text and rearrange controls on the forms to conform to the localized text.

Next I take you through an example that uses all the knowledge gained so far to make a localized resource editor. Chapter 7 is dedicated to making the editor and Chapter 8 is dedicated to localizing it.

Resource Editor Example

THIS CHAPTER IS WHERE YOU get down to brass tacks and write a resource editor. So far you have read (hopefully not waded) through quite a bit of explanation of the classes that make up the .NET globalization features. If you did not know too much about localizing software in general, perhaps you also learned something new on that subject.

Now it is time to put all that newfound knowledge to work while you still remember it. Together we write a Windows Forms resource editor application. As is the case with the rest of this book, I show you the code in both VB and C#.

When I started out thinking about a good example, a resource editor was the first one I came up with. At the time I thought it would be both applicable and useful to have a program like this. Having written the first six chapters of this book I find it even more so.

VS .NET has a few resource editors. They are reviewed in Table 7-1 and presented along with some of their shortcomings.

Table 7-1. Resource Editors in .NET

PROGRAM	NOTES
Windows IDE resource editor	Cannot enter graphics; only outputs XML, which is not good for translator.
Windows Forms designer	OK for small projects but gets unwieldy fast
Notepad	Only good for text-based resource files. Text-based resource files contain no graphics.

The resource editor I show you has the following capabilities:

- Tabbed pages to separate text resources and graphics resources.

- Grid control to view/edit/enter text resources.

- List view of graphical resources. Both keys and thumbnail pictures are shown.

- Input of any graphics file. Supports bmp, gif, jpg, and tif.

- Will read any size resource file in any of the three .NET resource file formats.

- Will read any number of resource files for single combination later.

- Build a new resource file name from supplied cultures.

- Output resources to any or all three resource file formats.

The ability to output a direct text resource file from input from an XML or binary resource file is important. This text format is easily handled by third-party translation services. Once the text resources are translated, you can use this tool to recombine the separate graphics and text resources back into a binary or XML resource file.

The program I show you here is quite involved. To make a sophisticated tool like this you need to use quite a bit of the .NET framework. This example is excellent for anyone interested in writing applications for .NET. Even if you have no interest in localization (although you should) this chapter shows you how to write a Windows application using most of the controls you are used to. Here is a list of some of what you see in the code in this chapter.

- Windows Forms

- Dialog boxes, modal dialogs, and dialog result codes

- Picture box controls

- Text and label controls, tabbed dialog controls, menus, frames, list boxes, check boxes, and buttons

- Class design—overloaded constructors, read/write/read-only properties, and nested classes

- Enums and constants

- Working with images

- File I/O

- Adding to the wizard-generated code

- Try-Catch exception handling

- User-defined exception class

- Single delegate for multiple events

- Delegate renaming

- Controls placed on forms at run time including: control arrays, and control positioning

- Grid control including: disconnected data sets in memory, table styles and collections, column styles and collections, filling in data table rows, and attaching data table to grid

- Using namespaces and aliases

- Calling VB 6 methods from C# and VB .NET

- CultureInfo class

- System.Resources namespace including: reading and writing XML, text, and binary resource files

As you can see, you are in for an in-depth discussion of localization and .NET programming in general. The next chapter takes the program you create here and globalize it. You use this program to generate resource files for itself!

Let's get started!

Starting the Project

As I've stated, this project will be written in VB and in C#. Since the VB code is a little easier to understand and not quite as complex as the C# code, I start out in VB .NET.

This project is a good illustration of the differences between the two languages. There are some basic differences in how you do things in C# as opposed to VB. Well, enough said. If you are anxious to see the C# version, hold on a bit; you'll get there.

Start up Visual Studio .NET and choose a VB Windows Forms project. Call it ResEditor.

You should have a single form on your screen. Before you get into writing code, the first order of business is to make all the forms and modules necessary for this project. These steps should help you along the way.

1. Rename the default form to frmResources.vb.

2. Add a new Windows Form called AskKey.vb.

3. Add a module called Consts.vb.

4. Add a class file called ResUtil.vb.

You now have all the files needed for this project. Build the project and .NET will add a few files of its own for you. If you are typing in the code this may also be the only time your program will compile the first time without errors. Figure 7-1 shows what the solution window should look like.

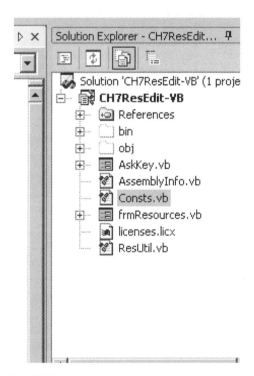

Figure 7-1. Solution with all files

To see all these files in Figure 7-1 click the "Show All Files" button on the Solution window.

Bring up the frmResources form and resize it to 824x504. Next go over to your toolbox and put the following controls on this form:

- Tab control. Name it tcResources. Size it to fit in the form. See Figure 7-5.

- Button. Name it cmdQuit.

- Status bar. Name it sbStatus and make sure that the "Show Panels" property is set to true.

- MainMenu control.

- Open File dialog. Name it OpenResFile.

Click the tab control and open the tab pages collection property. Add three tab pages. You should see the screen shown in Figure 7-2.

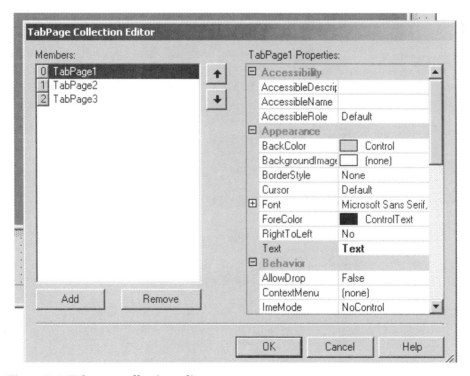

Figure 7-2. Tab page collection editor

The Text property for these pages should be "Text," "Pictures," and "Final. . ." respectively. Click OK to accept this. Next change the text property on the button to "Quit."

Click the status bar control and open the panels Collection property. Add three panels. You should see the screen shown in Figure 7-3.

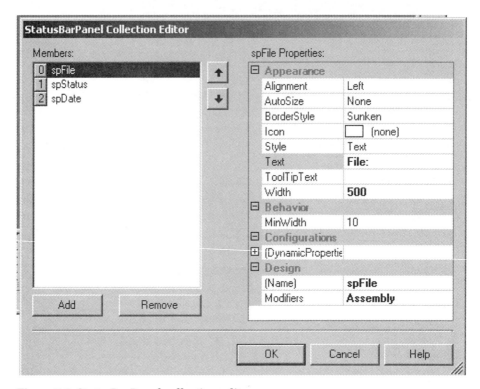

Figure 7-3. StatusBarPanel collection editor

The panels should be named spFile, spStatus, and spDate. Their text properties should be set to "File:," "Status:," and "Date:" respectively. Click OK to accept this.

Next, edit the menu and type the menu items as shown in Figure 7-4.

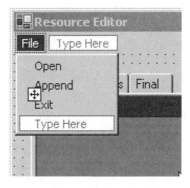

Figure 7-4. Menu items for the resource editor

Now you need to add a DataGrid control to the first page of the tab control. Drag this control from the toolbox and place it on the tab control's first page. This is the tab marked "Text." Set the grid controls Dock property to "Fill." This stretches the DataGrid control to fit the inside of the tab page. Rename this control dgStrings. You should now have a form that looks like the one shown in Figure 7-5.

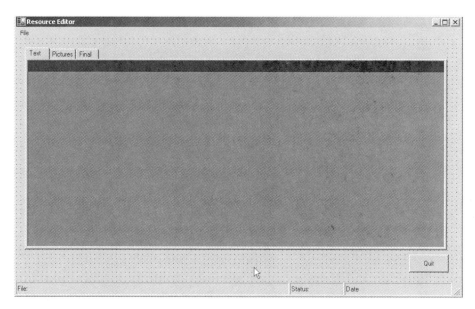

Figure 7-5. Complete ResEditor form showing the first tab

Now that you have the first tab page done, let's put the controls you need on the other tab pages as well. Click the second tab page (Pictures) and add the following controls with their properties changed as indicated:

- List box. Name it lstPictures.

- Button. Name it cmdAddPic. Text is "Add."

- Button. Name it cmdDelPic. Text is "Remove."

- PictureBox. Name it "pic" and change its BorderStyle to Fixed3D. I changed the back color to something other than gray so I could see it.

- Panel. Name it "PicPanel" and change its BorderStyle to Fixed3D.

- Two labels. Change the Text properties to "Key" and "Pictures" respectively. Center the text in each label.

Rearrange the screen to look like mine, as shown in Figure 7-6.

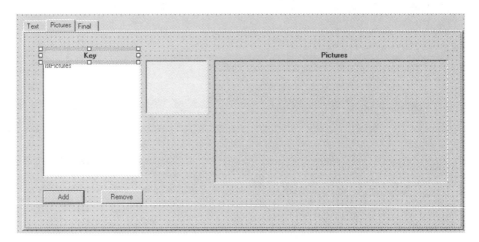

Figure 7-6. Pictures tab with all controls in place

Now you do the final tab page. There are quite a few controls on this page and their arrangement is important to the information flow. Place the following controls on the screen in the following order. Figure 7-7 shows the arrangement on the screen.

- Listbox. Name it lstCultures.

- Label. Change Text property to "Cultures" and center the text.

- GroupBox. Change Text property to "Basics."

- Label. Place it inside the Basics group box. Clear the Text property and set border to 3D. Name it lblInFilename.

- Label. Place it inside the Basics group box. Clear the Text property and set border to 3D. Name it lblResStringNum.

- Label. Place it inside the Basics group box. Clear the Text property and set border to 3D. Name it lblNumPics.

- Label. Place it inside the Basics group box. Text property is "Input File Name." Center the text.

- Label. Place it inside the Basics group box. Text property is "String Count." Center the text.

- Label. Place it inside the Basics group box. Text property is "Picture Count." Center the text.

- GroupBox. Place it on the tab. Text property is "Build Output File(s)."

- Button. Place inside "Output" group box. Name it cmdSave. Text is "Save."

- Label. Place inside "Output" group box. Text property is "Base Name."

- TextBox. Place inside "Output" group box. Name it txtBaseName. Text is cleared.

- CheckBox. Place inside "Output" group box. Name it chkCreateText. Text is "Create Text file for translator."

- CheckBox. Place inside "Output" group box. Name it chkCreateXML. Text is "Create XML Resource File."

- CheckBox. Place inside "Output" group box. Name it chkCreateBin. Text is "Create Binary Resource File."

- Label. Place inside the "Output" group box. Name it lblTxtFname. Text property is cleared. Set the border to 3D. Place the label below the chkCreateText check box control.

- Label. Place inside the "Output" group box. Name it lblXMLFname. Text property is cleared. Set the border to 3D. Place the label below the chkCreateXML check box control.

- Label. Place inside the "Output" group box. Name it lblBinFname. Text property is cleared. Set the border to 3D. Place the label below the chkCreateBin check box control.

Now that you have all the controls on the final tab screen, your screen should look something like mine (Figure 7-7).

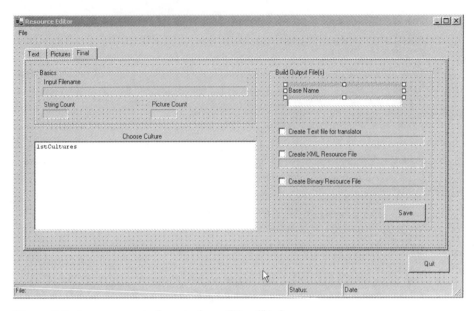

Figure 7-7. Arrangement of controls on "Final" tab screen

Where Is the Localization?

OK. Now you have your main form set up complete with all its constituent controls. You may be wondering why all the label controls have their default names. This is because they are not referenced anywhere in the code. Why bother giving them names? Well, if you have been paying attention to the previous chapters, this book is about localizing code. Every control should have a descriptive name and if it has a Text property that property should be set in code with a string pulled from a resource file.

Why didn't I follow my own rules for this program? Well, I want to show you what it is like to localize a program "after the fact." That's what I do in the next chapter. My philosophy is that localization needs to be designed into a program. However, in the real world you often need to localize an existing program. Chapter 8 illustrates how to do this. Writing a program that has localization designed in from the start is shown in Chapter 9.

Here Comes the Code

The first thing to do in any VB code page is to set the Option Strict = ON option. This eliminates all the "Evil Type Coercion" bugs that plagued VB 6. For all you VB'ers out there, this is not your usual VB. VB .NET is a powerful object-oriented language and all object-oriented rules apply. This includes strong type safety.

I recommend that you turn it on by default for every VB project you make so you will not forget to include it at the top of each file.

NOTE *Turn on Option Strict by right-clicking your project in the solution pane, select Properties, and choose the Option Strict ON choice. All forms, class files, and modules for this project will have Option Strict = ON at the top of the code.*

Start out by editing the Consts.vb file. This file includes some constants and an Enum that will be used to identify the type of resource file we are working with. It should look like Listing 7-1:

Listing 7-1. Constants and enumerators

```
Module Consts

    Public Const KeyCol As String = "Key"
    Public Const TextCol As String = "Text"
    Public Const CommentCol As String = "Comment"
    Public Const MaxKeyLen As Integer = 15
    Public Const CommentChar As Char = ";"c

    Public Enum ResTypes
      TextType = 1
      XMLType = 2
      BinType = 3
    End Enum

End Module
```

Now, on to the frmResources.vb form. To use many of the classes you need for the program, you must first include some namespaces.

```
Imports System
Imports System.Globalization
Imports System.Resources
Imports System.Threading
Imports System.IO
Imports MS = Microsoft.visualbasic.Strings
```

The Globalization namespace allows you to access the CultureInfo class. The Resources namespace allows you to access the resource Reader and Writer classes. The threading namespace allows you to change the default culture for the current thread. The IO namespace allows you to get file information. Finally, I have included an alias to the Microsoft.Visualbasic.Strings namespace. I use this later in the code to disambiguate the VB 6 "left" function.

Now you need to put in constants for use inside this form.

```
Const GridLineWidth As Integer = 1 'Pixel width of a grid line
'These names do not need to be in a resource file because they will
'never be seen by the user.
Const ResourceTableName As String = "Resources"

Const TEXT_TAB As Integer = 0
Const GRAPHICS_TAB As Integer = 1
Const FINAL_TAB As Integer = 2
Const PICSPACE As Int16 = 10
Const PICSIZE As Int16 = 64

Private m_StringTable As DataTable
Private m_ResFile As String
Private m_NewFname As String
Private m_ResType As ResTypes
Private m_Pictures As New Collection()
```

Notice that I use a collection here to hold all my pictures. I think collections are the greatest thing since sliced bread. The VB Collection class uses a hash table look up for extremely fast access to members. It is also much more versatile that the lowly array. You can even have collections of collections. This often comes in handy. However, I must say that the arrays in .NET are much better than in regular C++ or VB. You can iterate over arrays using the For Each syntax, for example.

NOTE *Try using collections to build a hierarchical tree or data objects. For example, a town has a collection of streets; a street has a collection of houses; a house has a collection of residents.*

You are at the point where you need to add the code that sets up the grid control for text strings. Listing 7-2 shows the form_load method and the supporting methods necessary to do this.

Listing 7-2. Loading the form and setting up the text grid control

```
Private Sub Form1_Load(ByVal sender As System.Object, _
                       ByVal e As System.EventArgs) Handles MyBase.Load

    InitStrings()

    SetupStringTable()
    dgStrings.DataSource = m_StringTable
    SetupStringResourceGrid()
    AlignColumns()

End Sub

Private Sub InitStrings()

    sbStatus.Panels(2).Text = Now.ToString
    sbStatus.Panels(1).Width = 100

End Sub

Private Sub AlignColumns()

    dgStrings.TableStyles(0).GridColumnStyles(0).Width = 100
    dgStrings.TableStyles(0).GridColumnStyles(1).Width = 300
    dgStrings.TableStyles(0).GridColumnStyles(2).Width = _
        dgStrings.Size.Width - dgStrings.TableStyles(0).GridColumnStyles(0). _
        Width - dgStrings.TableStyles(0).GridColumnStyles(1).Width - _
        dgStrings.RowHeaderWidth - 4 * GridLineWidth

End Sub

Private Sub SetupStringResourceGrid()
    Dim dgS As New DataGridTableStyle()
    Dim dgCKey As DataGridTextBoxColumn
    Dim dgCText As DataGridTextBoxColumn
    Dim dgCComment As DataGridTextBoxColumn
```

```vbnet
'Set up a table style first then add it to the grid
dgS.MappingName = ResourceTableName
dgS.PreferredColumnWidth = 300
dgS.SelectionBackColor = Color.Beige
dgS.SelectionForeColor = Color.Black
dgS.AllowSorting = True

'Make a column style for the first column and add it to the columnstyle
dgCKey = New DataGridTextBoxColumn()
dgCKey.MappingName = KeyCol
dgCKey.HeaderText = "Resource Key"
dgCKey.Width = 100
dgS.GridColumnStyles.Add(dgCKey)

'Make a column style for the second column and add it to the columnstyle
dgCComment = New DataGridTextBoxColumn()
dgCComment.MappingName = TextCol
dgCComment.HeaderText = "Resource Text"
dgCComment.Width = 300
dgS.GridColumnStyles.Add(dgCComment)

'Make a column style for the third column and add it to the columnstyle
dgCText = New DataGridTextBoxColumn()
dgCText.MappingName = CommentCol
dgCText.HeaderText = "Comment"
dgCText.Width = 400
dgS.GridColumnStyles.Add(dgCText)

'First purge all table styles from this grid then add the one that I want
dgStrings.TableStyles.Clear()
dgStrings.TableStyles.Add(dgS)

End Sub

Private Sub SetupStringTable()
    Dim dr As DataRow

    'Give this table a name so I can synchronize to it with the grid
    m_StringTable = New DataTable(ResourceTableName)

    'Add three columns to the table
    m_StringTable.Columns.Add(New DataColumn(KeyCol, _
                          Type.GetType("System.String")))
```

```
m_StringTable.Columns.Add(New DataColumn(TextCol, _
                          Type.GetType("System.String")))
m_StringTable.Columns.Add(New DataColumn(CommentCol, _
                          Type.GetType("System.String")))

End Sub
```

The first thing done in the load function is to initialize the strings. You are not localizing this code yet, so there is very little in the InitStrings method. Chapter 8 localizes this program and this method is where all the strings are pulled in from the resource file and assigned to the controls.

Next, in the SetupStringTable method I instantiate a new data table and give it the name defined at the top of the program "Resources." It is possible to have many tables that can be assigned to the same grid control. Then I assign three columns of type "String" to the data table. Table columns can also be assigned to Boolean values, which gives you a check box in each cell of that column.

The next step is to assign the new data table as the data source of the grid control. This effectively binds the table to the grid. Notice that even though I have bound the table to the grid there is still no direct correlation between the grid and the data that will show up in it. This is a great form of data abstraction.

Once the table is assigned to the grid, I call the method SetupStringResourceGrid. The table styles and column styles are set up with this method. A data grid, by default, has no table or column styles defined. The table style defines how the table looks as a whole. Each table style needs at least one column style. The column style defines how each column is shown in the table. The link between the column style and the table style is its mapping name. The link between the table style and the table is its mapping name. Just to be sure, I purge all existing table styles from the table and add the one that I just created.

The data grid and data table are prime examples of collections at work. The grid can have a collection of data tables, which has a collection of table styles, which has a collection of column styles.

The last task in the form_load method is to "pretty up" the display of the table within the grid. I do this by setting the size of the first two columns and using a little basic math to size the third column according to the width of the grid. If you use the anchoring capability of the control, this AlignColumns procedure is called during the resize event.

Build your project, and then press F5 to run it. You should see the table correctly resized in the grid. Figure 7-8 shows this screen.

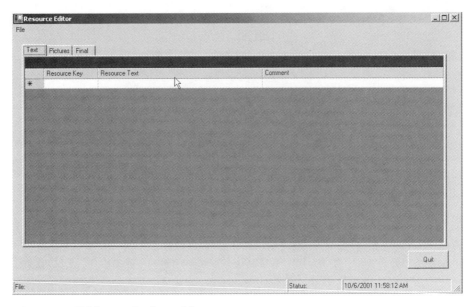

Figure 7-8. Table attached to grid

Other than pressing the "X" at the top of the screen, how do you exit the program gracefully? There are two ways: the Quit button and the File-Exit menu choice. Note the procedure in Listing 7-3.

Listing 7-3. Exit procedure

```
Private Sub ProgExit(ByVal sender As System.Object, _
                ByVal e As System.EventArgs) Handles cmdQuit.Click, _
                                        mnuExit.Click
    Me.Dispose()
    End
End Sub
```

The ProgExit sub handles the Quit button and the FileExit menu choice. Notice that I am calling the dispose method of this class, which is located in the Windows Forms Designer Generated Code section.

Generating the Resource Handler Class

What about filling the grid with text resources? There are two ways to do this. The first is to start typing in the cells. The second is to import the text from a resource file. This is where you go next.

Open the ResUtil.vb code. Change the ResUtil class definition from Public to Friend. This limits the scope of the class to those classes within this project. Also, import the following namespaces:

```
Imports System
Imports System.Globalization
Imports System.Resources
Imports System.IO
Imports System.Drawing
Imports System.Drawing.Imaging
```

Before you start on the ResUtil class, you need something to store an image in. Normally an image is its own container, but there are properties that you need to keep with the image. The main one is a name. This name is what is eventually displayed in the lstPictures list box. There is actually a property of an Image class that you can set up to hold any information you want. This is cumbersome so I prefer a Wrapper class.

Enter the code for the ResUtil class shown in Listing 7-4.

Listing 7-4. Image Wrapper class

```
Public Class ResImage

    Private img As Image
    Private imgName As String
    Private imgType As String

    Public Sub New(ByVal Key As Object, ByVal Value As Object)
        'Value is an object because of the way it is passed in
        img = CType(Value, Image)
        imgName = Key.ToString
        imgType = Value.GetType.ToString

    End Sub
    Public Sub New(ByVal Key As String, ByVal Value As Object)
        'Value is an object because of the way it is passed in
        img = CType(Value, Image)
        imgName = Key
        imgType = Value.GetType.ToString

    End Sub
```

```
Public Property Name() As String
  Get
     Return imgName
  End Get
  Set(ByVal Value As String)
     imgName = Value
  End Set
End Property
Public ReadOnly Property Image() As Image
  Get
     Return img
  End Get
End Property
Public ReadOnly Property Type() As String
  Get
     Return imgType
  End Get
End Property

End Class
```

This ResImage class holds an image of any type and has a name and a Type property. The Type property can be used to hold the original type of the image before any transformations. This information may or may not be useful.

Notice that the Image and Type properties are read-only. How can you get an image in here if the property is read-only? The answer lies in the constructors. There are two of them here. They both take a key and an image as arguments. One takes a key as an object and the other takes a key as a string. The constructor that takes a key as an object is used for passing the key object from the resource-reader enumerator. The key as a string is used when you import a new image into the program directly from a disk. The name of the image is defaulted to the key in each case. The name property is read/write in case you want to change the name later.

You may be wondering at this time why the image argument to the constructors is an object type rather than an Image type. The answer is that the resource reader passes in the image as an object. Normally a Wrapper class would enforce type safety by accepting only objects of a particular type. I could have changed the object type before I used this constructor but I chose not to.

NOTE *As you will see, I like to take advantage of overloaded constructors. It makes for much cleaner and more efficient code. I really like the idea of defining and assigning a variable all at once. This C++ way of doing things is something I really missed going to VB.*

Let's go back to the ResUtil class. This class will have the following attributes:

- An embedded exception class

- Three overloaded constructors

- An internal collection of images

- Four properties and two methods

- Six private methods

Listing 7-5 shows the constructors and public properties of this class. It also shows the custom Exception class you need.

Listing 7-5. ResUtil constructors and properties

```
Public Class InvalidTable
   Inherits System.Exception

   Sub New(ByVal Message As String)
      MyBase.New(Message)
   End Sub

End Class

Private m_ResFile As String
Private m_SaveFile As String
Private m_ResType As ResTypes
Private m_PicCol As Collection
```

```
'----- Constructors / Destructors --------
Public Sub New()

  'Default to binary file. Default name
  m_ResType = Consts.ResTypes.BinType
  m_ResFile = "BinResource.resources"
  m_SaveFile = m_ResFile
  m_PicCol = New Collection()

End Sub
Public Sub New(ByVal ResourceFilename As String)

  m_ResType = Consts.ResTypes.BinType
  m_ResFile = ResourceFilename
  m_SaveFile = m_ResFile
  m_PicCol = New Collection()

End Sub
Public Sub New(ByVal ResourceFilename As String, ByVal RType As ResTypes)

  m_ResType = RType
  m_ResFile = ResourceFilename
  m_SaveFile = m_ResFile
  m_PicCol = New Collection()

End Sub

'----- Public properties and functions --------
Public Property FileName() As String
  Get
    Return m_ResFile
  End Get
  Set(ByVal rhs As String)
    m_ResFile = rhs
  End Set
End Property
Public Property ResourceType() As ResTypes
  Get
    Return m_ResType
  End Get
  Set(ByVal rhs As ResTypes)
    m_ResType = rhs
  End Set
End Property
```

```
Public ReadOnly Property Pics() As Collection
   Get
      Return m_PicCol
   End Get
End Property
Public Property OutputFileName() As String
   Get
      Return m_SaveFile
   End Get
   Set(ByVal Value As String)
      m_SaveFile = Value
   End Set
End Property
```

Let's look first at the Exception class it inherits from System.Exception. It has just one method, which is the constructor. It takes the message passed in and fires off a new exception with this message.

```
Public Class InvalidTable
   Inherits System.Exception

   Sub New(ByVal Message As String)
      MyBase.New(Message)
   End Sub

End Class
```

The default constructor assumes a file name and file type of binary resource. The second constructor takes the file name as a string but still assumes the type is a binary resource file. The third constructor takes both the file name and resource type as arguments. Next come the properties. These allow you to:

- Get and Set the input file name.

- Get and Set the resource type.

- Get and Set the output file name.

- Get the collection of ResImage classes. This is read-only.

This ResUtil class is supposed to be a universal class to handle resource files. To accomplish this it must be able to read and write all resource file types. This class contains the following private methods:

- FillFromBinaryFile

- SaveToBinaryFile

- FillFromTextFile

- SaveToTextFile

- FillFromXMLFile

- SaveToXMLFile

Listing 7-6 shows the code for these functions. As you can see, the binary and XML resources are handled using the supplied resource file handlers. However, there are no native resource file handlers for a text resource file. For this, I use the StreamReader and StreamWrite classes.

Listing 7-6. Input/Output resource file methods for the ResUtil class

```
'----- private internal functions ---------
  Private Sub FillFromBinaryFile(ByRef ResData As DataTable)

    'Do not try anything if we are handed an invalid table
    'This is better than a try catch block. Avoid errors when possible.
    'Do not just catch them.
    If ResData Is Nothing Then
      Throw New InvalidTable("Data table was not defined")
      Exit Sub
    End If

    Try
      Dim ResReader As New ResourceReader(m_ResFile)
      Dim En As IDictionaryEnumerator = ResReader.GetEnumerator()

      'Iterate over the resource file
      'Add a row for each resource string and put key and value in
      'correct(columns)Don't forget! ResX resource files can contain
      'pictures. We only want the strings!
      While (En.MoveNext)
        If En.Value.GetType Is GetType(String) Then
          ResData.Rows.Add(ResData.NewRow)
          ResData.Rows(ResData.Rows.Count - 1)(KeyCol) = En.Key
          ResData.Rows(ResData.Rows.Count - 1)(TextCol) = En.Value
```

```vbnet
      ElseIf En.Value.GetType Is GetType(Bitmap) Then
         Dim rImg As New ResImage(En.Key, En.Value)
         m_PicCol.Add(rImg, En.Key.ToString())
      ElseIf En.Value.GetType Is GetType(Icon) Then
         Dim rImg As New ResImage(En.Key, En.Value)
         m_PicCol.Add(rImg, En.Key.ToString())
      ElseIf En.Value.GetType Is GetType(Image) Then
         Dim rImg As New ResImage(En.Key, En.Value)
         m_PicCol.Add(rImg, En.Key.ToString())
      End If
    End While

    ResReader.Close()

  Catch ex As Exception
    Throw ex

  End Try

End Sub
Private Sub SaveToBinaryFile(ByVal ResData As DataTable)
  Dim Fname As String
  Dim Pic As ResImage

  'Do not try anything if we are handed an invalid table
  'This is better than a try catch block. Avoid errors when possible.
  'Do not just catch them.
  If ResData Is Nothing Then
    Throw New InvalidTable("Data table was not defined")
    Exit Sub
  End If

  'Split the filename and make it a text file
  Dim File_Info As New FileInfo(m_SaveFile)
  Fname = File_Info.FullName + ".resources"

  Try
    'This will write over the existing file!
    Dim ResWriter As New ResourceWriter(Fname)
    Dim ResKey As String
    Dim ResVal As String
    Dim ResRow As DataRow
```

```vb
        'Iterate over the rows in the table and add to the resource file
        For Each ResRow In ResData.Rows
            ResKey = ResRow(KeyCol).ToString
            ResVal = ResRow(TextCol).ToString
            ResWriter.AddResource(ResKey, ResVal)
        Next

        'Save the pictures
        For Each Pic In m_PicCol
            ResWriter.AddResource(Pic.Name, Pic.Image)
        Next

        'Write out the resource file and close it.
        ResWriter.Generate()
        ResWriter.Close()

    Catch ex As Exception
        Throw ex

    End Try

End Sub
Private Sub FillFromTextFile(ByRef ResData As DataTable)
    Dim ResKey As String
    Dim ResVal As String
    Dim ResComment As String
    Dim ResRow As DataRow

    If ResData Is Nothing Then
        Throw New InvalidTable("Data table was not defined")
        Exit Sub
    End If

    Try
        Dim MyStream As New StreamReader(m_ResFile)
        Dim MyLine As String
        Dim pos As Integer

        'Any string with a comment marker is considered a comment.
        'Resgen thinks so too.
        While (True)
            MyLine = MyStream.ReadLine()
            If MyLine Is Nothing Then Exit While
            If MyLine <> "" Then
```

```vb
            pos = InStr(MyLine, ";")
            If pos < 2 Then    ' >=2 is an Ambiguous line
              If pos = 1 Then
                'This line is a comment so digest it as such
                ResComment = MyLine.ToString.TrimStart(CommentChar)
              End If

              If pos = 0 Then
                'This line is a string resource
                Dim str() As String = Split(MyLine, "=")
                ResKey = str(0).Trim()
                ResVal = str(1).Trim()

                'Add this info to the table
                ResData.Rows.Add(ResData.NewRow)
                ResData.Rows(ResData.Rows.Count - 1)(KeyCol) = ResKey
                ResData.Rows(ResData.Rows.Count - 1)(TextCol) = ResVal
                ResData.Rows(ResData.Rows.Count - 1)(CommentCol) = ResComment
              End If

          End If
        End If
      End While

  Catch ex As Exception
    Throw ex

  End Try

End Sub
Private Sub SaveToTextFile(ByVal ResData As DataTable)
  Dim fname As String
  Dim ResKey As String
  Dim ResVal As String
  Dim ResComment As String
  Dim ResRow As DataRow

  'Do not try anything if we are handed an invalid table
  'This is better than a try catch block. Avoid errors when possible.
  'Do not just catch them.
  If ResData Is Nothing Then
    Throw New InvalidTable("Data table was not defined")
    Exit Sub
  End If
```

```vb
        'Split the filename and make it a text file
        Dim File_Info As New FileInfo(m_SaveFile)
        fname = File_Info.FullName + ".txt"

    Try
        'Open up the new text file stream
        Dim MyStream As New StreamWriter(fname)

        'Iterate over the rows in the table and add to the text resource file
        For Each ResRow In ResData.Rows
            ResKey = ResRow(KeyCol).ToString.PadRight(MaxKeyLen + 1)
            ResVal = ResRow(TextCol).ToString
            ResComment = ResRow(CommentCol).ToString
            If Len(ResComment) > 0 Then
                MyStream.WriteLine(";" + ResComment)
            End If
            MyStream.WriteLine(ResKey + " = " + ResVal)
            MyStream.WriteLine()
        Next

        MyStream.Flush()
        MyStream.Close()

    Catch ex As Exception
        Throw ex

    End Try

End Sub
Private Sub FillFromXMLFile(ByRef ResData As DataTable)

    'Do not try anything if we are handed an invalid table
    'This is better than a try catch block. Avoid errors when possible.
    'Do not just catch them.
    If ResData Is Nothing Then
        Throw New InvalidTable("Data table was not defined")
        Exit Sub
    End If

    Try
        Dim ResXReader As New ResXResourceReader(m_ResFile)
        Dim En As IDictionaryEnumerator = ResXReader.GetEnumerator()
```

```
      'Iterate over the resource file
      'Add a row for each resource string and put key and value in correct
      'columns Don't forget! ResX resource files can contain pictures.
      'We only want the strings!
      While (En.MoveNext)
        If En.Value.GetType Is GetType(String) Then
          ResData.Rows.Add(ResData.NewRow)
          ResData.Rows(ResData.Rows.Count - 1)(KeyCol) = En.Key
          ResData.Rows(ResData.Rows.Count - 1)(TextCol) = En.Value

        ElseIf En.Value.GetType Is GetType(Bitmap) Then
          Dim rImg As New ResImage(En.Key, En.Value)
          m_PicCol.Add(rImg, En.Key.ToString())
        ElseIf En.Value.GetType Is GetType(Icon) Then
          Dim rImg As New ResImage(En.Key, En.Value)
          m_PicCol.Add(rImg, En.Key.ToString())
        ElseIf En.Value.GetType Is GetType(Image) Then
          Dim rImg As New ResImage(En.Key, En.Value)
          m_PicCol.Add(rImg, En.Key.ToString())
        End If
      End While

      ResXReader.Close()

    Catch ex As Exception
      Throw ex

    End Try

End Sub
Private Sub SaveToXMLFile(ByRef ResData As DataTable)
    Dim Fname As String
    Dim Pic As ResImage

    'Do not try anything if we are handed an invalid table
    'This is better than a try catch block. Avoid errors when possible.
    'Do not just catch them.
    If ResData Is Nothing Then
      Throw New InvalidTable("Data table was not defined")
      Exit Sub
    End If
```

```
'Split the filename and make it a text file
Dim File_Info As New FileInfo(m_SaveFile)
Fname = File_Info.FullName + ".resx"

Try
   'This will write over the existing file!
   Dim ResxWriter As New ResXResourceWriter(Fname)
   Dim ResKey As String
   Dim ResVal As String
   Dim ResRow As DataRow

   'Iterate over the rows in the table and add to the resource file
   For Each ResRow In ResData.Rows
     ResKey = ResRow(KeyCol).ToString
     ResVal = ResRow(TextCol).ToString
     ResxWriter.AddResource(ResKey, ResVal)
   Next

   'Save the pictures
   For Each Pic In m_PicCol
     ResxWriter.AddResource(Pic.Name, Pic.Image)
   Next

   'Write out the resource file and close it.
   ResxWriter.Generate()
   ResxWriter.Close()

Catch ex As Exception
   Throw ex

End Try

End Sub
```

Notice that in each method I first test to see if the data table argument has been initialized. If it hasn't, then I throw my new exception. The error message that is being sent should be localized. This happens in the next chapter.

The XML and binary reader methods test the resource type and redirect the resource to either the data table for strings, or add the image to the collection of images. In all reader methods, I generate a new row and fill the appropriate columns with the string resource data. The only resource file that can natively hold comments is the text file. It is possible to include comments in the XML and binary resource files but they are held as resources. I chose not to extend the native functionality of the XML and binary resource files.

Also notice that all the work in these methods is done inside a try-catch block. This is how all error handling should be done. In the interest of readability I did not include separate catch blocks for specific errors. Production code would include this finer level of error handling. Whatever error comes up I just re-throw it up the line.

How are these internal methods accessed? There are two more public methods to talk about here. They are the GetData and SaveData methods. The code is shown in Listing 7-7.

Listing 7-7. Getting and saving data

```
Public Sub GetData(ByRef ResData As DataTable, ByVal append As Boolean)

    If ResData Is Nothing Then
        Throw New InvalidTable("Data table was not defined")
        Exit Sub
    End If

    'Make sure that memory is clear
    If Not append Then
        ResData.Clear()
        While m_PicCol.Count > 0
            m_PicCol.Remove(1)
        End While
    End If

    Select Case m_ResType
        Case Consts.ResTypes.TextType
            Try
                FillFromTextFile(ResData)
            Catch ex As Exception
                Throw ex
            End Try

        Case Consts.ResTypes.XMLType
            Try
                FillFromXMLFile(ResData)
            Catch ex As Exception
                Throw ex
            End Try

        Case Consts.ResTypes.BinType
            Try
                FillFromBinaryFile(ResData)
```

```
        Catch ex As Exception
          Throw ex
        End Try
    End Select

End Sub
Public Sub SaveData(ByVal ResData As DataTable, ByVal Pics As Collection, _
                    ByVal ResType As ResTypes)

    If ResData Is Nothing Then
      Throw New InvalidTable("Data table was not defined")
      Exit Sub
    End If

    m_PicCol = Pics
    Select Case ResType
      Case Consts.ResTypes.TextType
        SaveToTextFile(ResData)
      Case Consts.ResTypes.XMLType
        SaveToXMLFile(ResData)
      Case Consts.ResTypes.BinType
        SaveToBinaryFile(ResData)
    End Select

End Sub
```

These two methods contain a select case block that redirects data to the appropriate resource file handler. Notice that the data table is passed by reference into the GetData method. Once this method is called, the data table is changed. No need to hand it back.

The ResUtil Class Completed

The complete code for this class module is shown in Listing 7-8. Make sure after typing in (or copying) this code that your program compiles. Fix any errors before you go on.

Listing 7-8. Complete ResUtil class module code

```
Option Strict On

Imports System
Imports System.Globalization
```

```vbnet
Imports System.Resources
Imports System.IO
Imports System.Drawing
Imports System.Drawing.Imaging


'Make it a friend because we do not want to expose it outside of this assembly.
'Like making a class private in COM
Friend Class ResUtil

  Public Class InvalidTable
    Inherits System.Exception

    Sub New(ByVal Message As String)
      MyBase.New(Message)
    End Sub

  End Class

  Private m_ResFile As String
  Private m_SaveFile As String
  Private m_ResType As ResTypes
  Private m_PicCol As Collection

  '----- Constructors / Destructors ---------
  Public Sub New()

    'Default to binary file. Default name
    m_ResType = Consts.ResTypes.BinType
    m_ResFile = "BinResource.resources"
    m_SaveFile = m_ResFile
    m_PicCol = New Collection()

  End Sub
  Public Sub New(ByVal ResourceFilename As String)

    m_ResType = Consts.ResTypes.BinType
    m_ResFile = ResourceFilename
    m_SaveFile = m_ResFile
    m_PicCol = New Collection()

  End Sub
  Public Sub New(ByVal ResourceFilename As String, ByVal RType As ResTypes)
```

```vbnet
    m_ResType = RType
    m_ResFile = ResourceFilename
    m_SaveFile = m_ResFile
    m_PicCol = New Collection()

End Sub


'----- Public properties and functions ----------
Public Property FileName() As String
  Get
    Return m_ResFile
  End Get
  Set(ByVal rhs As String)
    m_ResFile = rhs
  End Set
End Property
Public Property ResourceType() As ResTypes
  Get
    Return m_ResType
  End Get
  Set(ByVal rhs As ResTypes)
    m_ResType = rhs
  End Set
End Property
Public ReadOnly Property Pics() As Collection
  Get
    Return m_PicCol
  End Get
End Property
Public Property OutputFileName() As String
  Get
    Return m_SaveFile
  End Get
  Set(ByVal Value As String)
    m_SaveFile = Value
  End Set
End Property


Public Sub GetData(ByRef ResData As DataTable, ByVal append As Boolean)

  If ResData Is Nothing Then
    Throw New InvalidTable("Data table was not defined")
    Exit Sub
  End If
```

```
    'Make sure that memory is clear
    If Not append Then
      ResData.Clear()
      While m_PicCol.Count > 0
        m_PicCol.Remove(1)
      End While
    End If


    Select Case m_ResType
      Case Consts.ResTypes.TextType
        Try
          FillFromTextFile(ResData)
        Catch ex As Exception
          Throw ex
        End Try


      Case Consts.ResTypes.XMLType
        Try
          FillFromXMLFile(ResData)
        Catch ex As Exception
          Throw ex
        End Try


      Case Consts.ResTypes.BinType
        Try
          FillFromBinaryFile(ResData)
        Catch ex As Exception
          Throw ex
        End Try
    End Select

End Sub
Public Sub SaveData(ByVal ResData As DataTable, ByVal Pics As Collection, _
                    ByVal ResType As ResTypes)

    If ResData Is Nothing Then
      Throw New InvalidTable("Data table was not defined")
      Exit Sub
    End If

    m_PicCol = Pics
    Select Case ResType
      Case Consts.ResTypes.TextType
        SaveToTextFile(ResData)
```

```vb
        Case Consts.ResTypes.XMLType
          SaveToXMLFile(ResData)
        Case Consts.ResTypes.BinType
          SaveToBinaryFile(ResData)
      End Select

End Sub

'----- private internal functions ----------
Private Sub FillFromBinaryFile(ByRef ResData As DataTable)

  'Do not try anything if we are handed an invalid table
  'This is better than a try catch block. Avoid errors when possible.
  'Do not just catch them.
  If ResData Is Nothing Then
    Throw New InvalidTable("Data table was not defined")
    Exit Sub
  End If

  Try
    Dim ResReader As New ResourceReader(m_ResFile)
    Dim En As IDictionaryEnumerator = ResReader.GetEnumerator()

    'Iterate over the resource file
    'Add a row for each resource string and put key and value in
    'correct(columns)Don't forget! ResX resource files can contain
    'pictures. We only want the strings!
    While (En.MoveNext)
      If En.Value.GetType Is GetType(String) Then
        ResData.Rows.Add(ResData.NewRow)
        ResData.Rows(ResData.Rows.Count - 1)(KeyCol) = En.Key
        ResData.Rows(ResData.Rows.Count - 1)(TextCol) = En.Value

      ElseIf En.Value.GetType Is GetType(Bitmap) Then
        Dim rImg As New ResImage(En.Key, En.Value)
        m_PicCol.Add(rImg, En.Key.ToString())
      ElseIf En.Value.GetType Is GetType(Icon) Then
        Dim rImg As New ResImage(En.Key, En.Value)
        m_PicCol.Add(rImg, En.Key.ToString())
      ElseIf En.Value.GetType Is GetType(Image) Then
        Dim rImg As New ResImage(En.Key, En.Value)
        m_PicCol.Add(rImg, En.Key.ToString())
```

```vbnet
        End If
      End While

    ResReader.Close()

  Catch ex As Exception
      Throw ex

  End Try

End Sub
Private Sub SaveToBinaryFile(ByVal ResData As DataTable)
  Dim Fname As String
  Dim Pic As ResImage

  'Do not try anything if we are handed an invalid table
  'This is better than a try catch block. Avoid errors when possible.
  'Do not just catch them.
  If ResData Is Nothing Then
    Throw New InvalidTable("Data table was not defined")
    Exit Sub
  End If

  'Split the filename and make it a text file
  Dim File_Info As New FileInfo(m_SaveFile)
  Fname = File_Info.FullName + ".resources"

  Try
    'This will write over the existing file!
    Dim ResWriter As New ResourceWriter(Fname)
    Dim ResKey As String
    Dim ResVal As String
    Dim ResRow As DataRow

    'Iterate over the rows in the table and add to the resource file
    For Each ResRow In ResData.Rows
      ResKey = ResRow(KeyCol).ToString
      ResVal = ResRow(TextCol).ToString
      ResWriter.AddResource(ResKey, ResVal)
    Next
```

```vb
    'Save the pictures
    For Each Pic In m_PicCol
      ResWriter.AddResource(Pic.Name, Pic.Image)
    Next

    'Write out the resource file and close it.
    ResWriter.Generate()
    ResWriter.Close()

  Catch ex As Exception
    Throw ex

  End Try

End Sub
Private Sub FillFromTextFile(ByRef ResData As DataTable)
  Dim ResKey As String
  Dim ResVal As String
  Dim ResComment As String
  Dim ResRow As DataRow

  If ResData Is Nothing Then
    Throw New InvalidTable("Data table was not defined")
    Exit Sub
  End If

  Try
    Dim MyStream As New StreamReader(m_ResFile)
    Dim MyLine As String
    Dim pos As Integer

    'Any string with a comment marker is considered a comment.
    'Resgen thinks so too.
    While (True)
      MyLine = MyStream.ReadLine()
      If MyLine Is Nothing Then Exit While
      If MyLine <> "" Then
        pos = InStr(MyLine, ";")
        If pos < 2 Then    ' >=2 is an Ambiguous line
          If pos = 1 Then
            'This line is a comment so digest it as such
            ResComment = MyLine.ToString.TrimStart(CommentChar)
          End If
```

```vbnet
            If pos = 0 Then
              'This line is a string resource
              Dim str() As String = Split(MyLine, "=")
              ResKey = str(0).Trim()
              ResVal = str(1).Trim()

              'Add this info to the table
              ResData.Rows.Add(ResData.NewRow)
              ResData.Rows(ResData.Rows.Count - 1)(KeyCol) = ResKey
              ResData.Rows(ResData.Rows.Count - 1)(TextCol) = ResVal
              ResData.Rows(ResData.Rows.Count - 1)(CommentCol) = ResComment
            End If

          End If
        End If
      End While

    Catch ex As Exception
      Throw ex

    End Try

End Sub
Private Sub SaveToTextFile(ByVal ResData As DataTable)
    Dim fname As String
    Dim ResKey As String
    Dim ResVal As String
    Dim ResComment As String
    Dim ResRow As DataRow

    'Do not try anything if we are handed an invalid table
    'This is better than a try catch block. Avoid errors when possible.
    'Do not just catch them.
    If ResData Is Nothing Then
      Throw New InvalidTable("Data table was not defined")
      Exit Sub
    End If

    'Split the filename and make it a text file
    Dim File_Info As New FileInfo(m_SaveFile)
    fname = File_Info.FullName + ".txt"

    Try
      'Open up the new text file stream
      Dim MyStream As New StreamWriter(fname)
```

```vbnet
        'Iterate over the rows in the table and add to the text resource file
        For Each ResRow In ResData.Rows
          ResKey = ResRow(KeyCol).ToString.PadRight(MaxKeyLen + 1)
          ResVal = ResRow(TextCol).ToString
          ResComment = ResRow(CommentCol).ToString
          If Len(ResComment) > 0 Then
            MyStream.WriteLine(";" + ResComment)
          End If
          MyStream.WriteLine(ResKey + " = " + ResVal)
          MyStream.WriteLine()
        Next

        MyStream.Flush()
        MyStream.Close()

      Catch ex As Exception
        Throw ex

      End Try

End Sub
Private Sub FillFromXMLFile(ByRef ResData As DataTable)

    'Do not try anything if we are handed an invalid table
    'This is better than a try catch block. Avoid errors when possible.
    'Do not just catch them.
    If ResData Is Nothing Then
      Throw New InvalidTable("Data table was not defined")
      Exit Sub
    End If

    Try
      Dim ResXReader As New ResXResourceReader(m_ResFile)
      Dim En As IDictionaryEnumerator = ResXReader.GetEnumerator()

      'Iterate over the resource file
      'Add a row for each resource string and put key and value in correct
      'columns Don't forget! ResX resource files can contain pictures.
      'We only want the strings!
      While (En.MoveNext)
        If En.Value.GetType Is GetType(String) Then
          ResData.Rows.Add(ResData.NewRow)
          ResData.Rows(ResData.Rows.Count - 1)(KeyCol) = En.Key
          ResData.Rows(ResData.Rows.Count - 1)(TextCol) = En.Value
```

```
      ElseIf En.Value.GetType Is GetType(Bitmap) Then
        Dim rImg As New ResImage(En.Key, En.Value)
        m_PicCol.Add(rImg, En.Key.ToString())
      ElseIf En.Value.GetType Is GetType(Icon) Then
        Dim rImg As New ResImage(En.Key, En.Value)
        m_PicCol.Add(rImg, En.Key.ToString())
      ElseIf En.Value.GetType Is GetType(Image) Then
        Dim rImg As New ResImage(En.Key, En.Value)
        m_PicCol.Add(rImg, En.Key.ToString())
      End If
    End While

    ResXReader.Close()

  Catch ex As Exception
    Throw ex

  End Try

End Sub
Private Sub SaveToXMLFile(ByRef ResData As DataTable)
  Dim Fname As String
  Dim Pic As ResImage

  'Do not try anything if we are handed an invalid table
  'This is better than a try catch block. Avoid errors when possible.
  'Do not just catch them.
  If ResData Is Nothing Then
    Throw New InvalidTable("Data table was not defined")
    Exit Sub
  End If

  'Split the filename and make it a text file
  Dim File_Info As New FileInfo(m_SaveFile)
  Fname = File_Info.FullName + ".resx"

  Try
    'This will write over the existing file!
    Dim ResxWriter As New ResXResourceWriter(Fname)
    Dim ResKey As String
    Dim ResVal As String
    Dim ResRow As DataRow
```

```vbnet
                      'Iterate over the rows in the table and add to the resource file
                      For Each ResRow In ResData.Rows
                        ResKey = ResRow(KeyCol).ToString
                        ResVal = ResRow(TextCol).ToString
                        ResxWriter.AddResource(ResKey, ResVal)
                      Next

                      'Save the pictures
                      For Each Pic In m_PicCol
                        ResxWriter.AddResource(Pic.Name, Pic.Image)
                      Next

                      'Write out the resource file and close it.
                      ResxWriter.Generate()
                      ResxWriter.Close()

                  Catch ex As Exception
                      Throw ex

                  End Try

              End Sub

          End Class

'=========================== NEW CLASS =======================
Public Class ResImage

    Private img As Image
    Private imgName As String
    Private imgType As String

    Public Sub New(ByVal Key As Object, ByVal Value As Object)
        'Value is an object because of the way it is passed in
        img = CType(Value, Image)
        imgName = Key.ToString
        imgType = Value.GetType.ToString

    End Sub
    Public Sub New(ByVal Key As String, ByVal Value As Object)
        'Value is an object because of the way it is passed in
        img = CType(Value, Image)
        imgName = Key
        imgType = Value.GetType.ToString

    End Sub
```

```
Public Property Name() As String
  Get
    Return imgName
  End Get
  Set(ByVal Value As String)
    imgName = Value
  End Set
End Property
Public ReadOnly Property Image() As Image
  Get
    Return img
  End Get
End Property
Public ReadOnly Property Type() As String
  Get
    Return imgType
  End Get
End Property

End Class
```

Back to the Main Code

Now that you have a class that can handle resource files of any type, it's time to get back to making things happen on the screen.

When we last left our hero . . . So far you have code to set up and display a blank table on the screen. You also have code to kill the program either by the Quit button or a menu option. All you need to do is connect the open and append menu choices with the ResUtil class you just made and display the information on the screen. Easy huh? You'll see.

Enter the code shown in Listing 7-9. This method is an event handler for both the open and append menu functions. As you can guess the open menu clears out all resources and fills the form with resources from a particular file. The append menu choice adds to the existing resources. This choice is useful for adding a few resource files together into one.

Listing 7-9. Get resources for open and append

```vb
Private Sub GetResources(ByVal sender As Object, ByVal e As System.EventArgs) _
                    Handles mnuOpen.Click, mnuAppend.Click

    OpenResFile.Reset()
    OpenResFile.InitialDirectory = Directory.GetCurrentDirectory()
    OpenResFile.RestoreDirectory = True
    OpenResFile.Filter = "Text files (*.txt)|*.txt|XML files " + _
                    "(*.resx)|*.resx|Binary files" + _
                    "(*.resources)|*.resources"

    If (OpenResFile.ShowDialog() = DialogResult.OK) Then
      m_ResType = CType(OpenResFile.FilterIndex, ResTypes)
      m_ResFile = OpenResFile.FileName
      Dim Res As New ResUtil(m_ResFile, m_ResType)

      'clear the pictures
      lstPictures.Items.Clear()
      While lstPictures.Items.Count > 0
        lstPictures.Items.Remove(1)
      End While
      PicPanel.Controls.Clear()

      'Fill the string text box
      sbStatus.Panels(0).Text = m_ResFile
      If sender Is mnuOpen Then
        Res.GetData(m_StringTable, False)
        m_Pictures = Res.Pics
      ElseIf sender Is mnuAppend Then
        Res.GetData(m_StringTable, True)
        'Add to the pictures collection
        Dim NewPics As New Collection()
        Dim p As ResImage
        NewPics = Res.Pics
        For Each p In NewPics
          m_Pictures.Add(p)
        Next
      End If

      FillPicList()

    End If

End Sub
```

Let's look at this method. I set up an open file dialog box to look for the three resource file types. The user can choose a file or not. The function detects this based on the dialog result. If the user chooses OK, the method instantiates a new ResUtil object feeding it the file name and type. The method finds out who evoked it by looking at the sender object. Based on this, it either gets data and appends it to the existing resources in memory or it flushes existing memory resources and gets new data. The last thing in this method is a call to FillPicList. The FillPicList method is explained next.

The next three methods you enter are FillPicList, AddPic2Panel, and ArrangePictures. These functions are interesting in that they create new picture-box controls on the fly and place them in the picture panel. The pictures then get arranged in the panel based on the size of the panel. The ArrangePictures procedure makes sure that all pictures fit in the width of the panel. Therefore only a vertical scroll bar is ever needed. Listing 7-10 shows these three procedures.

Listing 7-10. Showing and arranging pictures in Tab 2

```
Private Sub FillPicList()
  Dim ResImg As ResImage

  PicPanel.AutoScroll = True
  pic.Image = Nothing
  For Each ResImg In m_Pictures
    lstPictures.Items.Add(ResImg.Name)
    'Make a new picture box and add it to the
    'panels control array
    AddPic2Panel(ResImg)
  Next
  ArrangePictures()

  If lstPictures.Items.Count > 0 Then
    lstPictures.SetSelected(0, True)
    cmdDelPic.Enabled = True
  Else
    cmdDelPic.Enabled = False
  End If

End Sub

Private Sub AddPic2Panel(ByVal ResImg As ResImage)
  Dim Pic As PictureBox

  Pic = New PictureBox()
  Pic.Size = New Size(PICSIZE, PICSIZE)
  Pic.Location = New Point(10, 10)
```

```
            Pic.SizeMode = PictureBoxSizeMode.StretchImage
            Pic.Image = ResImg.Image
            Pic.Tag = ResImg.Name
            PicPanel.Controls.Add(Pic)

    End Sub

    Private Sub ArrangePictures()
        Dim k As Int32
        Dim x As Int32
        Dim y As Int32

        'Number of pictures in a row.
        'DO not show a picture if it means we get a horizontal
        'scroll bar
        Dim NumPicsInWidth As Int32 = CType(((PicPanel.Size.Width - PICSPACE) / _
                                        (PICSIZE + PICSPACE)) - 1, Int32)
        'Control collections are zero based.
        'VB type collections are 1 based.
        For k = 0 To PicPanel.Controls.Count - 1
            'determine if we are in a new row
            If k Mod (NumPicsInWidth) = 0 Then
                x = PICSPACE
            Else
                x = PicPanel.Controls(k - 1).Location.X + PICSIZE + PICSPACE
            End If

            If k < NumPicsInWidth Then
                y = PICSPACE
            ElseIf k Mod (NumPicsInWidth) = 0 Then
                y = PicPanel.Controls(k - 1).Location.Y + PICSIZE + PICSPACE
            End If

            PicPanel.Controls(k).Location = New Point(x, y)
        Next

    End Sub
```

The first two methods FillPicList and AddPic2Panel make and fill picture boxes that end up on top of each other. The ArrangePictures method takes all the picture boxes and lines them up on the screen with a space of 10 pixels between each box.

The Import Functions at Work

You now have enough code to import resource files into this program and display the text and the graphics. Notice that I disable the Delete Pictures button if there are no pictures displayed. I also force a SelectedIndexChanged event in the lstPictures control. You have not done anything with this control yet, but that is coming.

Build the project and press F5 to run it. You should be able to pull in a resource file and show its resources on the screen.

It is easy enough for you to make a text resource file using NotePad. You already have made a binary and XML resource file that has a picture in it. You did this back in Chapter 5 in Listing 5-7. This was the example that added a bmp file to an XML resource file. Take this XML resource file and run it through ResGen.exe to create a binary resource file. The Apress web site will also have some resource files that you can play around with for this chapter.

Figures 7-9 and 7-10 show my screens after I opened a resource file. The file Imopened is from an example in Chapter 5.

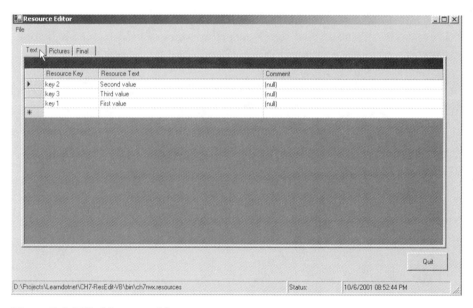

Figure 7-9. Filled in text grid

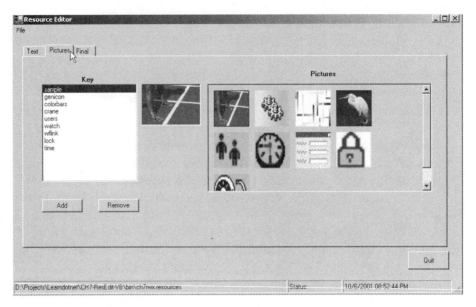

Figure 7-10. Graphics resources

It would be nice to scroll through the pictures and see which pictures belong to which key. Listing 7-11 shows the event handler for the SelectedIndexChanged event for the lstPictures list box.

Listing 7-11. Picture list box event handler

```
Private Sub PicList(ByVal sender As System.Object, _
                    ByVal e As System.EventArgs) _
                    Handles lstPictures.SelectedIndexChanged
    Dim rImg As ResImage

    rImg = CType(m_Pictures.Item(lstPictures.SelectedItem.ToString), ResImage)
    pic.Image = rImg.Image

    'Highlight the picture in question by
    'giving it a border. Don't foget to "unborder" the others.
    Dim pb As PictureBox
    For Each pb In PicPanel.Controls
      If pb.Tag.ToString = rImg.Name Then
        pb.BorderStyle = System.Windows.Forms.BorderStyle.FixedSingle
      Else
        pb.BorderStyle = System.Windows.Forms.BorderStyle.None
      End If
    Next

End Sub
```

This method does several things for display purposes. It detects which key is highlighted in the list and places the picture that belongs with it in the large picture box next to the list box. It then highlights the thumbnail in the panel by placing a border around it.

Removing a Picture

The next thing to do is attach some code to the remove and add buttons. First is the Remove button. Listing 7-12 shows the code for this button.

Listing 7-12. Remove button event handler

```
Private Sub RemovePic(ByVal sender As System.Object, _
                      ByVal e As System.EventArgs) Handles cmdDelPic.Click

  'Remove the picture from the pictures collection
  m_Pictures.Remove(lstPictures.SelectedItem.ToString)

  'Remove the picture from the panel and rearrange the rest
  Dim pb As PictureBox
  For Each pb In PicPanel.Controls
    If pb.BorderStyle = System.Windows.Forms.BorderStyle.FixedSingle Then
      PicPanel.Controls.Remove(pb)
      ArrangePictures()
      Exit For
    End If
  Next

  'Remove the name from the listbox of keys and
  'reselect the first one
  lstPictures.Items.Remove(lstPictures.SelectedItem)
  If lstPictures.Items.Count > 0 Then
    lstPictures.SetSelected(0, True)
  Else
    cmdDelPic.Enabled = False
    pic.Image = Nothing
  End If

End Sub
```

This method removes the name from the list box and removes the thumbnail from the panel. It then calls the ArrangePictures methods and reselects the first entry in the list box. If there are no more pictures the remove button is disabled. Easy enough. What about the add button?

Adding a Picture

Adding a picture should be fairly easy. All you need is a file open dialog and hook it up to the FillPic function. You want to do more than this though. You also need to give the picture a name. This name would be used as the key in the resource file.

The last project file you have left to touch is the AskKey.vb file. This is another form that you use to preview the picture you want to add and to give it a name.

Size this form to 298 x 178 and add the following controls :

- Label. Text property is "Picture Key."

- Text Box. Name it txtKey. Text property is clear.

- Button. Name is cmdOK. Text is "OK."

- Button. Name is cmdCancel. Text is "Cancel."

- PictureBox. Name is KeyPic.

Arrange your form to look something like mine, as shown in Figure 7-11.

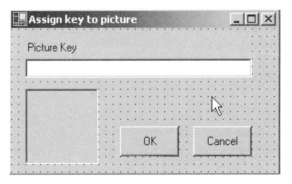

Figure 7-11. AskKey form with controls

Enter the following code in this class:

```
Private m_ResImg As ResImage

Private Sub AskKey_Load(ByVal sender As System.Object, _
                ByVal e As System.EventArgs) Handles MyBase.Load
```

```
   If Not m_ResImg Is Nothing Then
     KeyPic.Image = m_ResImg.Image
     txtKey.Text = m_ResImg.Name
     txtKey.SelectAll()
   End If

End Sub

Private Sub cmdOK_Click(ByVal sender As System.Object, _
                        ByVal e As System.EventArgs) Handles cmdOK.Click

   m_ResImg.Name = txtKey.Text
   DialogResult = DialogResult.OK

End Sub

Private Sub cmdCancel_Click(ByVal sender As System.Object, _
                        ByVal e As System.EventArgs) Handles cmdCancel.Click

   DialogResult = DialogResult.Cancel

End Sub
```

Nothing exciting here.

When you add a form in the IDE, the Forms wizard adds quite a bit of code for you. Every time you add, edit, or move a control on the form some of this code is automatically edited by the Windows Forms wizard. All this code is in the region called Windows Form Designer Generated Code. If you expand this code you will see comments to the effect of "Do not touch this code under extreme penalty because the forms designer will do it for you." — something along those lines anyway.

With this admonishment in mind, open this region and add the following code just below the default constructor.

```
Public Sub New(ByVal ResImg As ResImage)

   MyBase.New()

   'This call is required by the Windows Form Designer.
   InitializeComponent()

   m_ResImg = ResImg

End Sub
```

This is an overloaded form of the constructor that passes in the Image class to be displayed. Even though the Image class is defined as being passed by value, it is actually passed by reference. This is because the object being passed is a reference type. I encourage you to look up the nuances of reference type and value types in the documentation. It is important to know that something like this is happening behind the scenes.

Now that you have this form built, let's add some code to activate it. Add the following method in Listing 7-13. It is the event handler for the Add button.

Listing 7-13. Add picture button event handler

```
Private Sub AddPic(ByVal sender As System.Object, _
                   ByVal e As System.EventArgs) Handles cmdAddPic.Click

    OpenResFile.Reset()
    OpenResFile.InitialDirectory = Directory.GetCurrentDirectory()
    OpenResFile.RestoreDirectory = True
    OpenResFile.Filter = "Picture files " + _
                         "(*.jpg; *.bmp; *.gif)|*.jpg; *.bmp; *.gif"

    If (OpenResFile.ShowDialog() = DialogResult.OK) Then

        Dim fInfo As New FileInfo(OpenResFile.FileName)
        If fInfo.Extension.ToUpper = ".JPG" Or _
            fInfo.Extension.ToUpper = ".BMP" Or _
            fInfo.Extension.ToUpper = ".GIF" Then
          'Add the picture to the collection
          Dim rImg As New ResImage(OpenResFile.FileName, _
                             Image.FromFile(OpenResFile.FileName))
          Dim Keyform As New AskKey(rImg)
          If Keyform.ShowDialog(Me) = DialogResult.OK Then
            m_Pictures.Add(rImg, rImg.Name)
            'Add the picture to the panel and arrange
            AddPic2Panel(rImg)
            ArrangePictures()
            'Add the picture to the list and enable delete and select it
            lstPictures.Items.Add(rImg.Name)
            lstPictures.SetSelected(lstPictures.Items.Count - 1, True)
            cmdDelPic.Enabled = True
          End If
          Keyform.Dispose()
        End If
    End If


End Sub
```

This function opens a dialog box and allows the user to choose a graphics file. It loads the picture, puts it in the ResImage class along with the file name as the image name and passes this class to the AskKey form. The form is called using the ShowDialog method. This method as used here makes the AskKey form modal and assigns its parent property to this form. Once the user has assigned a new key (or not) and accepts the image, it is added to the list and displayed on the form. Figure 7-12 shows the AskForm in action.

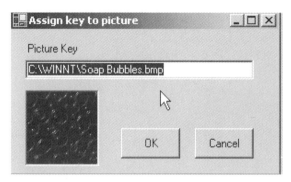

Figure 7-12. AskKey form

Saving the Data

You are now at the point where you need to save the resources in a resource file. So far you can import/add/remove/edit both text and graphics resources.

The first thing to do is fill the basic information fields on the third tab page. The basic information is a count of text and graphics resources and the input file name. While you are doing this, you might as well fill the lstCultures list box with all the cultures in the .NET world. Listing 7-14 shows the event code for the tab control.

Listing 7-14. Event code for the tab control

```
Private Sub tcResource_Click(ByVal sender As Object, _
                            ByVal e As System.EventArgs) _
                            Handles tcResource.Click

  If tcResource.SelectedIndex = FINAL_TAB Then
    lblInFilename.Text = m_ResFile
    lblResStringNum.Text = m_StringTable.Rows.Count.ToString
    lblNumPics.Text = m_Pictures.Count.ToString
```

```
    Dim AllCultures() As CultureInfo
    Dim ACulture As CultureInfo
    AllCultures = CultureInfo.GetCultures(CultureTypes.SpecificCultures)
    lstCultures.Items.Clear()
    lstCultures.Items.Add(" ".PadRight(10) + "(None)")
    lstCultures.Sorted = True
    For Each ACulture In AllCultures
      lstCultures.Items.Add(ACulture.Name.PadRight(15) + ACulture.DisplayName)
    Next
    chkCreateBin.Checked = True
  End If
  If tcResource.SelectedIndex = GRAPHICS_TAB Then
    If lstPictures.Items.Count < 1 Then
      cmdDelPic.Enabled = False
    End If

  End If

End Sub
```

You have seen some of this code in Listing 4-4. It is the code to enumerate through all the cultures in the CultureInfo class. By the way, it is best to change the font in the lstCultures list box to a fixed font such as courier. This eliminates the jagged display.

Add the following four methods to the code. They are event handlers for the check boxes, the text field, and the lstCultures list box. This code is found in Listing 7-15. This is the last code for this project.

Listing 7-15. Final code to handle controls on third tab page

```
Private Sub BuildCompleteName()

  m_NewFname = CStr(IIf(txtBaseName.Text = "", "?", txtBaseName.Text))
  If Not lstCultures.SelectedItem Is Nothing Then
    If lstCultures.SelectedItem.ToString.Trim <> "(None)" Then
      m_NewFname += "." + MS.Left(lstCultures.SelectedItem.ToString, 15).Trim
    End If
  End If

  If chkCreateText.Checked = True Then
    lblTxtFname.Text = m_NewFname + ".txt"
  Else
    lblTxtFname.Text = ""
```

```
     End If
     If chkCreateXML.Checked = True Then
       lblXMLfname.Text = m_NewFname + ".resx"
     Else
       lblXMLfname.Text = ""
     End If
     If chkCreateBin.Checked = True Then
       lblBinFname.Text = m_NewFname + ".resources"
     Else
       lblBinFname.Text = ""
     End If

End Sub


Private Sub CulturePick(ByVal sender As System.Object, _
                        ByVal e As System.EventArgs) _
                        Handles lstCultures.SelectedIndexChanged
   BuildCompleteName()
End Sub


Private Sub Create_Checked(ByVal sender As System.Object, _
                           ByVal e As System.EventArgs) _
                           Handles chkCreateText.CheckedChanged, _
                           chkCreateXML.CheckedChanged, _
                           chkCreateBin.CheckedChanged


   If chkCreateBin.Checked = False And chkCreateXML.Checked = False And _
                                      chkCreateText.Checked = False Then
     cmdSave.Enabled = False
   Else
     cmdSave.Enabled = True
   End If
   BuildCompleteName()

End Sub


Private Sub txtBaseName_TextChanged_1(ByVal sender As System.Object, _
                                      ByVal e As System.EventArgs) _
                                      Handles txtBaseName.TextChanged
   BuildCompleteName()
End Sub


Private Sub cmdSave_Click(ByVal sender As System.Object, _
                          ByVal e As System.EventArgs) Handles cmdSave.Click
```

```
Dim Res As New ResUtil(m_ResFile)

Res.OutputFileName = m_NewFname

If chkCreateText.Checked Then
    Res.SaveData(m_StringTable, m_Pictures, Consts.ResTypes.TextType)
End If
If chkCreateXML.Checked Then
    Res.SaveData(m_StringTable, m_Pictures, Consts.ResTypes.XMLType)
End If
If chkCreateBin.Checked Then
    Res.SaveData(m_StringTable, m_Pictures, Consts.ResTypes.BinType)
End If


End Sub
```

The check boxes enable the resource file name to be formed in the label below each check box as you type in the Base Name text field. The resource file name is built according to the culture you pick and the base name you type in the base name text box. Notice that the txtBaseName_TextChanged_1 method builds the resource file names on the fly as each letter is entered in the text box. Clicking in the lstCultures list box also changes the resource file names accordingly. The save method calls the ResUtil classes save method according to which check box is checked. Figure 7-13 shows this screen in action.

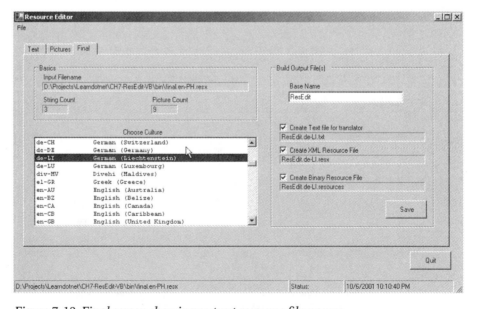

Figure 7-13. Final screen showing output resource file names

The VB Resource Editor Project in Summary

This completes the resource editor written in VB. This is a very useful tool in that it allows the user to make text resource files that can be sent to the translation service. It also allows the user to add and delete text as well as graphics resources. The number of resources that can fit in this editor is unlimited. Once resources are added, they can be combined into either an XML or binary resource file.

Making the C# Version of the Resource Editor

As I've done elsewhere in the book, now that I've shown the VB resource editor, this section explains the C# code. The explanation deals mostly with the code rather than the screens or output. Major differences between the VB code and C# code are pointed out and explained. I assume you have read the VB code and associated explanations.

Here we go!

Starting the _Project

The first thing to do is to bring up a new C# Windows Forms project. Name the project the same as the VB project: Reseditor. Rename your default form to frmResources. Add a new form called AskKey. Add two class files. Name one ResUtil and the other ResImages. Build the project. Your solution editor should look like mine, as in Figure 7-14.

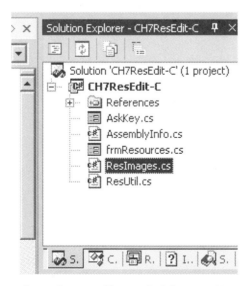

Figure 7-14. Solution Explorer showing files needed for ResEditor project in C#

C# has no such thing as a module file. I put all the constants and the enum in the ResUtil class. The constants are in their own class. Open the ResUtil class file and type in the following code below the namespace declaration. Listing 7-16 shows the classes for the constants and the enum.

Listing 7-16. Constants class

```csharp
public enum ResTypes
{
    TextType = 1,
    XMLType = 2,
    BinType = 3
}

public class ResUtilConsts
{
    public const string KeyCol = "Key";
    public const string TextCol = "Text";
    public const string CommentCol = "Comment";
    public const int MaxKeyLen = 15;
    public const char CommentChar = ';';
}
```

The constants defined in the ResUtilConsts class are static by default.

In the identical fashion to the VB code this file contains a ResUtil class and a ResImage class. It also contains the custom exception class defined in the VB version of this file. Let's start out with the ResImage class. It is shown in Listing 7-17. First, however let's import some namespaces.

```csharp
using System;
using System.Collections;
using System.Globalization;
using System.Resources;
using System.IO;
using System.Data;
using System.Drawing;
using System.Drawing.Imaging;
using System.Text.RegularExpressions;
```

Listing 7-17. ResImage class

```
public class ResImage
{
    private Image img;
    private string imgName;
    private string imgType;

    public ResImage(object key, object val)
    {
        img = (Image)val;
        imgName = key.ToString();
        imgType = val.GetType().ToString();
    }

    public ResImage(string key, object val)
    {
        img = (Image)val;
        imgName = key;
        imgType = val.GetType().ToString();
    }

    public string Name
    {
        get { return imgName; }
        set { imgName = value; }
    }

    public Image image
    {
        get { return img; }
    }

    public string type
    {
        get { return imgType; }
    }

}
```

An important difference to note here is how properties are defined. A read-only property in VB needs the Readonly keyword in the definition. In C#, a read-only property is implicit by not giving it a set property. Also, note the implicit value variable for the set property.

Entering Code for the ResUtil Class

The complete code for the ResUtil class is shown in Listing 7-18. One thing to note in this class is that it has a data type of ResImages. This is a custom collection class that I defined and that replaces the VB collection class. Do not worry if after typing in this code it will not compile. You get to the ResImages class after this.

Listing 7-18. ResUtil class code

```
public class ResUtil
{
private string m_ResFile;
private string m_SaveFile;
private ResTypes m_ResType;
private ResImages m_PicCol;

public ResUtil()
{
  //Default to binary file. Default name
  m_ResType = ResTypes.BinType;
  m_ResFile = "BinResource.resources";
  m_SaveFile = m_ResFile;
  m_PicCol = new ResImages();
}
public ResUtil(string ResourceFilename)
{
  m_ResType = ResTypes.BinType;
  m_ResFile = ResourceFilename;
  m_SaveFile = m_ResFile;
  m_PicCol = new ResImages();
}
public ResUtil(string ResourceFilename, ResTypes ResourceType)
{
  m_ResType = ResourceType;
  m_ResFile = ResourceFilename;
  m_SaveFile = m_ResFile;
  m_PicCol = new ResImages();
}

public string FileName
{
  get { return m_ResFile; }
  set { m_ResFile = value; }
}
```

```csharp
public ResTypes ResourceType
{
  get { return m_ResType; }
  set { m_ResType = value; }
}
public ResImages Pics
{
  get { return m_PicCol; }
}

public string OutputFileName
{
  get { return m_SaveFile; }
  set { m_SaveFile = value; }
}

public void GetData(DataTable ResData, bool append)
{
  if ( ResData == null )
  {
    throw new InvalidTable("Data table was not defined");
    return;
  }

  //Make sure that memory is clear
  if (!append )
  {
    ResData.Clear();
    while ( m_PicCol.Count > 0 )
        m_PicCol.Remove(1);
  }

  switch ( m_ResType )
  {
    case ResTypes.TextType:
      try
      {
        FillFromTextFile(ResData);
      }
      catch (Exception ex)
      {
        throw ex;
      }
```

```csharp
                break;
        case ResTypes.XMLType:
          try
          {
            FillFromXMLFile(ResData);
          }
          catch (Exception ex)
          {
            throw ex;
          }
          break;
        case ResTypes.BinType:
          try
          {
            FillFromBinaryFile(ResData);
          }
          catch (Exception ex)
          {
            throw ex;
          }
          break;
    }
}

public void SaveData(DataTable ResData, ResImages Pics, ResTypes ResType)
{
  if ( ResData == null )
  {
    throw new InvalidTable("Data table was not defined");
    return;
  }

  m_PicCol = Pics;
  switch ( ResType )
  {
    case ResTypes.TextType:
        SaveToTextFile(ResData);
        break;
    case ResTypes.XMLType:
        SaveToXMLFile(ResData);
        break;
    case ResTypes.BinType:
        SaveToBinaryFile(ResData);
        break;
```

```
  }
}

private void FillFromBinaryFile(DataTable ResData)
{
  //Do not try anything if we are handed an invalid table
  //This is better than a try catch block. Avoid errors when possible.
  //Do not just catch them.
  if ( ResData == null )
  {
    throw new InvalidTable("Data table was not defined");
    return;
  }
  try
  {
    ResourceReader ResReader = new  ResourceReader(m_ResFile);
    IDictionaryEnumerator En = ResReader.GetEnumerator();

    //Iterate over the resource file
    //Add a row for each resource string and put key and value in
    // correct columns Don't forget! ResX resource files can contain
    //pictures. We only want the strings!
    while (En.MoveNext())
    {

      if ( En.Value.GetType() == typeof(string))
      {
        ResData.Rows.Add(ResData.NewRow());
        ResData.Rows[ResData.Rows.Count - 1][ResUtilConsts.KeyCol] = En.Key;
        ResData.Rows[ResData.Rows.Count - 1][ResUtilConsts.TextCol] = En.Value;
      }
      else if (En.Value.GetType() == typeof(Bitmap))
      {
        ResImage rImg = new ResImage(En.Key, En.Value);
        m_PicCol.Add(rImg, En.Key.ToString());
      }
      else if (En.Value.GetType() == typeof(Icon))
      {
        ResImage rImg = new ResImage(En.Key, En.Value);
        m_PicCol.Add(rImg, En.Key.ToString());
      }
```

```
          else if ( En.Value.GetType() == typeof(Image) )
          {
            ResImage rImg = new ResImage(En.Key, En.Value);
            m_PicCol.Add(rImg, En.Key.ToString());
          }
        }
        ResReader.Close();
      }
      catch (Exception ex)
      {
        throw ex;
      }
    }

    private void SaveToBinaryFile(DataTable ResData )
    {
      string Fname;

      if ( ResData == null )
      {
        throw new InvalidTable("Data table was not defined");
        return;
      }

      //Split the filename and make it a text file
      FileInfo File_Info = new FileInfo(m_SaveFile);
      Fname = File_Info.FullName + ".resources";
      try
      {
        //This will write over the existing file!
        ResourceWriter ResWriter = new ResourceWriter(Fname);
        string ResKey;
        string ResVal;

        //Iterate over the rows in the table and add to the resource file
        foreach ( DataRow ResRow in ResData.Rows )
        {
          ResKey = ResRow[ResUtilConsts.KeyCol].ToString();
          ResVal = ResRow[ResUtilConsts.TextCol].ToString();
          ResWriter.AddResource(ResKey, ResVal);
        }
```

```csharp
      //Save the pictures
      foreach ( ResImage Pic in m_PicCol )
      {
        ResWriter.AddResource(Pic.Name, Pic.image);
      }

      //Write out the resource file and close it.
      ResWriter.Generate();
      ResWriter.Close();
    }
    catch (Exception ex)
    {
      throw ex;
    }
  }


  private void FillFromTextFile(DataTable ResData )
  {
    string ResKey;
    string ResVal;
    string ResComment;
    //     Dim ResRow As DataRow

    if ( ResData == null )
    {
      throw new InvalidTable("Data table was not defined");
      return;
    }
    try
    {
      StreamReader MyStream = new StreamReader(m_ResFile);
      string MyLine;

      //Any string with a comment marker is considered a comment.
      //Resgen thinks so too.
      while (true)
      {
        if ((MyLine = MyStream.ReadLine()) == null )
          break;

        if (MyLine != "" )
        {
          // Instantiate a new Regular expression object
          Regex r = new Regex(";");
```

```csharp
            // Find a single match in the string.
            Match m = r.Match(MyLine);
            if (m.Index < 2 )    // >=2 is an Ambiguous line
            {
              ResComment = "";
              //This line is a comment so digest it as such
              if (m.Index == 1 )
                ResComment = MyLine.ToString().
                                    TrimStart(ResUtilConsts.CommentChar);

              if (m.Index == 0 )
              {
                //This line is a string resource
                string[] str = MyLine.Split('=');
                ResKey = str[0].Trim();
                ResVal = str[1].Trim();

                //Add this info to the table
                ResData.Rows.Add(ResData.NewRow());
                ResData.Rows[ResData.Rows.Count - 1]
                          [ResUtilConsts.KeyCol] = ResKey;
                ResData.Rows[ResData.Rows.Count - 1]
                          [ResUtilConsts.TextCol] = ResVal;
                ResData.Rows[ResData.Rows.Count - 1]
                          [ResUtilConsts.CommentCol] = ResComment;
              }
            }
          }
        }
      }
      catch (Exception ex)
      {
        throw ex;
      }
    }

    private void SaveToTextFile(DataTable ResData)
    {
      string fname;
      string ResKey;
      string ResVal;
      string ResComment;
```

```csharp
  if ( ResData == null )
  {
    throw new InvalidTable("Data table was not defined");
    return;
  }

  //Split the filename and make it a text file
  FileInfo File_Info = new FileInfo(m_SaveFile);
  fname = File_Info.FullName + ".txt";

  try
  {
    //Open up the new text file stream
    StreamWriter MyStream = new StreamWriter(fname);

    //Iterate over the rows in the table and add to the text resource file
    foreach ( DataRow ResRow in ResData.Rows )
    {
      ResKey = ResRow[ResUtilConsts.KeyCol].ToString().
                      PadRight(ResUtilConsts.MaxKeyLen + 1);
      ResVal = ResRow[ResUtilConsts.TextCol].ToString();
      ResComment = ResRow[ResUtilConsts.CommentCol].ToString();
      if (ResComment.Length > 0 )
        MyStream.WriteLine(";" + ResComment);

      MyStream.WriteLine(ResKey + " = " + ResVal);
      MyStream.WriteLine();
    }

    MyStream.Flush();
    MyStream.Close();
  }
  catch (Exception ex)
  {
    throw ex;
  }
}

private void FillFromXMLFile(DataTable ResData)
{
  //Do not try anything if we are handed an invalid table
  //This is better than a try catch block. Avoid errors when possible.
  //Do not just catch them.
  if ( ResData == null )
  {
```

```
                throw new InvalidTable("Data table was not defined");
                return;
            }
            try
            {
                ResXResourceReader ResXReader = new  ResXResourceReader(m_ResFile);
                IDictionaryEnumerator En = ResXReader.GetEnumerator();

                while (En.MoveNext())
                {
                    if ( En.Value.GetType() == typeof(string))
                    {
                        ResData.Rows.Add(ResData.NewRow());
                        ResData.Rows[ResData.Rows.Count - 1][ResUtilConsts.KeyCol] = En.Key;
                        ResData.Rows[ResData.Rows.Count - 1][ResUtilConsts.TextCol] = En.Value;
                    }
                    else if (En.Value.GetType() == typeof(Bitmap))
                    {
                        ResImage rImg = new ResImage(En.Key, En.Value);
                        m_PicCol.Add(rImg, En.Key.ToString());
                    }
                    else if (En.Value.GetType() == typeof(Icon))
                    {
                        ResImage rImg = new ResImage(En.Key, En.Value);
                        m_PicCol.Add(rImg, En.Key.ToString());
                    }
                    else if ( En.Value.GetType() == typeof(Image) )
                    {
                        ResImage rImg = new ResImage(En.Key, En.Value);
                        m_PicCol.Add(rImg, En.Key.ToString());
                    }
                }
                ResXReader.Close();
            }
            catch (Exception ex)
            {
                throw ex;
            }
        }

        private void SaveToXMLFile(DataTable ResData)
        {
            string Fname;
```

```csharp
      if ( ResData == null )
      {
        throw new InvalidTable("Data table was not defined");
        return;
      }

      //Split the filename and make it a resx file
      FileInfo File_Info = new FileInfo(m_SaveFile);
      Fname = File_Info.FullName + ".resx";

      try
      {
        //This will write over the existing file!
        ResXResourceWriter ResxWriter = new ResXResourceWriter(Fname);
        string ResKey;
        string ResVal;

        //Iterate over the rows in the table and add to the resource file
        foreach ( DataRow ResRow in ResData.Rows )
        {
          ResKey = ResRow[ResUtilConsts.KeyCol].ToString();
          ResVal = ResRow[ResUtilConsts.TextCol].ToString();
          ResxWriter.AddResource(ResKey, ResVal);
        }

        //Save the pictures
        foreach ( ResImage Pic in m_PicCol )
        {
          ResxWriter.AddResource(Pic.Name, Pic.image);
        }

        //Write out the resource file and close it.
        ResxWriter.Generate();
        ResxWriter.Close();
      }
      catch (Exception ex)
      {
        throw ex;
      }
    }
}
```

This code is functionally similar to the VB ResUtil code. There are minor differences due to syntactical differences between C# and VB. It is instructive to compare this code to the VB code and see what those differences really are. As an example, if you look carefully you see that instead of using the VB Instr function I use the regular expression object to detect the presence of a substring within a string. Regular expressions are a very potent way to parse text.

NOTE   *I used to use regular expressions all the time in my DOS and Unix days. I have a friend who can still come up with the most amazing regular expression code I have ever seen. All by heart!*

Making a Custom Collection Class

This section deals with the ResImages file. The file contains code for a Custom Collection class that holds all the images.

Visual Basic 6 has a collection object and likewise VB .NET mimics this functionality with the Collection class. The problem with the VB Collection class is that it is not type safe. It allows you to put anything in the collection and possibly end up with a jumble of objects. There are ways around this by making your own Collection-class wrapper in VB. I did not do this for the VB code in the example. Instead I do it in the C# code. Another reason for making your own Collection class is to control who gets to add and remove objects. The VB Collection class has the add and remove methods exposed. If you write an assembly that exposes a VB collection, anyone could connect to that collection and add or remove objects without your assembly knowing about it. This is not a good idea.

A normal collection has the following basic functionalities:

- Add. This method adds an item to the collection.

- Remove. This method removes an item from the collection.

- Count. This property retrieves the count of items in the collection.

- Enumerator. This property allows for each iteration of the collection objects.

- Item. This property retrieves an item based on a key or index.

At times you will find a specialized collection that has a Clear method. This method wipes out all data in the collection. An example of a collection that has this method is the Nodes collection in a tree view control.

C# does not have a generic collection similar to VB. It has an abstract CollectionBase class that you can inherit from to provide your own collection. It also has quite a few specialized collections. For more information look in the MSDN Help under the Icollection interface.

The Collection class in this project uses a sorted list. I use this form of internal storage because it maintains a list of your objects based on both a key and an index. This allows retrieval of an object based on either of these two parameters. This is similar to the VB collection.

One thing to note about collection naming convention. It is common to name a Collection class based on the object it is supposed to hold. All you do is add an "s" to the end of the name. The object contained in our collection is ResImage. The collection will be called ResImages.

Listing 7-19 shows the complete code for this class.

Listing 7-19. ResImages collection class

```csharp
using System;
using System.Collections;

namespace CH7ResEdit_C
{
  /// <summary>
  /// This is the collection class that handles a collection of
  /// ResImage objects. Traditionally a collection of objects is
  /// named that object with an 's' on the end.
  /// </summary>
  public class ResImages : IEnumerable
  {
    //Slower than Hash table but more flexible
    //Can get item by index number or by key.
    //Most like VB type collection
    private SortedList mCol;

    public ResImages()
     {
       mCol = new  SortedList();
    }

    // enables foreach processing
    private mEnum GetEnumerator()
    {
      return new mEnum(this);
    }
```

```csharp
        //Property count
        public int Count
        {
          get { return mCol.Count; }
        }

        // ---- overloaded add method ----
        public void Add(ResImage w)
        {
            mCol.Add( w.Name, w);
        }
        public void Add(ResImage w, string key)
        {
          mCol.Add(key,w);
        }

        // ---- overloaded remove method ----
        public void Remove(int Index)
        {
          mCol.RemoveAt(Index);
        }
        public void Remove(string key)
        {
          mCol.Remove(key);
        }

        // ---- overloaded item method ----
        public ResImage Item(int index)
        {
          return (ResImage) mCol.GetByIndex(index);
        }
        public ResImage Item(string key)
        {
          return (ResImage) mCol[key];
        }

//--------- Below is where I implement the IEnumerator interface ----

        // Implement the GetEnumerator() method:
        IEnumerator IEnumerable.GetEnumerator()
        {
            return GetEnumerator();
        }
```

```csharp
    // Declare the enumerator and implement the IEnumerator interface:
    private class mEnum: IEnumerator
    {
      private int nIndex;
      private ResImages collection;

      // constructor. make the collection
      public mEnum(ResImages coll)
      {
        collection = coll;
        nIndex = -1;
      }

      // start over
      public void Reset()
      {
        nIndex = -1;
      }

      // bump up the index
      public bool MoveNext()
      {
        nIndex++;
        return(nIndex < collection.mCol.Count);
      }

      // get the current object
      public ResImage Current
      {
        get {return (ResImage) collection.mCol.GetByIndex(nIndex); }
      }

      // The current property on the IEnumerator interface:
      object IEnumerator.Current
      {
        get { return(Current); }
      }
    }
  }
}
```

This class contains all the methods necessary for a collection. Notice that the item method is overloaded. You can get an item from the collection based on a string key or an index. I do both in the frmResources code.

This class implements the IEnumerable interface. This interface is what gives this collection the ability to be iterated with the C# for each construct. The concept of an interface is extremely important in .NET

Notice the Add method. This method provides the type safety and type checking necessary for this class. Only an object of type ResImage can be added to this collection.

Finishing Off the Code

So far you have all the support code for this C# version of the ResEditor. Now it is time to provide the display and resources manipulation code. You will find that this code is very similar to the VB ResEditor code. The code is provided in Listing 7-20. This code listing does not contain the Windows generated code.

Listing 7-20. Code for the frmResources form

```csharp
using System;
using System.Globalization;
using System.Drawing;
using System.Collections;
using System.ComponentModel;
using System.Windows.Forms;
using System.Data;
using System.IO;
using MS = Microsoft.VisualBasic.Strings;

namespace CH7ResEdit_C
{
    /// <summary>
    /// Summary description for Form1.
    /// </summary>
    public class frmResources : System.Windows.Forms.Form
    {
... Windows code ...
        /// <summary>
        /// Required designer variable.
        /// </summary>
        private System.ComponentModel.Container components = null;
```

```csharp
        // Programmer generated code!
        const int GridLineWidth=1; //Pixel width of a grid line
        const string ResourceTableName  = "Resources";

        const int TEXT_TAB = 0;
        const int GRAPHICS_TAB = 1;
        const int FINAL_TAB = 2;
        const int PICSPACE = 10;
        const int PICSIZE = 64;

        private DataTable m_StringTable;
        private String m_ResFile;
        private String m_NewFname;

        private System.Windows.Forms.MenuItem mnuAppend;
        private System.Windows.Forms.MenuItem mnuOpen;
        private System.Windows.Forms.MenuItem mnuExit;
        private System.Windows.Forms.OpenFileDialog OpenResFile;
        private ResTypes m_ResType;
        private System.Windows.Forms.TabControl tcResources;
        private System.Windows.Forms.CheckBox chkCreateBin;
        private System.Windows.Forms.Label lblInFilename;
        private System.Windows.Forms.Label lblResStringNum;
        private System.Windows.Forms.Label lblNumPics;
        private System.Windows.Forms.Button cmdSave;
        private System.Windows.Forms.CheckBox chkCreateXML;
        private System.Windows.Forms.CheckBox chkCreateText;
        private ResImages m_Pictures = new ResImages();

    public frmResources()
    {
//
        // Required for Windows Form Designer support
        //
        InitializeComponent();

    //Set up the delegates for events here
    this.mnuExit.Click +=
            new System.EventHandler(this.ProgExit);
    this.mnuOpen.Click +=
            new System.EventHandler(this.GetResources);
    this.mnuAppend.Click +=
            new System.EventHandler(this.GetResources);
```

```
                this.lstPictures.SelectedIndexChanged +=
                        new System.EventHandler(this.PicList);
                this.tcResources.Click +=
                        new System.EventHandler(this.TabChange);
                this.cmdAddPic.Click +=
                        new System.EventHandler(this.AddPic);
                this.cmdDelPic.Click +=
                        new System.EventHandler(this.RemovePic);
                this.txtBaseName.TextChanged +=
                        new System.EventHandler(this.NameChanged);
                this.lstCultures.SelectedIndexChanged +=
                        new System.EventHandler(this.CulturePick);
                this.chkCreateBin.CheckStateChanged +=
                        new System.EventHandler(this.Create_Checked);
                this.chkCreateText.CheckStateChanged +=
                        new System.EventHandler(this.Create_Checked);
                this.chkCreateXML.CheckStateChanged +=
                        new System.EventHandler(this.Create_Checked);
                this.cmdSave.Click +=
                        new System.EventHandler(this.SaveIt);
        }
    [STAThread]
     static void Main()
       {
            Application.Run(new frmResources());
       }

        private void Form1_Load(object sender, System.EventArgs e)
        {
          InitStrings();
          SetupStringTable();
          dgStrings.DataSource = m_StringTable;
          SetupStringResourceGrid();
          AlignColumns();
        }

        private void InitStrings()
        {
          sbStatus.Panels[2].Text = DateTime.Now.ToString();
          sbStatus.Panels[1].Width = 100;
        }

        private void SetupStringTable()
        {
```

```
        //Give this table a name so I can synchronize to it with the grid
        m_StringTable = new DataTable(ResourceTableName);

        //Add three columns to the table
        m_StringTable.Columns.Add(new DataColumn(ResUtilConsts.KeyCol,
                                Type.GetType("System.String")));
        m_StringTable.Columns.Add(new DataColumn(ResUtilConsts.TextCol,
                                Type.GetType("System.String")));
        m_StringTable.Columns.Add(new DataColumn(ResUtilConsts.CommentCol,
                                Type.GetType("System.String")));
}

private void SetupStringResourceGrid()
{
    DataGridTableStyle dgS = new DataGridTableStyle();
    DataGridTextBoxColumn dgCKey;
    DataGridTextBoxColumn dgCText;
    DataGridTextBoxColumn dgCComment;

    //Set up a table style first then add it to the grid
    dgS.MappingName = ResourceTableName;
    dgS.PreferredColumnWidth = 300;
    dgS.SelectionBackColor = Color.Beige;
    dgS.SelectionForeColor = Color.Black;
    dgS.AllowSorting = true;

    //Make a column style for the first column and add it to the columnstyle
    dgCKey = new DataGridTextBoxColumn();
    dgCKey.MappingName = ResUtilConsts.KeyCol;
    dgCKey.HeaderText = "Resource Key";
    dgCKey.Width = 100;
    dgS.GridColumnStyles.Add(dgCKey);

    //Make a column style for the second column and add it to the columnstyle
    dgCComment = new DataGridTextBoxColumn();
    dgCComment.MappingName = ResUtilConsts.TextCol;
    dgCComment.HeaderText = "Resource Text";
    dgCComment.Width = 300;
    dgS.GridColumnStyles.Add(dgCComment);

    //Make a column style for the third column and add it to the columnstyle
    dgCText = new DataGridTextBoxColumn();
    dgCText.MappingName = ResUtilConsts.CommentCol;
```

```
    dgCText.HeaderText = "Comment";
    dgCText.Width = 400;
    dgS.GridColumnStyles.Add(dgCText);

    //First purge all table styles from this grid then add the one that I want
    dgStrings.TableStyles.Clear();
    dgStrings.TableStyles.Add(dgS);
}

private void AlignColumns()
{
    dgStrings.TableStyles[0].GridColumnStyles[0].Width = 100;
    dgStrings.TableStyles[0].GridColumnStyles[1].Width = 300;
    dgStrings.TableStyles[0].GridColumnStyles[2].Width =
        dgStrings.Size.Width - dgStrings.TableStyles[0].GridColumnStyles[0].Width
        - dgStrings.TableStyles[0].GridColumnStyles[1].Width
        - dgStrings.RowHeaderWidth - 4 * GridLineWidth;
}

private void FillPicList()
{
    PicPanel.AutoScroll = true;
    pic.Image = null;
    foreach(ResImage ResImg in m_Pictures)
    {
        lstPictures.Items.Add(ResImg.Name);
        //Make a new picture box and add it to the
        //panels control array
        AddPic2Panel(ResImg);
    }
    ArrangePictures();

    if (lstPictures.Items.Count > 0 )
    {
        lstPictures.SetSelected(0, true);
        cmdDelPic.Enabled = true;
    }
    else
        cmdDelPic.Enabled = false;
}
```

```
private void AddPic2Panel(ResImage ResImg)
{
  PictureBox Pic;

  Pic = new PictureBox();
  Pic.Size = new Size(PICSIZE, PICSIZE);
  Pic.Location = new Point(10, 10);
  Pic.SizeMode = PictureBoxSizeMode.StretchImage;
  Pic.Image = ResImg.image;
  Pic.Tag = ResImg.Name;
  PicPanel.Controls.Add(Pic);
}
private void ArrangePictures()
{
  int x;
  int y = 0;

  //Number of pictures in a row.
  //DO not show a picture if it means we get a horizontal
  //scroll bar
  int NumPicsInWidth  = (int)((PicPanel.Size.Width - PICSPACE) /
                              (PICSIZE + PICSPACE)) - 1;
  //Control collections are zero based.
  //VB type collections are 1 based.
  for (int k = 0; k<= PicPanel.Controls.Count - 1; k++)
  {
    //determine if we are in a new row
    if (k % (NumPicsInWidth) == 0 )
        x = PICSPACE;
    else
        x = PicPanel.Controls[k - 1].Location.X + PICSIZE + PICSPACE;

    if (k < NumPicsInWidth )
        y = PICSPACE;
    else if (k % (NumPicsInWidth) == 0 )
        y = PicPanel.Controls[k - 1].Location.Y + PICSIZE + PICSPACE;

    PicPanel.Controls[k].Location = new Point(x, y);
  }
}

public void BuildCompleteName()
{
  m_NewFname = txtBaseName.Text == ""? "?": txtBaseName.Text;
```

```
                 if ( lstCultures.SelectedItem !=null )
                 {
                   if (lstCultures.SelectedItem.ToString().Trim() != "(None)" )
                     m_NewFname += "." + MS.Left(lstCultures.SelectedItem.ToString(),15)
                                                   .Trim();

                 }

                 if (chkCreateText.Checked == true )
                   lblTxtFname.Text = m_NewFname + ".txt";
                 else
                   lblTxtFname.Text = "";

                 if (chkCreateXML.Checked == true )
                   lblXMLfname.Text = m_NewFname + ".resx";
                 else
                   lblXMLfname.Text = "";

                 if (chkCreateBin.Checked == true )
                   lblBinFname.Text = m_NewFname + ".resources";
                 else
                   lblBinFname.Text = "";
               }

               private void NameChanged(object sender, System.EventArgs e)
               {
                 BuildCompleteName();
               }
               private void CulturePick(object sender, System.EventArgs e)
               {
                 BuildCompleteName();
               }
               private void Create_Checked(object sender, System.EventArgs e)
               {
                 if( chkCreateBin.Checked == false && chkCreateXML.Checked == false &&
                     chkCreateText.Checked == false )
                   cmdSave.Enabled = false;
                 else
                   cmdSave.Enabled = true;
```

```csharp
    BuildCompleteName();
}
private void SaveIt(object sender, System.EventArgs e)
{
  ResUtil Res = new ResUtil(m_ResFile);
  Res.OutputFileName = m_NewFname;

  if (chkCreateText.Checked )
    Res.SaveData(m_StringTable, m_Pictures, ResTypes.TextType);

  if (chkCreateXML.Checked )
    Res.SaveData(m_StringTable, m_Pictures, ResTypes.XMLType);

  if (chkCreateBin.Checked )
    Res.SaveData(m_StringTable, m_Pictures, ResTypes.BinType);
}
private void PicList(object sender, System.EventArgs e)
{
  ResImage rImg;

  rImg = (ResImage) m_Pictures.Item(lstPictures.SelectedItem.ToString());
  pic.Image = rImg.image;

  //Highlight the picture in question by
  //giving it a border. Don't foget to "unborder" the others.
  foreach(PictureBox pb in PicPanel.Controls)
  {
    if (pb.Tag.ToString() == rImg.Name )
      pb.BorderStyle = System.Windows.Forms.BorderStyle.FixedSingle;
    else
      pb.BorderStyle = System.Windows.Forms.BorderStyle.None;
  }
}
private void GetResources(object sender, System.EventArgs e)
{
  OpenResFile.Reset();
  OpenResFile.InitialDirectory = Directory.GetCurrentDirectory();
  OpenResFile.RestoreDirectory = true;
  OpenResFile.Filter = "Text files (*.txt)|*.txt|XML files " +
                       "(*.resx)|*.resx|Binary files (*.resources)|" +
                       "*.resources";
```

```
    if (OpenResFile.ShowDialog() == DialogResult.OK)
   {
     m_ResType = (ResTypes) OpenResFile.FilterIndex;
     m_ResFile = OpenResFile.FileName;
     ResUtil Res = new ResUtil(m_ResFile, m_ResType);

     //clear the pictures
     lstPictures.Items.Clear();
     while (lstPictures.Items.Count > 0)
       lstPictures.Items.Remove(1);

     PicPanel.Controls.Clear();

     //Fill the string text box
     sbStatus.Panels[0].Text = m_ResFile;
     if (sender == mnuOpen )
     {
       Res.GetData(m_StringTable, false);
       m_Pictures = Res.Pics;
     }
     else if (sender == mnuAppend )
     {
       Res.GetData(m_StringTable, true);
       //Add to the pictures collection
       ResImages NewPics;

       NewPics = Res.Pics;
       foreach(ResImage p in NewPics)
         m_Pictures.Add(p);
     }
     FillPicList();
   }
}

private void TabChange(object sender, System.EventArgs e)
{
  if (tcResources.SelectedIndex == FINAL_TAB )
  {
    lblInFilename.Text = m_ResFile;
    lblResStringNum.Text = m_StringTable.Rows.Count.ToString();
    lblNumPics.Text = m_Pictures.Count.ToString();
```

```csharp
        CultureInfo[] AllCultures;
        AllCultures = CultureInfo.GetCultures(CultureTypes.SpecificCultures);
        lstCultures.Items.Clear();
        lstCultures.Items.Add(" ".PadRight(10) + "(None)");
        lstCultures.Sorted = true;
        foreach(CultureInfo ACulture in AllCultures)
            lstCultures.Items.Add(ACulture.Name.PadRight(15) +
                                    ACulture.DisplayName);

        chkCreateBin.Checked = true;
      }
    if (tcResources.SelectedIndex == GRAPHICS_TAB )
    {
      if( lstPictures.Items.Count < 1 )
        cmdDelPic.Enabled = false;
    }
}


private void AddPic(object sender, System.EventArgs e)
{
  OpenResFile.Reset();
  OpenResFile.InitialDirectory = Directory.GetCurrentDirectory();
  OpenResFile.RestoreDirectory = true;
  OpenResFile.Filter =  "Picture files (*.jpg; *.bmp; *.gif)|" +
                        "*.jpg; *.bmp; *.gif";

  if (OpenResFile.ShowDialog() == DialogResult.OK)
  {

    FileInfo fInfo = new FileInfo(OpenResFile.FileName);
    if ((fInfo.Extension.ToUpper() == ".JPG") ||
        (fInfo.Extension.ToUpper() == ".BMP") ||
        (fInfo.Extension.ToUpper() == ".GIF") )
    {
      //Add the picture to the collection
      ResImage rImg = new ResImage(OpenResFile.FileName,
                                    Image.FromFile(OpenResFile.FileName));
      AskKey Keyform = new AskKey(rImg);
      if (Keyform.ShowDialog(this) == DialogResult.OK )
      {
        m_Pictures.Add(rImg, rImg.Name);
        //Add the picture to the panel and arrange
        AddPic2Panel(rImg);
```

```
                ArrangePictures();
                //Add the picture to the list and enable delete and select it
                lstPictures.Items.Add(rImg.Name);
                lstPictures.SetSelected(lstPictures.Items.Count - 1, true);
                cmdDelPic.Enabled = true;
            }
            Keyform.Dispose();
          }
        }
      }
      private void ProgExit(object sender, System.EventArgs e)
      {
        this.Dispose();
      }

      private void RemovePic(object sender, System.EventArgs e)
      {
        //Remove the picture from the picture collection
        m_Pictures.Remove(lstPictures.SelectedItem.ToString());

        //Remove the picture from the panel and rearrange the rest
        foreach( PictureBox pb in PicPanel.Controls)
        {
          if (pb.BorderStyle == System.Windows.Forms.BorderStyle.FixedSingle )
          {
            PicPanel.Controls.Remove(pb);
            ArrangePictures();
            break;
          }
        }

        //Remove the name from the listbox of keys and
        //reselect the first one
        lstPictures.Items.Remove(lstPictures.SelectedItem);
        if (lstPictures.Items.Count > 0 )
          lstPictures.SetSelected(0, true);
        else
        {
          cmdDelPic.Enabled = false;
          pic.Image = null;
        }
      }
    }
  }
}
```

Handling Events in C#

The most notable thing about this code is the difference between how control events are handled in C# as opposed to VB. In VB .NET you just double-click a control on your form and a method is generated for you in your code that handles the event. You know this code is connected to the control because of the "Handles" keyword at the end of the method definition. You can change the name of the VB method and you still know that it is tied to this event. Here is a sample VB event definition.

```
Private Sub CulturePick(ByVal sender As System.Object,
ByVal e As System.EventArgs) _
                        Handles lstCultures.SelectedIndexChanged
```

As you can see, this method handles the SelectedIndexChanged event of the lstCultures list box. The name of the method has been changed from its original name.

The same thing is true for C# but with a caveat. If you double-click a control in a C# form, you are taken to an event handler that was generated for you. Same as VB. However, there is no way to know by inspecting this event code that it is tied to your control. There is no "Handles <event>" code. The only guess you can make is by the name of the method. As you know, you can change the name of an event handler. If this is true, there must be something in the code somewhere that connects this event handler to the control. Well there is. It is way up in the Windows Generated code.

My advice to you is to never double-click a control to get an event unless you want the default event. You will end up having to go into the Windows Generated code and deleting the delegate definition. It is better to hand-code the event delegate yourself. You will also be able to program one method that handles multiple events. Following is the delegate method definition and method code that handles the check boxes. Listing 7-21 shows how to create a single delegate for many events. This code is extracted from Listing 7-20.

Lisitng 7-21. Single delegate for all check box events

```
this.chkCreateBin.CheckStateChanged +=
        new System.EventHandler(this.Create_Checked);
this.chkCreateText.CheckStateChanged +=
        new System.EventHandler(this.Create_Checked);
this.chkCreateXML.CheckStateChanged +=
        new System.EventHandler(this.Create_Checked);
```

```
private void Create_Checked(object sender, System.EventArgs e)
{
  if( chkCreateBin.Checked == false && chkCreateXML.Checked == false &&
      chkCreateText.Checked == false )
    cmdSave.Enabled = false;
  else
    cmdSave.Enabled = true;

  BuildCompleteName();
}
```

Summary

This has been an interesting chapter in that you made a full-featured resource editor in both VB and C#. You saw how to generate a windows forms project and add code to read and write resources to any of the standard resource formats. You also saw how to add picture box controls to a panel control at runtime. This gave the ability to show an unlimited number of graphic resources in the panel.

As a contrast to the VB version of this project you saw the exact same functionality written in C#. This gives you a good idea of the advantages and disadvantages of both languages.

Next, you use this resource editor to create a resource file for itself. You then use this resource file to help localize this project.

CHAPTER 8

Let's Localize

CHAPTER 7 INCLUDED AN example of a full-fledged resource editor. This chapter uses the resource editor to localize itself. If you remember, when you built the screens and the code, you did not pay any attention to localization. There are unnamed controls and default text in all the labels. Error messages are hard-coded as is any output to text boxes.

As you go through this chapter and correct the lack of localization, you may wonder "Why didn't I do this from the start?" You will experience first-hand that it is easier to design with localization in mind.

Laying Out the Task

The localization task has several steps. No particular order is required for some of the steps. They just happen to be ordered in the way I usually attack a "fix it so it can be sold overseas" project. The gross steps to take for this project are listed next.

- Rearrange the GUI controls so translated text fits in the allotted space.

- Internalize the assignment of static strings from the controls into one method.

- Make sure that all images are displayed by code settings rather than through the design mode.

- Make sure all dates and times are displayed using internationally aware functions.

- Make sure that currency and numbers are displayed using internationally-aware functions.

- Use the resource editor to make a resource file with all strings and images needed for this example.

- Use the .NET resource manager classes to get all strings from the appropriate resource file.

The languages you'll use for this example are English (default) and German. Now that you know what to do, let's start.

Revisiting the GUI

Open the ResEdit project from Chapter 7. I'll go over both VB and C# at the same time, so open either project. The first thing you are going to do is give names to all the controls that still have their default names. There are a few of them. Typically in a project such as this, most of the controls that have default names are the label controls. This is the case here as well. Rename the controls listed in Table 8-1 as described.

Table 8-1. Renaming Controls in ResEdit

LOCATION	CONTROL DESCRIPTION	NEW NAME
Pictures Tab	Label that says "Key"	lblPicKey
Pictures Tab	Label that says "Pictures"	lblPictures
Final Tab	Basics frame	fraBasics
Final Tab	Output frame	fraOutput
Final Tab	Label "Input Filename"	lblInputFname
Final Tab	Label "Base Name"	lblBaseName
Final Tab	Label "String Count"	lblStrCnt
Final Tab	Label "Picture Count"	lblPicCnt
Final Tab	Label "Choose Culture"	lblCulture

Once you have done this, the controls in this project should have a name. The only ones that don't are the tab pages themselves. This is OK because I refer to them by index rather than by name.

Initializing the Controls with Strings

OK, now you have names for all the controls. Big deal. The thing to do now is to make a method that initializes the text in all static controls. You already have that method—InitStrings(). This method should be one of the first methods called in any program. Listing 8-1 shows the new InitStrings() method for both the VB and C# ResEditor.

Listing 8-1. New InitString method

VB

```vb
Private Sub InitStrings()

    'Status Panel
    sbStatus.Panels(2).Text = Now.ToString
    sbStatus.Panels(1).Width = 100

    'Tab Pages
    tcResource.TabPages(TEXT_TAB).Text = "Text"
    tcResource.TabPages(GRAPHICS_TAB).Text = "Pictures"
    tcResource.TabPages(FINAL_TAB).Text = "Final..."

    'Form Controls
    cmdQuit.Text = "Quit"
    mnuFile.Text = "File"
    mnuOpen.Text = "Open"
    mnuAppend.Text = "Append"
    mnuExit.Text = "Exit"

    'do picture tab
    lblPicKey.Text = "Key"
    lblPictures.Text = "Pictures"
    cmdAddPic.Text = "Add"
    cmdDelPic.Text = "Remove"

    'Do Final tab
    fraBasics.Text = "Basics"
    lblInputFname.Text = "Input Filename"
    lblStrCnt.Text = "String Count"
    lblPicCnt.Text = "Picture Count"
    lblCulture.Text = "Choose Culture"
    fraOutput.Text = "Build Output File(s)"
    lblBaseName.Text = "Base Name"
    cmdSave.Text = "Save"
      chkCreateText.Text = "Create Text file for translator"
      chkCreateXML.Text = "Create XMl File"
      chkCreateBin.Text = "Create Binary File"

End Sub
```

C#

```csharp
private void InitStrings()
{
  sbStatus.Panels[2].Text = DateTime.Now.ToString();
  sbStatus.Panels[1].Width = 100;

  //Tab Pages
  tcResources.TabPages[TEXT_TAB].Text = "Text";
  tcResources.TabPages[GRAPHICS_TAB].Text = "Pictures";
  tcResources.TabPages[FINAL_TAB].Text = "Final...";

  //Form Controls
  cmdQuit.Text = "Quit";
  mnuFile.Text = "File";
  mnuOpen.Text = "Open";
  mnuAppend.Text = "Append";
  mnuExit.Text = "Exit";

  //do picture tab
  lblPicKey.Text = "Key";
  lblPictures.Text = "Pictures";
  cmdAddPic.Text = "Add";
  cmdDelPic.Text = "Remove";

  //Do Final tab
  fraBasics.Text = "Basics";
  lblInputFname.Text = "Input Filename";
  lblStrCnt.Text = "String Count";
  lblPicCnt.Text = "Picture Count";
  lblCulture.Text = "Choose Culture";
  fraOutput.Text = "Build Output File(s)";
  lblBaseName.Text = "Base Name";
  cmdSave.Text = "Save";
  chkCreateText.Text = "Create Text file for translator";
  chkCreateXML.Text = "Create XMl File";
  chkCreateBin.Text = "Create Binary File";
}
```

A little later you bring in all these strings from a resource file.

Enhancing the ResImage Class

Most programs have at least one icon. This program is supposed to save graphics in a resource file for later use in a real program. If you have been paying attention, you should have noticed that this program only saves graphics of the bitmap type. You cannot load a bitmap as an icon in a .NET program. Therefore, you need to make a little side trip and add some functionality to the ResImage class to be able to hold an icon.

What is an icon? You can think of an icon as a small transparent bitmap. The machine displaying it usually sets the size of an icon. A regular bitmap image has a defined size.

Loading and saving icons in resource files is not difficult. The dilemma is how to display it. I display images in a picture box, which does not display an icon. I could have a separate control that shows just an icon when necessary but I like generality and it would be nice to display an icon and any other kind of image in the same control. The method I came up with converts an icon to a bitmap for display purposes, but stores it as an icon internally. This method allows me to read and save icons but display them as bitmaps.

Remember the Type property in the ResImage class? I said in Chapter 7 that this might come in handy. Although I did not use this property in Chapter 7, I use it here. An image type in .NET does not hold an icon and does not convert between the two. It is, however, possible to convert an icon to a bitmap. I take advantage of this fact as I modify the ResImage class to hold an icon. Let's go ahead and change the ResImage class. You find this class in the ResUtil.vb file for the VB project and in the ResUtil.cs file for C#.

Within this class you need to add a private member of type Icon. You also need to change the constructors to store the image as an icon if necessary. Finally you need to change the Type property.

Presently the Type property is a string. This is rather inconvenient for comparisons so I changed it to return a type of Type. Listing 8-2 shows the new ResImage class in both C# and VB.

Listing 8-2. New ResImage class that now holds an icon

VB

```
Public Class ResImage

    Private img As Image
    Private m_Icon As Icon
    Private imgName As String
    Private imgType As Type
```

```vbnet
Public Sub New(ByVal Key As Object, ByVal Value As Object)
  'Value is an object because of the way it is passed in
  If Value.GetType Is GetType(Icon) Then
    m_Icon = CType(Value, Icon)
    img = m_Icon.ToBitmap()
  Else
    img = CType(Value, Image)
  End If
  imgName = Key.ToString
  imgType = Value.GetType

End Sub
Public Sub New(ByVal Key As String, ByVal Value As Object)
  'Value is an object because of the way it is passed in
  If Value.GetType Is GetType(Icon) Then
    m_Icon = CType(Value, Icon)
    img = m_Icon.ToBitmap()
  Else
    img = CType(Value, Image)
  End If
  imgName = Key
  imgType = Value.GetType

End Sub

Public Property Name() As String
  Get
    Return imgName
  End Get
  Set(ByVal Value As String)
    imgName = Value
  End Set
End Property
Public ReadOnly Property Image() As Image
  Get
    Return img
  End Get
End Property
Public ReadOnly Property Icon() As Icon
  Get
    Return m_Icon
  End Get
End Property
```

```vbnet
   Public ReadOnly Property Type() As Type
      Get
         Return imgType
      End Get
   End Property
End Class
```

C#

```csharp
   public class ResImage
   {
      private Image img;
      private Icon m_Icon;
      private string imgName;
      private Type imgType;

      public ResImage(object key, object val)
      {
         if ( val.GetType() == typeof(Icon) )
         {
            m_Icon = (Icon)val;
            img = m_Icon.ToBitmap();
         }
         else
            img = (Image)val;

         imgName = key.ToString();
         imgType = val.GetType();
      }

      public ResImage(string key, object val)
      {
         if ( val.GetType() == typeof(Icon) )
         {
            m_Icon = (Icon)val;
            img = m_Icon.ToBitmap();
         }
         else
            img = (Image)val;
         imgName = key;
         imgType = val.GetType();
      }
```

```
    public string Name
    {
      get { return imgName; }
      set { imgName = value; }
    }

    public Image image
    {
      get { return img; }
    }
    public Icon Icon
    {
      get { return m_Icon; }
    }

    public Type type
    {
      get { return imgType; }
    }
  }
```

This class is now able to hold virtually any type of image you would want in a resource file. If the image is an icon, the class holds this information internally but allows access to it as if it were a bitmap. This makes it easy to display the image on the resource editor screen. In order to get the icon back out, I have added a new property called Icon. Any method can query the ResImage object for its type and retrieve the image if it is an icon.

Try compiling and running the program now. You should not get any errors and you should be able to load the resource editor with pictures as before. So far nothing seems to have changed as far as the editor itself goes.

The loading of graphical resources does not need to change. The two methods FillFromXMLFile and FillFromBinaryFile send images to ResImage constructors, which take care of deciding if the image is a bitmap or an icon. That is the point of a class like this. Do as much as possible internally and hide the implementation details from the outside.

Let's make one more change to the ResUtil file before you move on to the main code. This change involves saving the files. If the save methods were not changed, everything would still work except that the icons would be saved as bitmaps. Once the images are in the resource file you lose the original type information. Fortunately, icons can be saved in a resource file.

All you need to add to the save methods is a test to see if the image being saved is an icon or a bitmap. If it is an icon then save the icon, otherwise save the bitmap. Listing 8-3 shows the new SaveToXMLFile and SaveToBinaryFile methods for both the VB and C# projects.

Listing 8-3. The new save methods for both VB and C# projects

VB

```
Private Sub SaveToXMLFile(ByRef ResData As DataTable)
   Dim Fname As String
   Dim Pic As ResImage

   'Do not try anything if we are handed an invalid table
   'This is better than a try catch block. Avoid errors when possible.
   'Do not just catch them.
   If ResData Is Nothing Then
     Throw New InvalidTable("Data table was not defined")
     Exit Sub
   End If

   'Split the filename and make it a text file
   Dim File_Info As New FileInfo(m_SaveFile)
   Fname = File_Info.FullName + ".resx"

   Try
      'This will write over the existing file!
      Dim ResxWriter As New ResXResourceWriter(Fname)
      Dim ResKey As String
      Dim ResVal As String
      Dim ResRow As DataRow

      'Iterate over the rows in the table and add to the resource file
      For Each ResRow In ResData.Rows
        ResKey = ResRow(KeyCol).ToString
        ResVal = ResRow(TextCol).ToString
        ResxWriter.AddResource(ResKey, ResVal)
      Next

      'Save the pictures
      For Each Pic In m_PicCol
        If Pic.Type Is GetType(Icon) Then
          ResxWriter.AddResource(Pic.Name, Pic.Icon)
        Else
          ResxWriter.AddResource(Pic.Name, Pic.Image)
```

```
            End If
        Next

        'Write out the resource file and close it.
        ResxWriter.Generate()
        ResxWriter.Close()

    Catch ex As Exception
        Throw ex
    End Try
End Sub

Private Sub SaveToBinaryFile(ByVal ResData As DataTable)
    Dim Fname As String
    Dim Pic As ResImage

    'Do not try anything if we are handed an invalid table
    'This is better than a try catch block. Avoid errors when possible.
    'Do not just catch them.
    If ResData Is Nothing Then
        Throw New InvalidTable("Data table was not defined")
        Exit Sub
    End If

    'Split the filename and make it a text file
    Dim File_Info As New FileInfo(m_SaveFile)
    Fname = File_Info.FullName + ".resources"

    Try
        'This will write over the existing file!
        Dim ResWriter As New ResourceWriter(Fname)
        Dim ResKey As String
        Dim ResVal As String
        Dim ResRow As DataRow

        'Iterate over the rows in the table and add to the resource file
        For Each ResRow In ResData.Rows
            ResKey = ResRow(KeyCol).ToString
            ResVal = ResRow(TextCol).ToString
            ResWriter.AddResource(ResKey, ResVal)
        Next
```

```
      'Save the pictures
      For Each Pic In m_PicCol
        If Pic.Type Is GetType(Icon) Then
          ResWriter.AddResource(Pic.Name, Pic.Icon)
        Else
          ResWriter.AddResource(Pic.Name, Pic.Image)
        End If
      Next

      'Write out the resource file and close it.
      ResWriter.Generate()
      ResWriter.Close()

    Catch ex As Exception
      Throw ex
    End Try
  End Sub
```

C#

```csharp
private void SaveToXMLFile(DataTable ResData)
{
  string Fname;

  if ( ResData == null )
  {
    throw new InvalidTable("Data table was not defined");
    return;
  }

  //Split the filename and make it a resx file
  FileInfo File_Info = new FileInfo(m_SaveFile);
  Fname = File_Info.FullName + ".resx";

  try
  {
    //This will write over the existing file!
    ResXResourceWriter ResxWriter = new ResXResourceWriter(Fname);
    string ResKey;
    string ResVal;
```

```
          //Iterate over the rows in the table and add to the resource file
          foreach ( DataRow ResRow in ResData.Rows )
          {
            ResKey = ResRow[ResUtilConsts.KeyCol].ToString();
            ResVal = ResRow[ResUtilConsts.TextCol].ToString();
            ResxWriter.AddResource(ResKey, ResVal);
          }

          //Save the pictures
          foreach ( ResImage Pic in m_PicCol )
          {
            if ( Pic.type == typeof(Icon) )
              ResxWriter.AddResource(Pic.Name, Pic.Icon);
            else
              ResxWriter.AddResource(Pic.Name, Pic.image);
          }

          //Write out the resource file and close it.
          ResxWriter.Generate();
          ResxWriter.Close();
        }
        catch (Exception ex)
        {
          throw ex;
        }
      }

      private void SaveToBinaryFile(DataTable ResData )
      {
        string Fname;

        if ( ResData == null )
        {
          throw new InvalidTable("Data table was not defined");
          return;
        }

        //Split the filename and make it a text file
        FileInfo File_Info = new FileInfo(m_SaveFile);
        Fname = File_Info.FullName + ".resources";

        try
        {
```

```
    //This will write over the existing file!
    ResourceWriter ResWriter = new ResourceWriter(Fname);
    string ResKey;
    string ResVal;

    //Iterate over the rows in the table and add to the resource file
    foreach ( DataRow ResRow in ResData.Rows )
    {
      ResKey = ResRow[ResUtilConsts.KeyCol].ToString();
      ResVal = ResRow[ResUtilConsts.TextCol].ToString();
      ResWriter.AddResource(ResKey, ResVal);
    }

    //Save the pictures
    foreach ( ResImage Pic in m_PicCol )
    {
      if ( Pic.type == typeof(Icon) )
        ResWriter.AddResource(Pic.Name, Pic.Icon);
      else
        ResWriter.AddResource(Pic.Name, Pic.image);
    }

    //Write out the resource file and close it.
    ResWriter.Generate();
    ResWriter.Close();
  }
  catch (Exception ex)
  {
    throw ex;
  }
}
```

Notice that as I iterate through the image collection I test for the image type and save the image resource correctly.

Manually Adding an Icon to the Resource Editor

There is one last change you need to make to properly handle icons. That change involves adding an icon manually. So far I have altered the ResUtil and ResImage classes to load, display, and save icons correctly. The last thing that needs to be done is to change the AddPic method in the main code. This is the method that allows the user to click the Add button in the "Pictures" tab and add a graphic image to the resource set.

The change involves allowing the user to choose a file with the extension of ICO and reading the file from disk as either an image or an icon. Listing 8-4 shows the new AddPic method for both the VB and C# projects.

Listing 8-4. New AddPic method to allow manual entry of icon graphics

VB

```
Private Sub AddPic(ByVal sender As System.Object, _
                    ByVal e As System.EventArgs) Handles cmdAddPic.Click
  Dim rImg As ResImage

  OpenResFile.Reset()
  OpenResFile.InitialDirectory = Directory.GetCurrentDirectory()
  OpenResFile.RestoreDirectory = True
  OpenResFile.Filter = "Picture files " + _
              "(*.jpg; *.bmp; *.gif; *.ico)|*.jpg; *.bmp; *.gif; *.ico"

  If (OpenResFile.ShowDialog() = DialogResult.OK) Then
    Dim fInfo As New FileInfo(OpenResFile.FileName)
    If fInfo.Extension.ToUpper = ".JPG" Or _
        fInfo.Extension.ToUpper = ".BMP" Or _
        fInfo.Extension.ToUpper = ".ICO" Or _
        fInfo.Extension.ToUpper = ".GIF" Then
      'Add the picture to the collection
      If fInfo.Extension.ToUpper = ".ICO" Then
        rImg = New ResImage(OpenResFile.FileName, _
                                  New Icon(OpenResFile.FileName))
      Else
        rImg = New ResImage(OpenResFile.FileName, _
                                  Image.FromFile(OpenResFile.FileName))
      End If
      Dim Keyform As New AskKey(rImg)
      If Keyform.ShowDialog(Me) = DialogResult.OK Then
        m_Pictures.Add(rImg, rImg.Name)
        'Add the picture to the panel and arrange
        AddPic2Panel(rImg)
        ArrangePictures()
        'Add the picture to the list and enable delete and select it
        lstPictures.Items.Add(rImg.Name)
        lstPictures.SetSelected(lstPictures.Items.Count - 1, True)
```

```
            cmdDelPic.Enabled = True
        End If
        Keyform.Dispose()
      End If
      End If
  End Sub
```

C#

```csharp
    private void AddPic(object sender, System.EventArgs e)
    {
      OpenResFile.Reset();
      OpenResFile.InitialDirectory = Directory.GetCurrentDirectory();
      OpenResFile.RestoreDirectory = true;
      OpenResFile.Filter = "Picture files " +
                  "(*.jpg; *.bmp; *.gif; *.ico)|*.jpg; *.bmp; *.gif; *.ico";

      if (OpenResFile.ShowDialog() == DialogResult.OK)
      {

        FileInfo fInfo = new FileInfo(OpenResFile.FileName);
        if ((fInfo.Extension.ToUpper() == ".JPG") ||
          (fInfo.Extension.ToUpper() == ".BMP") ||
          (fInfo.Extension.ToUpper() == ".ICO") ||
          (fInfo.Extension.ToUpper() == ".GIF") )
        {

          ResImage rImg;

          if ( fInfo.Extension.ToUpper() == ".ICO" )
          {
            rImg = new ResImage(OpenResFile.FileName,
              new Icon(OpenResFile.FileName));
          }
          else
          {
            rImg = new ResImage(OpenResFile.FileName,
              Image.FromFile(OpenResFile.FileName));
          }

          AskKey Keyform = new AskKey(rImg);
          if (Keyform.ShowDialog(this) == DialogResult.OK )
```

```
            {
                m_Pictures.Add(rImg, rImg.Name);
                //Add the picture to the panel and arrange
                AddPic2Panel(rImg);
                ArrangePictures();
                //Add the picture to the list and enable delete and select it
                lstPictures.Items.Add(rImg.Name);
                lstPictures.SetSelected(lstPictures.Items.Count - 1, true);
                cmdDelPic.Enabled = true;
            }
            Keyform.Dispose();
        }
    }
}
```

This last change allowed the program to accept icons manually if the user chooses. Now that you have this capability, let's use it for this program.

Most Windows programs have an icon that represents that program in a minimized state. You can also see the icon in Windows Explorer and on the upper-left corner of the program's screen. The icon you have for this program is the default one given by .NET. Go into the InitStrings method and add the following line of code. Substitute any icon you wish for the argument.

VB

```
Me.Icon = New Icon("usa.ico")
```

C#

```
this.Icon=new Icon("USA.ico");
```

At this point all the static GUI strings and graphics for the program are initialized in this function. Later you add a resource manager to get all these resources from a resource file.

Finishing the Internationalization Portion

You need to do a few things to make sure the program will work correctly in other Western languages.

- Make sure that numbers are displayed correctly.

- Make sure that currency is displayed correctly.

- Make sure that dates and times are displayed correctly.

The best way to test this capability is to change the current culture in the thread you are working in. If you do this, you can start the program and go through all the screens to see if the dates, times, numbers, and so forth are displayed correctly for that culture. While you are doing this if you have any date and numeric entry fields, check to see that these fields accept input in the correct format.

Open the frmResources file and enter the following code in the constructor before the InitializeComponent call. Make sure that you are importing the System.Threading namespace.

VB

```
Thread.CurrentThread.CurrentCulture = New CultureInfo("de-DE")
```

C#

```
Thread.CurrentThread.CurrentCulture = New CultureInfo("de-DE");
```

Run the program and you should see the European date and time format on the status bar. Figure 8-1 shows my screen after I changed the current threads culture.

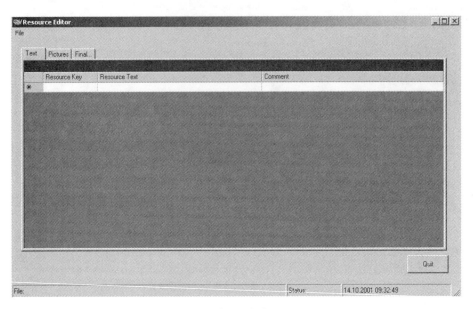

Figure 8-1. Screen showing European date and time

As far as this small program goes, that is pretty much it for testing the dates and times, and so on. There are no currency, number, or input fields to test.

Comment out the test code you added and open the tcResource_Click method. It would be nice to be able to display the culture name in the native language of that culture. The CultureInfo class allows you to do that. The code in this method iterates over the cultures and displays the name of the culture in the list box using the DisplayName method. The CultureInfo class allows you to use a method called NativeName instead. This method displays the name of the culture in that culture's language. It also displays that culture's name in the font necessary to display the correct characters.

There is one problem with doing this. The GetCultures method gets all the cultures that .NET knows about. There are not enough fonts natively available to Windows for it to display all the characters. The easy way around this (and you will take the easy way for this project) is to get only the cultures that Windows knows about. This pretty much guarantees that you will have the fonts necessary for display.

To do this you change the GetCultures argument from CultureTypes.SpecificCultures to CultureTypes.InstalledWin32Cultures. Listing 8-5 shows the new tc_Resource_Click method.

Listing 8-5. Change tcResource_Click to display cultures in native language

VB

```vb
Private Sub tcResource_Click(ByVal sender As Object, _
                            ByVal e As System.EventArgs) _
                            Handles tcResource.Click, _
                            tcResource.SelectedIndexChanged, _
                            tcResource.DoubleClick

    If tcResource.SelectedIndex = FINAL_TAB Then
        lblInFilename.Text = m_ResFile
        lblResStringNum.Text = m_StringTable.Rows.Count.ToString
        lblNumPics.Text = m_Pictures.Count.ToString

        Dim AllCultures() As CultureInfo
        Dim ACulture As CultureInfo
        AllCultures = CultureInfo.GetCultures(CultureTypes.InstalledWin32Cultures)
        lstCultures.Items.Clear()
        lstCultures.Items.Add(" ".PadRight(10) + "(None)")
        lstCultures.Sorted = True
        For Each ACulture In AllCultures
            lstCultures.Items.Add(ACulture.Name.PadRight(15) + ACulture.NativeName)
        Next
        chkCreateBin.Checked = True
    End If
    If tcResource.SelectedIndex = GRAPHICS_TAB Then
        If lstPictures.Items.Count < 1 Then
            cmdDelPic.Enabled = False
        End If
    End If
End Sub
```

C#

```csharp
private void TabChange(object sender, System.EventArgs e)
{
    if (tcResources.SelectedIndex == FINAL_TAB )
    {
        lblInFilename.Text = m_ResFile;
        lblResStringNum.Text = m_StringTable.Rows.Count.ToString();
        lblNumPics.Text = m_Pictures.Count.ToString();
```

```
CultureInfo[] AllCultures;
AllCultures =
      CultureInfo.GetCultures(CultureTypes.InstalledWin32Cultures);
lstCultures.Items.Clear();
lstCultures.Items.Add(" ".PadRight(10) + "(None)");
lstCultures.Sorted = true;
foreach(CultureInfo ACulture in AllCultures)
    lstCultures.Items.Add(ACulture.Name.PadRight(15) +
                              ACulture.NativeName);

  chkCreateBin.Checked = true;
}
if (tcResources.SelectedIndex == GRAPHICS_TAB )
{
  if( lstPictures.Items.Count < 1 )
    cmdDelPic.Enabled = false;
}
}
```

Compile and start the program. Go to the third tab and scroll through the cultures. You should see fewer cultures than before but the ones you see are displayed in their native languages.

Making a New Resource File

Now that our program is internationalized, it is time to localize it by allowing for multiple languages. It is time to put your resource editor to use. Start it and enter in the strings necessary for this program. Table 8-2 shows all the text resources you need.

Table 8-2. Text Resources Needed for the ResEditor Program

KEY	TEXT
QUIT	Quit
FILE	File
OPEN	Open
APPEND	Append
EXIT	Exit
KEY	Key
PICTURES	Pictures
ADD	Add
REMOVE	Remove
BASICS	Basics
INPUT FNAME	Input Filename
STRING COUNT	String Count
PIC COUNT	Picture Count
CULTURE	Choose Culture
OUTPUT	Build Output File(s)
BASE NAME	Base Name
RESOURCE KEY	Resource Key
RESOURCE TEXT	Resource Text
COMMENT	Comment
DATA ERR	Data table was not defined
CREATE TEXT	Create Text File for Translator
CREATE XML	Create XML File
CREATE BIN	Create Binary file
SAVE	Save

Figure 8-2 shows my screen after I input this information. Remember that comments are not saved in XML or binary resource files. They are only saved in the .txt resource file format. When you make the .resources file and bring it back in to the ResEditor the comment field is (null).

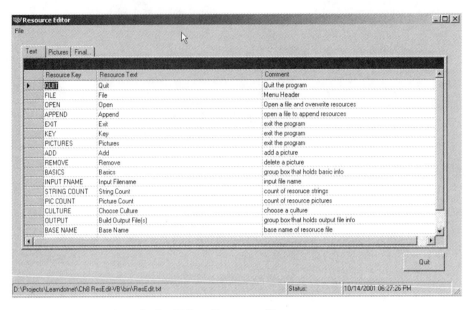

Figure 8-2. Text strings for ResEditor Resource file

Next are the pictures you need for this program. Since the only pictures are icons, this is what you will enter. Switch over to the second tab and click on the Add button. Search for icons you want to represent your program in English and in German. I used some icon flags I found in the .NET samples directory. Figure 8-3 shows this screen with the default icon for my program.

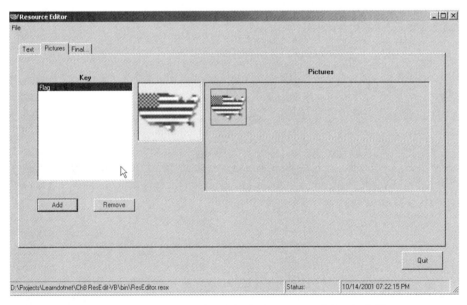

Figure 8-3. Icons used to represent the default language of the ResEditor program

Switch to the third tab (Final. . .) and save the resource file. Choose "None" for the culture because the resource file you are saving is the default resource file. You can choose to save the XML resource file. We do not make use of it here. Figure 8-4 shows my screen before saving the file.

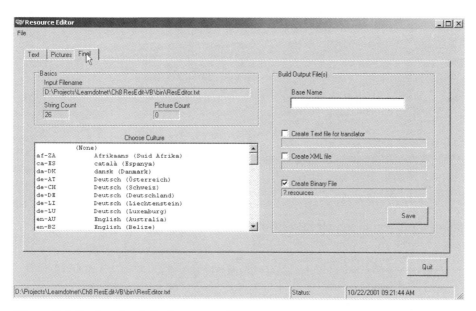

Figure 8-4. Saving the default resource file

The secondary language is German for this example.

Normally you would send the text resource file out to be translated into German. You would then import the text file into this program and combine it with a graphics resource file to make a single resource file for the German language.

This project does not have translated strings. Instead, your translation consists of preceding each text string with a "G–." Now is the time to make the German resource file. Go back to the Text tab on the screen and precede each string with a "G–." Figure 8-5 shows my German text input screen. You may get a different order of text if you pull up my screen. This is because I have the sort order of my first column set to ascending.

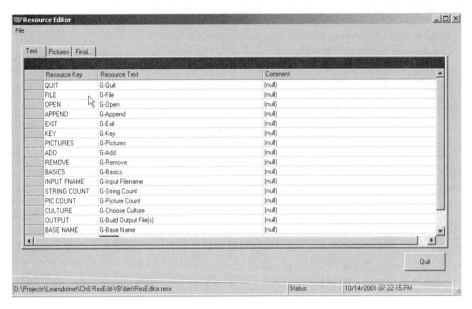

Figure 8-5. German text for ResEditor program

Next go to the Pictures screen and find another icon to represent Germany. Figure 8-6 shows my screen with a German flag.

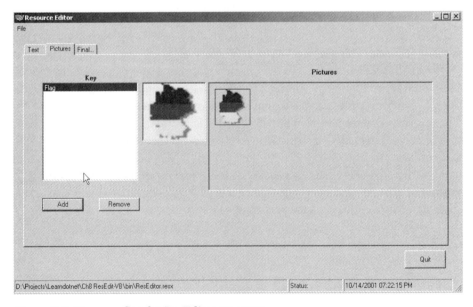

Figure 8-6. German flag for ResEditor program

Now go to the third screen (Final. . .) and save these resources as a German resource file. Figure 8-7 shows my "Final" screen.

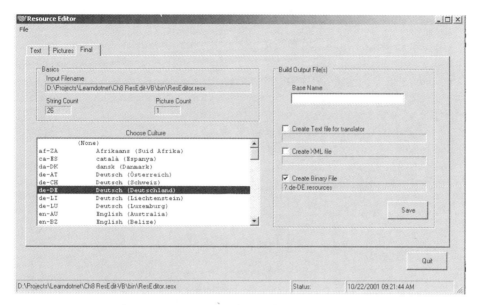

Figure 8-7. Saving the German resource file

Finalizing the Code

You are now at the last point in this example. You will add a resource manager to the program so it can get all strings and icons from the proper resource file.

You will not be using "loose" resources or a resource set. Instead, you use the capability of the resource manager to find the correct resource file in the correct directory, and to use fallback if necessary. This is the method most of your projects will use.

Before you change the code to use a resource manager, you need to do the following:

- Make sure that the executable you are making is called ResEditor.

- Make two directories under the root of the executable called "en-US" and "de-DE."

- Make a satellite file for each resource file in the proper directory.

Make Sure the Names Are Correct

Right-click the project name in the Solutions window. Bring up the Properties window. The assembly name should be ResEditor. Why is this important, you ask? The resource manager gets its name information from the assembly manifest. If you have a different name for your resource file than the name contained in the assembly manifest, you get an error. The error you get makes it seem as if the resource file is there but the resource is not.

If you use C# the root your project runs from is .\bin\debug_. If you use VB then the root your project runs from is .\bin without the debug directory. The resource files belong in a directory placed under the root of where your program runs from.

Create the directory called "en-US" and "de-DE." The default culture for my machine is US English. Figure 8-8 shows my directory structure for both projects.

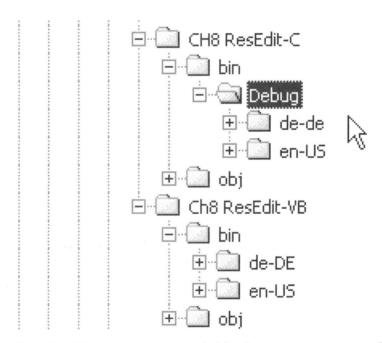

Figure 8-8. Directory structure needed for the resource manager to find resource files

Generate the Satellite Files

You need to put the resource satellite files in these subdirectories. The ResEditor program does not generate the satellite DLLs necessary for this, so you have to do it by hand. Here's my suggestion of the steps you can follow to accomplish this.

1. Put the ResEditor.de-DE.resources resource file in the de-DE directory.

2. Put the ResEditor.resources resource file in the en-US directory and rename it to ResEditor.en-US.resources.

3. Generate a build.bat file in each of the directories that will make the satellite DLL file.

4. Run the build.bat file in each directory.

What the build.bat file should look like for each directory follows:

de-DE

```
al /out:reseditor.Resources.Dll /v:1.0.0.0 /c:de-DE /embed:ResEditor.de-
DE.resources,ResEditor.de-DE.resources,Private
```

En-US

```
al /out:ResEditor.Resources.Dll /v:1.0.0.0 /c:en-US /embed:ResEditor.en-
US.resources,ResEditor.en-US.resources,private
```

As you can see, this invokes the AL.exe program and generates a satellite DLL with the resource file embedded in it.

Before you can run the build.bat file, you need to run the corvars.bat file that comes with .NET. This file is found in C:\Program Files\Microsoft.NET\ FrameworkSDK\Bin.

You should now have ResEditor.en-US.dll and ResEditor.de-DE.dll files in their respective directories. Everything is now set up to run properly.

Last Changes to the Code

Since the resource manager is used in several files, it needs to be global to this project. The resource manager is put in the Consts.vb file for the VB project, and in the ResUtilConsts class in the ResUtil.cs file for the C# project. Listing 8-6 shows the code to make resource managers in VB and in C#.

Listing 8-6. Making a resource manager

VB. Resource Manager in Consts.vb File

```
Option Strict On

Imports System.Resources

Module Consts

  Public Const KeyCol As String = "Key"
  Public Const TextCol As String = "Text"
  Public Const CommentCol As String = "Comment"
  Public Const MaxKeyLen As Integer = 15
  Public Const CommentChar As Char = ";"c

  Public Enum ResTypes
    TextType = 1
    XMLType = 2
    BinType = 3
  End Enum

  Public rm As ResourceManager

End Module
```

C#. Resource Manager in ResUtilConsts Class

```
public class ResUtilConsts
{
  public const string KeyCol = "Key";
  public const string TextCol = "Text";
  public const string CommentCol = "Comment";
  public const int MaxKeyLen = 15;
  public const char CommentChar = ';';

  public static ResourceManager rm;
}
```

Now you need to instantiate it. You do this in the InitStrings method. This is the same for each project. The reason you do it here is so this method can be called when the language is changed either by computer setting or programmatically.

VB

```
rm = New ResourceManager("ResEditor", Me.GetType().Assembly)
```

C#

```
ResUtilConsts.rm = new ResourceManager("ResEditor", this.GetType().Assembly);
```

Once you have done this it is time to alter the rest of the code in the InitStrings method to get all its strings and the icon from the resource file. Use the ResourceManager.GetString and ResourceManager.GetObject methods to do this.

Listing 8-7 shows the InitStrings methods for both the C# and VB projects.

Listing 8-7. New InitStrings method to get strings and icon from the resource file

VB

```
  Private Sub InitStrings()

    rm = New ResourceManager("ResEditor", Me.GetType().Assembly)

    'Status Panel
    sbStatus.Panels(2).Text = Now.ToString
    sbStatus.Panels(1).Width = 100

    'Tab Pages
    tcResource.TabPages(TEXT_TAB).Text = rm.GetString("TEXT")
    tcResource.TabPages(GRAPHICS_TAB).Text = rm.GetString("PICTURES")
    tcResource.TabPages(FINAL_TAB).Text = rm.GetString("FINAL")

    'Form Controls
    cmdQuit.Text = rm.GetString("QUIT")
    mnuFile.Text = rm.GetString("FILE")
    mnuOpen.Text = rm.GetString("OPEN")
    mnuAppend.Text = rm.GetString("APPEND")
    mnuExit.Text = rm.GetString("EXIT")

    'do picture tab
    lblPicKey.Text = rm.GetString("KEY")
    lblPictures.Text = rm.GetString("PICTURES")
    cmdAddPic.Text = rm.GetString("ADD")
    cmdDelPic.Text = rm.GetString("REMOVE")
```

```vb
'Do Final tab
fraBasics.Text = rm.GetString("BASICS")
lblInputFname.Text = rm.GetString("INPUT FNAME")
lblStrCnt.Text = rm.GetString("STRING COUNT")
lblPicCnt.Text = rm.GetString("PIC COUNT")
lblCulture.Text = rm.GetString("CULTURE")
fraOutput.Text = rm.GetString("OUTPUT")
lblBaseName.Text = rm.GetString("BASE NAME")
cmdSave.Text = rm.GetString("SAVE")
chkCreateText.Text = rm.GetString("CREATE TEXT")
chkCreateXML.Text = rm.GetString("CREATE XML")
chkCreateBin.Text = rm.GetString("CREATE BIN")

Me.Icon = CType(rm.GetObject("Flag"), Icon)

End Sub
```

C#

```csharp
private void InitStrings()
{

    ResUtilConsts.rm = new ResourceManager("ResEditor", this.GetType().Assembly);

    sbStatus.Panels[2].Text = DateTime.Now.ToString();
    sbStatus.Panels[1].Width = 100;

    //Tab Pages
    tcResources.TabPages[TEXT_TAB].Text = ResUtilConsts.rm.GetString("TEXT");
    tcResources.TabPages[GRAPHICS_TAB].Text =
            ResUtilConsts.rm.GetString("PICTURES");
    tcResources.TabPages[FINAL_TAB].Text = ResUtilConsts.rm.GetString("FINAL");

    //Form Controls
    cmdQuit.Text = ResUtilConsts.rm.GetString("QUIT");
    mnuFile.Text = ResUtilConsts.rm.GetString("FILE");
    mnuOpen.Text = ResUtilConsts.rm.GetString("OPEN");
    mnuAppend.Text = ResUtilConsts.rm.GetString("APPEND");
    mnuExit.Text = ResUtilConsts.rm.GetString("EXIT");
```

```
//do picture tab
lblPicKey.Text = ResUtilConsts.rm.GetString("KEY");
lblPictures.Text = ResUtilConsts.rm.GetString("PICTURES");
cmdAddPic.Text = ResUtilConsts.rm.GetString("ADD");
cmdDelPic.Text = ResUtilConsts.rm.GetString("REMOVE");

//Do Final tab
fraBasics.Text = ResUtilConsts.rm.GetString("BASICS");
lblInputFname.Text = ResUtilConsts.rm.GetString("INPUT FNAME");
lblStrCnt.Text = ResUtilConsts.rm.GetString("STRING COUNT");
lblPicCnt.Text = ResUtilConsts.rm.GetString("PIC COUNT");
lblCulture.Text = ResUtilConsts.rm.GetString("CULTURE");
fraOutput.Text = ResUtilConsts.rm.GetString("OUTPUT");
lblBaseName.Text = ResUtilConsts.rm.GetString("BASE NAME");
cmdSave.Text = ResUtilConsts.rm.GetString("SAVE");
chkCreateText.Text = ResUtilConsts.rm.GetString("CREATE TEXT");
chkCreateXML.Text = ResUtilConsts.rm.GetString("CREATE XML");
chkCreateBin.Text = ResUtilConsts.rm.GetString("CREATE BIN");

this.Icon = (Icon)ResUtilConsts.rm.GetObject("Flag");

}
```

The last thing to do before you test this localization is to change the hard-coded error strings in the following methods in the ResUtil code.

- GetData

- SaveData

- FillFromBinaryFile

- SaveToBinaryFile

- FillFromTextFile

- SaveToTextFile

- FillFromXMLFile

- SaveToXMLFile

Listing 8-8 shows how this should be done.

Listing 8-8. Loading error text from the resource file

VB

```
If ResData Is Nothing Then
  Throw New InvalidTable(rm.GetString("DATA ERR"))
  Exit Sub
End If
```

C#

```
if ( ResData == null )
{
  throw new InvalidTable(ResUtilConsts.rm.GetString("DATA ERR"));
  return;
}
```

Testing the Program

Here you are at the end of your localization project. It is time to test the code and see how it works. Before you do that, let's recap how this will work.

A resource manager is instantiated when the program starts. The resource file obtained by the resource manager is based on the current culture set by the machine. This allows the program to auto-sense the culture and display the correct strings and graphics.

To test this program press F5 and you should see all the English strings and the U.S. flag icon. Now add the following code to the form load event in both projects.

VB

```
Thread.CurrentThread.CurrentCulture = New CultureInfo("de-DE")
Thread.CurrentThread.CurrentUICulture = New CultureInfo("de-DE")
```

C#

```
Thread.CurrentThread.CurrentCulture = new CultureInfo("de-DE");
Thread.CurrentThread.CurrentUICulture = new CultureInfo("de-DE");
```

Run the program again and you should see the same screen as mine, shown in Figure 8-9.

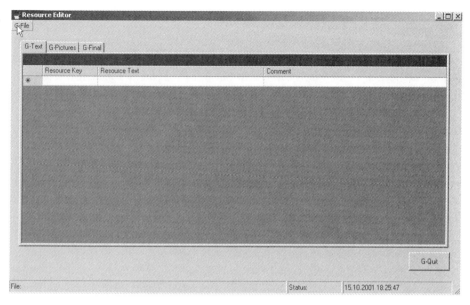

Figure 8-9. German language screen

Summary

What you did in this chapter was to use the resource editor you made in Chapter 7 to generate a resource file to help in localizing itself! Pretty neat, huh?

You started out with a program that was designed without the intention of having it localized, with the exception of longer than necessary fields. You then needed to make this program work in Germany. Here is what you did to make it work.

- You added icon capability to the program. This lets the user know it is intended for his or her country.

- You added the ResEditor program to generate text strings and an icon for itself. You made one resource file for U.S. use, and one for Germany.

- You changed the code to eliminate all hard-coded strings. All string assignments were put in one method that can be easily called.

- You made satellite resource files and installed them in the proper directories.

- You added a resource manager to get strings from the proper resource file depending on the culture that was set.

After all this, you tested the code by changing the default culture. All dates, times, text, and graphics for the program changed according to the culture set.

This is a rather lightweight program to localize but all the concepts discussed in Chapters 4, 5, and 6 are demonstrated here. The program is not quite as robust as it could be, but I toned down the error handling for clarity's sake. If you find the program useful and want to extend it, feel free.

Next I take you through a small ASP.NET program that includes localization from the start.

CHAPTER 9

Localization in ASP.NET

THIS CHAPTER IS WHERE YOU MAKE a foray into the next stage of .NET localization—the Internet.

One of the major changes and advancements that .NET offers web programmers is a better and more programmer-friendly ASP development model. No longer are your ASP pages a jumble of HTML text and VB code. The HTML text is now on one page and the code is behind the scenes in its own class file.

Traditionally ASP pages were written using VB script. ASP.NET allows you to write ASP code in any of the .NET languages. With this in mind, I provide the code in both C# and VB .NET for this final example. This example is also designed from the start with localization. If you remember, the resource editor in Chapter 7 was intentionally written with no localization in mind. Chapter 8 was where you went back and localized the resource editor program.

 NOTE   *If you are using the source from the Apress web site, you need to install it in the InetPubs directory on your C: drive. Also the solution files need to be installed in a different directory than the InetPubs directory. They need to be installed in your .\mydocuments\visual studio projects directory.*

The Coldest Hotel Application

The example I show in this chapter is a simple ASP page that takes a customer through booking a hotel room. When I say simple, I mean simple. The purpose of this ASP page is not to teach you ASP programming but to show you what needs to be done to localize a web application. There are some differences and pitfalls to localizing a web application than to localizing a Windows Forms application.

Start out by opening a new VB or C# ASP.NET web application. The default name is WebApplication1. Rename the project "ColdHotel." Press OK to accept this. .NET grinds away and makes a web application template for you.

The ASP page will be called "WebForm1.aspx." In the Solution window, rename this form "ColdHotel.aspx." Your Solution window should look like mine (Figure 9-1).

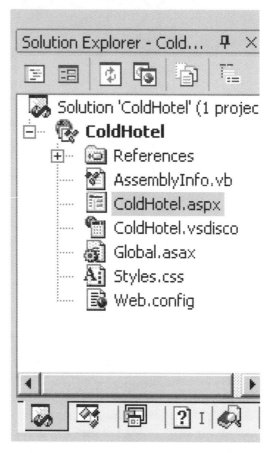

Figure 9-1. Solution window showing all files for the ColdHotel project

The form you are presented with is kind of blah. I changed the background color of my form to silver. This makes it stand out a little bit when debugging starts.

The next thing to do is to start adding controls to the form. There are two basic ways to do this. One is to use HTML controls and the other is to use web controls. I chose web controls because they are server-side controls. This means that the server, not the client, decides how the controls are rendered. It also allows you to manage the controls programmatically just like the normal Windows Forms.

The controls I chose for this example demonstrate most things you change during localization. I show text, numbers, dates, times, and a calendar.

Open your WebForms toolbox and put the following controls on your form.

- Label. Name it lblChooseLang.

- DropDownList. Name it cmbChooseLang. Make sure the AutoPostback property is set to True.

- Label. Name it lblWelcome. Make the Font property X-Large.

- Label. Name it lblInstructions. Make the Font property Medium.

- Calendar. Name it calReservation.

- Label. Name it lblTodaysDate.

- Label. Name it lblCurrentDate. Change the BorderStyle property to Inset.

- Label. Name it lblConfirm.

- Label. Name it lblArriveDate. Change the BorderStyle property to Inset.

- Label. Name it lblHitText.

- Label. Name it lblHitCount. Change the BorderStyle property to Inset.

That's it for controls. Make all the text controls about twice as long as the text that fits in them. Place them on the screen in a similar fashion to what I show in Figure 9-2.

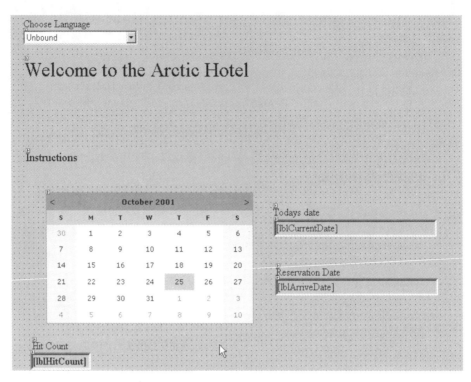

Figure 9-2. ASP web page showing all controls

The calendar control I use will look different than yours by default. You can change the appearance by right-clicking the control and choosing the AutoFormat property. There are seven schemes you can choose from.

Notice that all the controls have a small green arrow at the top left of the control. This lets you know that the control is a server control. The other way to tell is to right-click the form and choose View HTML Source. The definition of each control says: runat="server."

You can also go back and forth between the HTML view and the design view using the navigation buttons at the bottom left of the screen.

Writing the Code

Open the code pane to this form you just made. If you are in VB make sure that the first line of code is the Option Strict On statement. This disallows any implicit type conversions.

Next add the necessary lines to include the following namespaces.

- System.Globalization

- System.Resources

- System.Threading

The definition of the class, along with the control declarations, are shown in Listing 9-1.

Listing 9-1. Class and control definitions

VB

```
Option Strict On

Imports System
Imports System.Globalization
Imports System.Resources
Imports System.Threading

Public Class ColdHotel
  Inherits System.Web.UI.Page
  Protected WithEvents lblCurrentDate As System.Web.UI.WebControls.Label
  Protected WithEvents lblWelcome As System.Web.UI.WebControls.Label
  Protected WithEvents lblInstructions As System.Web.UI.WebControls.Label
  Protected WithEvents lblTodaysDate As System.Web.UI.WebControls.Label
  Protected WithEvents lblArriveDate As System.Web.UI.WebControls.Label
  Protected WithEvents lblConfirm As System.Web.UI.WebControls.Label
  Protected WithEvents calReservation As System.Web.UI.WebControls.Calendar
  Protected WithEvents lblHitText As System.Web.UI.WebControls.Label
  Protected WithEvents lblHitCount As System.Web.UI.WebControls.Label
  Protected WithEvents cmbChooseLang As System.Web.UI.WebControls.DropDownList
. . .
```

C#

```
using System;
using System.Collections;
using System.ComponentModel;
using System.Data;
using System.Drawing;
using System.Web;
```

```
using System.Web.SessionState;
using System.Web.UI;
using System.Web.UI.WebControls;
using System.Web.UI.HtmlControls;
using System.Globalization;
using System.Resources;
using System.Threading;

namespace ColdHotel_c
{
    /// <summary>
    /// Summary description for WebForm1.
    /// </summary>
    public class ColdHotel : System.Web.UI.Page
    {
     protected System.Web.UI.WebControls.Label lblChooseLang;
     protected System.Web.UI.WebControls.DropDownList cmbChooseLang;
     protected System.Web.UI.WebControls.Label lblWelcome;
     protected System.Web.UI.WebControls.Label lblInstructions;
     protected System.Web.UI.WebControls.Calendar calReservations;
     protected System.Web.UI.WebControls.Label lblTodaysDate;
     protected System.Web.UI.WebControls.Label lblCurrentDate;
     protected System.Web.UI.WebControls.Label lblArriveDate;
     protected System.Web.UI.WebControls.Label lblHitCount;
     protected System.Web.UI.WebControls.Label lblHitText;
     protected System.Web.UI.WebControls.Label lblConfirm;
  . . .
```

The next thing to do is add a couple of class variables and an Enum. The Enum is a list of languages that can be used in this program. The variable HitCnt is necessary to show a large number whose group and decimal separators change according to culture.

Add this code just below the definitions of the controls.

VB

```
Private HitCnt As Long = 5442367
Private Enum Languages_tag
    English
    German
    Spanish
    French
End Enum
Private rm As ResourceManager
```

C#

```
private long HitCnt = 5442367;
private enum Languages_tag
{
  English,
  German,
  Spanish,
  French
};
private ResourceManager rm;
```

Notice that I added a resource manager to get the text resources from the resource files. You use the resource manager in two different ways in this example. One way is with loose resources and the other way is the traditional satellite resource file method. Although both ways are valid, I will show you why one way is much better than the other when it comes to ASP pages.

For demonstration's sake there is one set of text strings that I am not localizing. Those strings make up the set of languages supported by the web page. Normally in a program like this you would have the set of languages appear in the language that the user's computer is set to.

You need to make a method to fill the drop-down list with the languages that this program supports. Listing 9-2 shows this method.

Listing 9-2. Method to load all the language strings in the drop-down list box

VB

```
Private Sub FillLanguages()

  If cmbChooseLang.Items.Count = 0 Then
    cmbChooseLang.Items.Clear()
    cmbChooseLang.Items.Add("English")
    cmbChooseLang.Items.Item(cmbChooseLang.Items.Count - 1).Value = _
                                        CStr(Languages_tag.English)
    cmbChooseLang.Items.Add("German")
    cmbChooseLang.Items.Item(cmbChooseLang.Items.Count - 1).Value = _
                                        CStr(Languages_tag.German)
    cmbChooseLang.Items.Add("Spanish")
    cmbChooseLang.Items.Item(cmbChooseLang.Items.Count - 1).Value = _
                                        CStr(Languages_tag.Spanish)
    cmbChooseLang.Items.Add("French")
    cmbChooseLang.Items.Item(cmbChooseLang.Items.Count - 1).Value = _
                                        CStr(Languages_tag.French)
```

```
        End If

    LanguageWasSelected(cmbChooseLang, Nothing)

End Sub
```

C#

```
private void FillLanguages()
{
  if ( cmbChooseLang.Items.Count == 0 )
  {
    cmbChooseLang.Items.Clear();
    cmbChooseLang.Items.Add("English");
    cmbChooseLang.Items[cmbChooseLang.Items.Count - 1].Value =
                          ((int)Languages_tag.English).ToString();
    cmbChooseLang.Items.Add("German");
    cmbChooseLang.Items[cmbChooseLang.Items.Count - 1].Value =
                          ((int)Languages_tag.German).ToString();
    cmbChooseLang.Items.Add("Spanish");
    cmbChooseLang.Items[cmbChooseLang.Items.Count - 1].Value =
                          ((int)Languages_tag.Spanish).ToString();
    cmbChooseLang.Items.Add("French");
    cmbChooseLang.Items[cmbChooseLang.Items.Count - 1].Value =
                          ((int)Languages_tag.French).ToString();
  }

  LanguageWasSelected(cmbChooseLang, null);
}
```

I use the Value property of each choice to hold the value of the enum that corresponds to the language. The Value property is a string, so I cast the enum to a string before I store it. The reason I store the enum value of the language is to make the language chosen by the user independent of the index chosen in the drop-down box. I can then change the order of the languages and any code that I add without affecting the user's choice. Also, since I compare what the user chose to a number, I can localize the strings in this drop-down list without changing the code that determines what the user picked.

Handling the Events

Before I take you through the resource manager code I think that it is best that the event-handling code be generated first.

Two events are of interest. The first is when the user chooses a new language, and the other is when the user picks a date from the calendar.

The drop-down list contains several languages the user can choose. If the user chooses a new language it would be nice if the text, dates, number format, and calendar change accordingly. For this to happen you need to post an event to the server. The event that needs to be handled is the SelectedIndexChanged event. The VB code for this is relatively easy and is shown in Listing 9-3.

Listing 9-3. VB code to handle the cmbChooseLang.SelectedIndexChanged event

```
Private Sub LanguageWasSelected(ByVal sender As System.Object, _
                                ByVal e As System.EventArgs) _
                                Handles cmbChooseLang.SelectedIndexChanged


    Select Case cmbChooseLang.Items(cmbChooseLang.SelectedIndex).Value
      Case CStr(Languages_tag.French)
        Thread.CurrentThread.CurrentCulture = New CultureInfo("fr-FR")
      Case CStr(Languages_tag.German)
        Thread.CurrentThread.CurrentCulture = New CultureInfo("de-DE")
      Case CStr(Languages_tag.Spanish)
        Thread.CurrentThread.CurrentCulture = New CultureInfo("es-ES")
      Case Else
        Thread.CurrentThread.CurrentCulture = New CultureInfo("en-US")
    End Select


    Thread.CurrentThread.CurrentUICulture = Thread.CurrentThread.CurrentCulture


End Sub
```

This is fairly simple code. It takes the Value property of the current selection and compares it to the enum list. If the choice is in the list, then I change the current thread to the correct culture. The last thing I do is set the CurrentUICulture to the CurrentCulture. This is good practice as there are very few times when you want them to be different.

Notice that I explicitly cast the enum value to a string before comparing it to the Value property of the drop-down list. This is because the Value property is a string.

The C# code for the same event handler is almost identical. However, as you saw with the ResourceEditor project, C# requires that you explicitly declare a delegate for each event.

Open the Web Form Designer Generated Code region of the C# project. Add the following line of code to the InitializeComponent method.

```
this.cmbChooseLang.SelectedIndexChanged +=
                  new System.EventHandler(this.LanguageWasSelected);
```

Now add the method in Listing 9-4 to your C# project

Listing 9-4. C# code to handle the cmbChooseLang.SelectedIndexChanged event

```
private void LanguageWasSelected(object sender, EventArgs e)
{
  switch (Convert.ToInt32(cmbChooseLang.Items
                           [cmbChooseLang.SelectedIndex].Value))
  {
    case (int)Languages_tag.French:
      Thread.CurrentThread.CurrentCulture = new CultureInfo("fr-FR");
      break;
    case (int)Languages_tag.German:
      Thread.CurrentThread.CurrentCulture = new CultureInfo("de-DE");
      break;
    case (int)Languages_tag.Spanish:
      Thread.CurrentThread.CurrentCulture = new CultureInfo("es-ES");
      break;
    default:
      Thread.CurrentThread.CurrentCulture = new CultureInfo("en-US");
      break;
  }

  Thread.CurrentThread.CurrentUICulture=Thread.CurrentThread.CurrentCulture;
}
```

If you look at the code, you see that I am casting the Value property from a string to an integer in the switch statement. Each of the case statements casts the enum to an integer as well. Why? Well I need to compare an integer to an integer. This is not VB 6 with evil typecasting going on behind the scenes converting one type to another. C# forces you to know what you want to do.

You need to take a couple of steps before you can test the code for the first time. They include adding code to the PageLoad method to call various functions and stubbing out the InitStrings method. Listing 9-5 shows almost the complete code you need to run this example. Note that the InitStrings method is virtually empty. After you test this code, I take you through what you need in the InitStrings method.

Listing 9-5. Complete code for the ASP example without the complete InitStrings method

VB Code with Web Form Designer Generated Code Expanded

```
Option Strict On

Imports System
Imports System.Globalization
Imports System.Resources
Imports System.Threading

Public Class ColdHotel
  Inherits System.Web.UI.Page
  Protected WithEvents lblCurrentDate As System.Web.UI.WebControls.Label
  Protected WithEvents lblWelcome As System.Web.UI.WebControls.Label
  Protected WithEvents lblInstructions As System.Web.UI.WebControls.Label
  Protected WithEvents lblTodaysDate As System.Web.UI.WebControls.Label
  Protected WithEvents lblArriveDate As System.Web.UI.WebControls.Label
  Protected WithEvents lblConfirm As System.Web.UI.WebControls.Label
  Protected WithEvents calReservation As System.Web.UI.WebControls.Calendar
  Protected WithEvents lblHitText As System.Web.UI.WebControls.Label
  Protected WithEvents lblHitCount As System.Web.UI.WebControls.Label
  Protected WithEvents cmbChooseLang As System.Web.UI.WebControls.DropDownList

#Region " Web Form Designer Generated Code "

  'This call is required by the Web Form Designer.
  <System.Diagnostics.DebuggerStepThrough()> Private Sub InitializeComponent()

  End Sub

  Private Sub Page_Init(ByVal sender As System.Object, _
              ByVal e As System.EventArgs) Handles MyBase.Init
    'CODEGEN: This method call is required by the Web Form Designer
    'Do not modify it using the code editor.
    InitializeComponent()

  End Sub
```

```
#End Region

   Private HitCnt As Long = 5442367
   Private Enum Languages_tag
     English
     German
     Spanish
     French
   End Enum
   Private rm As ResourceManager

   Private Sub Page_Load(ByVal sender As System.Object, _
                            ByVal e As System.EventArgs) Handles MyBase.Load

     FillLanguages()
     InitStrings()
     lblCurrentDate.Text = Today().ToString("D")
   End Sub

   Private Sub InitStrings()

     lblHitCount.Text = HitCnt.ToString("n")
     If lblArriveDate.Text <> "" Then
       lblArriveDate.Text = calReservation.SelectedDate.ToString("D")
     End If

   End Sub

   Private Sub FillLanguages()

     If cmbChooseLang.Items.Count = 0 Then
       cmbChooseLang.Items.Clear()
       cmbChooseLang.Items.Add("English")
       cmbChooseLang.Items.Item(cmbChooseLang.Items.Count - 1).Value = _
                                           CStr(Languages_tag.English)
       cmbChooseLang.Items.Add("German")
       cmbChooseLang.Items.Item(cmbChooseLang.Items.Count - 1).Value = _
                                           CStr(Languages_tag.German)
       cmbChooseLang.Items.Add("Spanish")
       cmbChooseLang.Items.Item(cmbChooseLang.Items.Count - 1).Value = _
                                           CStr(Languages_tag.Spanish)
       cmbChooseLang.Items.Add("French")
       cmbChooseLang.Items.Item(cmbChooseLang.Items.Count - 1).Value = _
```

```vb
                                      CStr(Languages_tag.French)
        End If
        LanguageWasSelected(cmbChooseLang, Nothing)
    End Sub


    Private Sub Reservation(ByVal sender As System.Object, _
                            ByVal e As System.EventArgs) _
                                  Handles calReservation.SelectionChanged


        lblArriveDate.Text = calReservation.SelectedDate.ToString("D")


    End Sub


    Private Sub LanguageWasSelected(ByVal sender As System.Object, _
                                  ByVal e As System.EventArgs) _
                                  Handles cmbChooseLang.SelectedIndexChanged


        Select Case cmbChooseLang.Items(cmbChooseLang.SelectedIndex).Value
          Case CStr(Languages_tag.French)
            Thread.CurrentThread.CurrentCulture = New CultureInfo("fr-FR")
          Case CStr(Languages_tag.German)
            Thread.CurrentThread.CurrentCulture = New CultureInfo("de-DE")
          Case CStr(Languages_tag.Spanish)
            Thread.CurrentThread.CurrentCulture = New CultureInfo("es-ES")
          Case Else
            Thread.CurrentThread.CurrentCulture = New CultureInfo("en-US")
        End Select


        Thread.CurrentThread.CurrentUICulture = Thread.CurrentThread.CurrentCulture


    End Sub

End Class
```

C#

```csharp
using System;
using System.Collections;
using System.ComponentModel;
using System.Data;
using System.Drawing;
using System.Web;
```

```csharp
using System.Web.SessionState;
using System.Web.UI;
using System.Web.UI.WebControls;
using System.Web.UI.HtmlControls;
using System.Globalization;
using System.Resources;
using System.Threading;

namespace ColdHotel_c
{
  /// <summary>
  /// Summary description for WebForm1.
  /// </summary>
  public class ColdHotel : System.Web.UI.Page
  {
    protected System.Web.UI.WebControls.Label lblChooseLang;
    protected System.Web.UI.WebControls.DropDownList cmbChooseLang;
    protected System.Web.UI.WebControls.Label lblWelcome;
    protected System.Web.UI.WebControls.Label lblInstructions;
    protected System.Web.UI.WebControls.Label lblTodaysDate;
    protected System.Web.UI.WebControls.Label lblCurrentDate;
    protected System.Web.UI.WebControls.Label lblArriveDate;
    protected System.Web.UI.WebControls.Label lblHitCount;
    protected System.Web.UI.WebControls.Label lblHitText;
    protected System.Web.UI.WebControls.Label lblConfirm;

    private long HitCnt = 5442367;
    protected System.Web.UI.WebControls.Calendar calReservation;

    private enum Languages_tag
    {
      English,
      German,
      Spanish,
      French
    };

    private ResourceManager rm;

    public ColdHotel()
    {
      Page.Init += new System.EventHandler(Page_Init);
    }
```

```
  private void Page_Load(object sender, System.EventArgs e)
  {
    FillLanguages();
    InitStrings();
    lblCurrentDate.Text = DateTime.Today.ToString("D");

  }

  private void Page_Init(object sender, EventArgs e)
  {
    //
    // CODEGEN: This call is required by the ASP.NET Web Form Designer.
    //
    InitializeComponent();
  }

#region Web Form Designer generated code
  /// <summary>
  /// Required method for Designer support - do not modify
  /// the contents of this method with the code editor.
  /// </summary>
  private void InitializeComponent()
  {
    this.cmbChooseLang.SelectedIndexChanged +=
                new System.EventHandler(this.LanguageWasSelected);
    this.calReservation.SelectionChanged +=
                new System.EventHandler(this.Reservation);
    this.Load += new System.EventHandler(this.Page_Load);

  }
#endregion

  private void InitStrings()
  {
    lblHitCount.Text = HitCnt.ToString("n");
    if (lblArriveDate.Text != "" )
      lblArriveDate.Text = calReservation.SelectedDate.ToString("D");
  }

  private void FillLanguages()
  {
    if ( cmbChooseLang.Items.Count == 0 )
    {
```

```csharp
        cmbChooseLang.Items.Clear();
        cmbChooseLang.Items.Add("English");
        cmbChooseLang.Items[cmbChooseLang.Items.Count - 1].Value =
                                ((int)Languages_tag.English).ToString();
        cmbChooseLang.Items.Add("German");
        cmbChooseLang.Items[cmbChooseLang.Items.Count - 1].Value =
                                ((int)Languages_tag.German).ToString();
        cmbChooseLang.Items.Add("Spanish");
        cmbChooseLang.Items[cmbChooseLang.Items.Count - 1].Value =
                                ((int)Languages_tag.Spanish).ToString();
        cmbChooseLang.Items.Add("French");
        cmbChooseLang.Items[cmbChooseLang.Items.Count - 1].Value =
                                ((int)Languages_tag.French).ToString();
    }

    LanguageWasSelected(cmbChooseLang, null);
}

private void Reservation(object sender, EventArgs e)
{
    lblArriveDate.Text = calReservation.SelectedDate.ToString("D");
}

private void LanguageWasSelected(object sender, EventArgs e)
{
    switch (Convert.ToInt32(cmbChooseLang.Items
                        [cmbChooseLang.SelectedIndex].Value))
    {
        case (int)Languages_tag.French:
            Thread.CurrentThread.CurrentCulture = new CultureInfo("fr-FR");
            break;
        case (int)Languages_tag.German:
            Thread.CurrentThread.CurrentCulture = new CultureInfo("de-DE");
            break;
```

```
    case (int)Languages_tag.Spanish:
      Thread.CurrentThread.CurrentCulture = new CultureInfo("es-ES");
      break;
    default:
      Thread.CurrentThread.CurrentCulture = new CultureInfo("en-US");
      break;
  }

    Thread.CurrentThread.CurrentUICulture =
Thread.CurrentThread.CurrentCulture;
    }

  }
}
```

Now it is time to test the example.

There are a couple of ways to test this code. You can test it in a browser or you can "Build and Browse," which tests the code in the IDE.

The Build and Browse method is invoked one of two ways. One way is to right-click the form definition in the Solution window and choose "Build and Browse" from the drop-down menu. The other way is to choose "Build and Browse" from the File menu.

I prefer the browser method. If it works here you know it will work on someone else's browser. The procedure for testing in a browser is the same as for a Windows Forms project. Press F5.

Have you pressed F5 yet? If not, do it. Your screen should look like mine, as shown in Figure 9-3. Do not worry about the text right now. You reconcile your programs later when I explain the InitStrings function. Be sure to click a date in the calendar. If you have loaded the code from the web site instead of typing it, you may get an error indicating that you should set a start page first. If so, right-click the page in the Solution Explorer and choose "Set as Start Page."

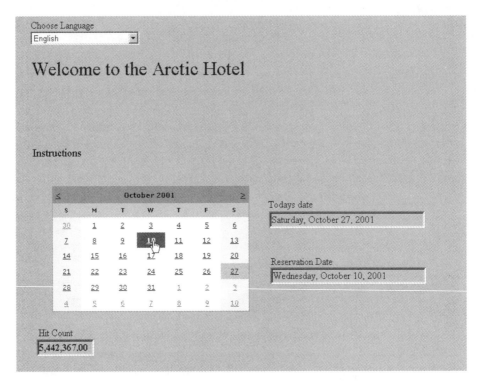

Figure 9-3. First test of ColdHotel project in a browser

OK. Now everything is in the default culture, which in my case is American English. You see today's date, the calendar in English, and the hit count number displayed as it would be in the United States.

The test comes when you choose another language. Choose German for example. Your browser should now change to look like mine (Figure 9-4).

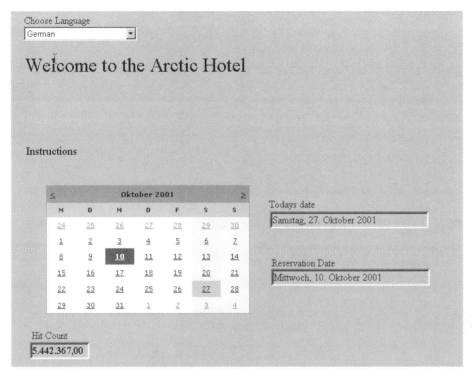

Figure 9-4. ColdHotel program in German

If your code worked, you should see a German calendar. You will also notice that the dates are in German and the hit count number is displayed as it would be in Germany.

This is pretty cool I think. All I needed to do in the code was to change the current threads culture to German and use the ToString method to display the values.

The ToString method is culturally aware. The Calendar control provided by .NET is also culturally aware.

Play around with other languages. Scroll through the calendar and choose other dates. It should all work without any problems.

Displaying the Strings

Now it is time to fill in the InitStrings method. I cover this last because there are a couple of ways to get strings in a web form. There are some caveats.

Generating Strings with the Resource Editor

First you need a resource file. Open the Resource Editor you built in Chapters 7 and 8. Enter the following key/text pairs.

- *Key* = HIT COUNT. *Text* = Hit Count.

- *Key* = INSTRUCTIONS. *Text* = Using the calendar, please choose a date that you would like to stay with us.

- *Key* =TODAYS DATE. *Text* = Today's date.

- *Key* =RESERVATION DATE. *Text* = Reservation date.

- *Key* = WELCOME. *Text* = Welcome to the Arctic Hotel. You may stay at one of our various Igloos, Polar bear dens or in the Hotel itself.

Save the file as both a text resource file and a binary resource file. The base name for the file should be "ColdHotel."

While you are here, make the German, Spanish, and French resource files as well. Similar to the ResourceEditor project, you do not translate the strings but just denote that they belong to a particular language. For German, prefix each text string with the character (G). For Spanish use (S). For French use (F).

The Spanish resource files should have the basename/culturename of "ColdHotel.es-ES." The German resource files should have the basename/culturename of "ColdHotel.de-DE." The French resource files should have the basename/culturename of "ColdHotel.fr-FR."

You need to put these files somewhere your ColdHotel program can access them. But where? Do you know where .NET put your project?

When .NET creates a web project it puts it under a directory called Inetpub\wwwroot. This directory is usually located on your C: drive. Figure 9-5 shows my directory structure for both the VB and C# examples.

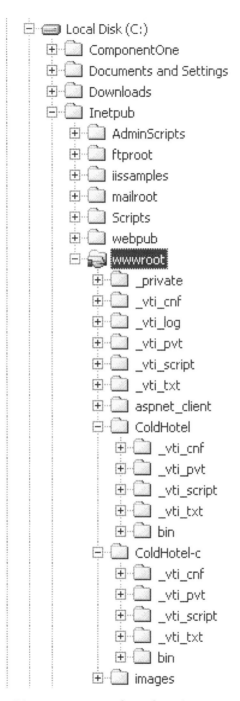

Figure 9-5. Directory structure for web projects

You get resources using the "loose resources" method to start. The default directory for loose resource files in a web project is C:\WINNT\System32. Put your ColdHotel.resources file here.

A loose resources approach uses the GetFileBasedResourceManager method. Listing 9-6 shows the complete InitStrings method. This includes retrieving the strings and displaying them.

Listing 9-6. IntiStrings *method using loose resources*

VB

```
Private Sub InitStrings()

  'Loose resources with default resource set
  rm = ResourceManager.CreateFileBasedResourceManager("ColdHotel", ".", Nothing)

  lblWelcome.Text = rm.GetString("WELCOME")
  lblInstructions.Text = rm.GetString("INSTRUCTIONS")
  lblHitText.Text = rm.GetString("HIT COUNT")
  lblTodaysDate.Text = rm.GetString("TODAYS DATE")
  lblConfirm.Text = rm.GetString("RESERVATION DATE")
  lblHitCount.Text = HitCnt.ToString("n")
  If lblArriveDate.Text <> "" Then
    lblArriveDate.Text = calReservation.SelectedDate.ToString("D")
  End If
End Sub
```

C#

```
private void InitStrings()
{
  //Loose resources with default resource set
  rm = ResourceManager.CreateFileBasedResourceManager("ColdHotel",".",null);

  lblWelcome.Text = rm.GetString("WELCOME");
  lblInstructions.Text = rm.GetString("INSTRUCTIONS");
  lblHitText.Text = rm.GetString("HIT COUNT");
  lblTodaysDate.Text = rm.GetString("TODAYS DATE");
  lblConfirm.Text = rm.GetString("RESERVATION DATE");
```

```
lblHitCount.Text = HitCnt.ToString("n");
if (lblArriveDate.Text != "" )
  lblArriveDate.Text = calReservation.SelectedDate.ToString("D");
}
```

Now that you have this method in your code, test it by pressing F5. You should see the English strings appear no matter which language you choose. For now, this is OK.

End the debugging session. Now what is the procedure for editing the resource file? Well you go back into the ResourceEditor, make your changes, and save the file. You then save the file to the C:\WINNT\System32 directory so the web program can use it.

Try this experiment. Copy the "ColdHotel.resources" file to the C:\WINNT\System32 directory. What happens? You should get an error saying that this file is locked and is being used by another application. You could kill all programs on your machine and you still would not be able to copy over this file. The only recourse is to reboot . . . or is it?

ASP.NET locks resource files that are used in a ResourceSet. The GetFileBasedResourceManager method uses the default ResourceSet provided by .NET.

There is a way around this. You can release the resources by using the ReleaseAllResources method. Put the following line of code as the last line of your InitStrings method.

VB

```
rm.ReleaseAllResources()
```

C#

```
rm.ReleaseAllResources();
```

Now run your program and exit. Try copying the "ColdHotel.resources" to the C:\WINNT\System32 directory. The process will be successful.

This method is OK but it has a major drawback. Can you guess what it is? The fact that I had to release the resources means that the file was locked during the time I was using it. What happens if you have a large web application that opens a resource set at the start but does not release the resource file until the program stops? You would never be able to update the resource file while the program is working. If you had to shut your web server down every time you wanted to update the resource file you would make some surfers pretty mad. This method of resource file utilization effectively breaks XCOPY deployment.

So what is the answer? Well, the best way is to use satellite resource files. These files are put in memory when accessed because they are DLLs. You are then able to copy over the DLL with a new version while it is in use. The next time you load the DLL in your web program, you get all the newest resources. No need to shut down the program.

Using the Fallback Method

It's time to change the InitStrings method to work with satellite resource files. First, you need to turn the .resources files into DLLs. Locate your bin directory within your project directory tree. Refer to Figure 9-5 to see where mine is. Yours should be similar.

Make four subdirectories off this bin directory. They are listed here.

- en-US: Put the ColdHotel.resources file in here.

- es-ES: Put the ColdHotel.es-ES.resources file in here.

- fr-FR: Put the ColdHotel.fr-FR.resources file in here.

- de-DE: Put the ColdHotel.de-DE.resources file in here.

These directories are where your DLL resource files will be located. It is best to make a build.bat file and put it in each of these directories. The contents of this batch file is slightly different for each resource file. Put this line of code in each of the five batch files respectively. Make sure that you type this as one line of code; not two.

en-US Build.bat File Contents

```
al /out:ColdHotel.Resources.Dll /v:1.0.0.0 /c:en-US
/embed:ColdHotel.en-US.resources,ColdHotel.en-US.resources,Private
```

es-ES Build.bat File Contents

```
al /out:ColdHotel.Resources.Dll /v:1.0.0.0 /c:es-ES
/embed:ColdHotel.es-ES.resources,ColdHotel.es-ES.resources,Private
```

en-US Build.bat File Contents

```
al /out:ColdHotel.Resources.Dll /v:1.0.0.0 /c:en-US
/embed:ColdHotel.en-US.resources,ColdHotel.en-US.resources,Private
```

fr-FR Build.bat File Contents

```
al /out:ColdHotel.Resources.Dll /v:1.0.0.0 /c:fr-FR
/embed:ColdHotel.fr-FR.resources,ColdHotel.fr-FR.resources,Private
```

de-DE Build.bat File Contents

```
al /out:ColdHotel.Resources.Dll /v:1.0.0.0 /c:de-DE
/embed:ColdHotel.de-DE.resources,ColdHotel.de-DE.resources,Private
```

You should now have a .resources file and a build.bat file in each of these directories.

To run these batch files you need to run the corvars.bat file first. This is best done in DOS so you can run the batch file immediately afterward.

Open a DOS box. Run the corvars.bat file. Go to each of these directories and run the build.bat file in each. You should now have three files in each of these directories. They are a build.bat file, .resources file, and ColdHotel.Resources.dll.

Making the Final Change to the InitStrings Method

Now that you have the correct directories set up with the correct files, it is time to change the InitStrings method to take advantage of these satellite resource files.

First, get rid of the private resource manager. There is no need to scope the resource manager for the whole class. You will be using one internal to the InitStrings method. Now change the InitStrings method to look like mine, as in Listing 9-7.

Listing 9-7. InitStrings method using satellite resource files

VB

```
Private Sub InitStrings()

    'The best way is to use satellite assemblies
    Dim rm As ResourceManager = New ResourceManager("ColdHotel", _
                           GetType(ColdHotel).Module.Assembly)
```

```
      lblWelcome.Text = rm.GetString("WELCOME")
      lblInstructions.Text = rm.GetString("INSTRUCTIONS")
      lblHitText.Text = rm.GetString("HIT COUNT")
      lblTodaysDate.Text = rm.GetString("TODAYS DATE")
      lblConfirm.Text = rm.GetString("RESERVATION DATE")
      lblHitCount.Text = HitCnt.ToString("n")
      If lblArriveDate.Text <> "" Then
        lblArriveDate.Text = calReservation.SelectedDate.ToString("D")
      End If
    End Sub
```

C#

```
  private void InitStrings()
  {
    //The best way is to use satellite assemblies
    ResourceManager rm = new ResourceManager("ColdHotel",
                            typeof(ColdHotel).Module.Assembly);

    lblWelcome.Text = rm.GetString("WELCOME");
    lblInstructions.Text = rm.GetString("INSTRUCTIONS");
    lblHitText.Text = rm.GetString("HIT COUNT");
    lblTodaysDate.Text = rm.GetString("TODAYS DATE");
    lblConfirm.Text = rm.GetString("RESERVATION DATE");
    lblHitCount.Text = HitCnt.ToString("n");
    if (lblArriveDate.Text != "" )
      lblArriveDate.Text = calReservation.SelectedDate.ToString("D");
  }
```

Now press F5 to test the program. Change languages and you should see the correct text, numbers, dates, and calendar.

Summary

This is the last big example in this book. You have made a simple ASP.NET program that is localized. No doubt it can be improved tremendously. However teaching you web design is not really the goal. The intent is to show you how localization is done in ASP.NET.

ASP is a big subject worthy of several books in its own right. I suggest you pick up a copy of one of the Apress ASP.NET books.

You saw that although you could use loose resources it is not a good idea in ASP programming. Instead it is best to use satellite resource files.

Here are some points to remember when localizing ASP pages:

- Using a resource set locks the resource file. This breaks XCOPY deployment and prevents you from copying over a new resource file.

- You can use ReleaseAllResources to release the resource file but it will still be locked while you use it.

- It is best to use the Satellite resource file capability of .NET for localizing ASP programs.

The remaining chapters are dedicated to miscellaneous aspects of .NET programming and localization design in general.

CHAPTER 10

Versioning Resource Files in .NET

IN THIS CHAPTER YOU LOOK AT actions you need to do to properly deploy resource files for your .NET programs.

As you peruse .NET books on VB and C# you will invariably find a general chapter on .NET security and versioning. This can be quite a large topic. I look into security and versioning with an eye toward the interaction between resource files and the programs that use them.

What is security in .NET? Well, there are several kinds of security.

- Role-based security: This is where access to a program or resource is based on the user or an identity.

- Code-based security: This is where access is given to a program based on the accessing program's identity.

- Client-certificate-based security: This is used within the ASP.NET world.

- Version security: This is where your program demands a particular version of another assembly to work with.

- No security: Anything goes and anyone can access your program.

Version security is what I deal with in this chapter. I show you the details of how to version a resource file and use that resource file while assuring that it was you who actually wrote it.

On your trip through the versioning process there are a few stops you need to make along the way. There are some concepts and tools you need to fully understand the versioning process.

Implicit Security

There is another kind of security in .NET that you have been using throughout the examples in this book. You may not have realized it but by keeping your DLLs and programs in certain directories, you are keeping them private to your program.

How would you implicitly make them public? You put them in the GAC. No, GAC is not the sound your cat sometimes makes; it is the Global Assembly Cache.

A very loose interpretation of the GAC is to think of it like the registry. All you COM programmers know that the registry is where all the GUIDs and related program information is stored. The registry is where COM looks to find the location of a program when your COM application tries to instantiate an interface.

That being said the registry is open to anyone with a programmer's license to store any information he or she wants. It is amazing to see how much, and what, information is stored in the registry. Some of it belongs in configuration files . . . but I digress.

The GAC differs from the registry in that it is only used to keep .NET DLLs. The GAC is actually a folder on your C:\ drive. Point your browser to C:\WINNT\Assembly.

Note that what you see in the right pane is not the usual information. Figure 10-1 shows my GAC as seen through Windows Explorer.

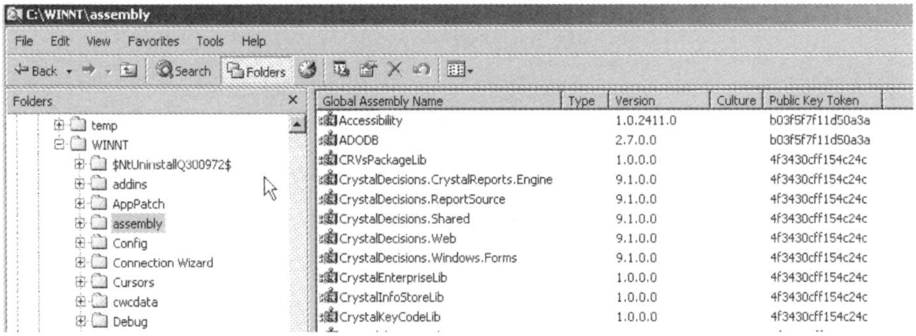

Figure 10-1. The GAC as shown with Windows Explorer

Here you see all the global assemblies that .NET knows about. The information in the right pane shows the name, type, Culture, and Public Key Token.

You know about the Culture (or should by now). The type refers to whether or not the code is pre-jitted. The version is the version of the program, and the Public Key Token uniquely identifies the program.

So what is pre-jitted? The short answer is that .NET programs are compiled to Intermediate Language, or IL code. When the program runs, it is just-in-time compiled for your machine. The compiled version of code is then kept in memory. Hence the name JIT compiler. Pre-jitted code means that you have used a .NET program called ngen.exe to precompile your code to native machine code. The advantage of this is loading speed (no need to JIT compile). The disadvantage is that the code is compiled to a generic machine. It does not take advantage of any advanced machine properties that your computer may have. Pre-jitted code also is compiled for a particular platform. If the .NET CLR is ever ported over to another platform – say Linux – then your pre-jitted code will not work.

How about this Public Key Token? What's that all about? Part of the answer lies in Microsoft's answer to DLL hell. A program that you develop in .NET can be given a strong name. This strong name is a unique name, part of which consists of a public and private key. Cryptography is out of the scope of this book but suffice it to say the public key is the signature of your program. The private key is what generated this signature. No one else can regenerate your program without the private key (that only you have). Most companies would store their private keys in a safe place so they can't be used to spoof your program. This is what makes your program unique. The public key allows you to access information that was encrypted with the corresponding private key.

The public key token is actually a hash of the public key. Hashing allows you to get a signature of the public key that is embedded in the assembly. This token is sufficient to determine if the dependent assembly is the exact one you want. It is virtually impossible for two different public keys to generate the same hash token. The reverse is also true. It is also impossible to reverse engineer the public key from the hash value. One thing the public/private key system does not do is identify the author. It is an anonymous system. To identify an author of an assembly you need a sign code system, such as Authenticode, to sign the program. This subject is beyond what I want to talk about.

By the way, did you notice that all the programs in the GAC have public keys? What does this tell you? It means that to be in the GAC your program must have a strong name. This is after all a common area for .NET programs and there must be a unique way to identify each one.

Did you also notice that most of all the .NET assemblies have the same public key token? This should tell you that they were signed with the same public key file.

Installing Your Program in the GAC

Now that you know about strong names, how do you give a strong name to a program? There is a tool called sn.exe. This program generates a public/private key pair that you can use to sign your assembly. If you have a resource file in the form of a satellite DLL you may want to install it in the GAC so more than one program can access the resources. It is the sn.exe tool that you use to generate the keys that allows you to put your program there.

It is good practice to use the same public/private key pair to sign all your files within the same assembly. With that in mind, suppose you were writing several modules that needed to access the resource file you put in the GAC. You finished your resource file but not the rest of the files. This means you probably do not have access to the final public/private key pair with which to sign your resource DLL. What to do?

There is a method to handle this situation—delayed signing. Delayed signing means that the compiler inserts the public key into the assembly manifest and space is reserved in your assembly portable executable (PE) file for the strong name at final build. It is possible to delay-sign an assembly, install it in the GAC, and sign it properly later.

 NOTE *By the way, if a program does not have a strong name what kind of name does it have? A weak one? No, Microsoft probably did not like the connotation of weak. The opposite of a strong name is a simple name.*

Start a small VB Windows Forms project. I named mine CH10SNVB. Place two labels on the form and change the label BorderStyle to 3D so you can see them. Those are all the forms and controls you need for this project. My form is shown in Figure 10-2.

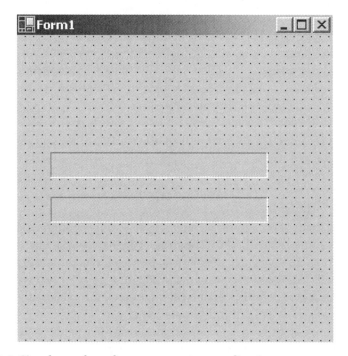

Figure 10-2. Simple test form for a strong name application

Press F5 to build and run the program. Once you do this, .NET makes some directories and files for you. Using Windows Explorer, make a new directory under the bin directory called "en-US." This is the familiar culture directory.

> **NOTE** *This program is so trivial that it does not warrant a mirror in C#.*

Open your NotePad editor and make a text resource file called CH10SNVB.en-US.txt. Put in the following lines of code to make up the resources.

```
HELLO = Hello
PUBLIC = Public
```

This is not the most comprehensive resource file but it serves the purpose. Save the file and turn it into a satellite resource file. Let's review the steps for this.

1. Open a DOS box in this directory.

2. Run the CorVars.bat file to get the paths set correctly.

3. Type "resgen CH10SNVB.en-US.txt" to generate the binary .resources file.

4. Use the AL assembly generation tool to make a satellite resource file DLL. Type "al /out:CH10SNVB.Resources.Dll /v:1.0.0.0 /c:en-US /embed:CH10SNVB.en-US.resources,CH10SNVB.en-US.resources,private."

You should now have three files in your en-US directory. They are:

• CH10SNVB.en-US.txt

• CH10SNVB.en-US.resources

• CH10SNVB.Resources.dll

Return to your VB project (without closing the DOS box) and add code to have a fallback resource manager connect to the resource file and fill in the labels on the form. The reason I use the fallback method in this example is that it forces .NET to find the resource file. If you use a resource set, you would be telling .NET where to find it. This is important when you install the resource file in the GAC. Listing 10-1 shows the code in the form necessary to do this.

Listing 10-1. Form code to read resource file and fill in label fields

```
Option Strict On

Imports System.Resources
Imports System.IO

Public Class Form1
  Inherits System.Windows.Forms.Form

Windows Form Designer generated code

  Private Sub Form1_Load(ByVal sender As System.Object, _
             ByVal e As System.EventArgs) Handles MyBase.Load
    Dim rm As ResourceManager = New ResourceManager _
               ("CH10SNVB", Me.GetType().Assembly)

    Label1.Text = rm.GetString("HELLO")
    Label2.Text = rm.GetString("PUBLIC")

  End Sub
End Class
```

I did not include the Windows-generated code in this listing. There is nothing special there as far as this example is concerned.

Press F5 and run the program. It should work and you should see a form similar to mine, as shown in Figure 10-3.

Figure 10-3. Working form showing text obtained from the resource file

Now it is time to delay-sign the resource file and install it in the GAC. Once that is done you will make some minor code alterations and run the program again. The resources will then be obtained from the resource file in the GAC.

You use two new command-line utilities here. They are sn.exe and gacutil.exe. The sn.exe program creates a strong name file that contains a public/private key pair. The gacutil.exe program installs and removes programs from the GAC.

Go back to your DOS box in the en-US directory. Type the following command making sure to use a lower case "k" for the switch:

```
sn -k key.snk
```

This makes a new file called key.snk. It is a binary file and cannot be read with NotePad. Next, type the following command:

```
sn -p key.snk pubkey.snk
```

What this does is extract the public key from the key.snk file and put it in a file called pubkey.snk. It is this file that you use to delay-sign your assembly. Now it is time to rebuild your satellite resource file DLL giving it a delayed strong name based on the public key. Type the following line at your DOS command prompt. Make sure that the next three lines are typed as just one line.

```
al /out:CH10SNVB.Resources.Dll /v:1.0.0.0 /c:en-US
/embed:CH10SNVB.en-US.resources,CH10SNVB.en-US.resources /delay+
/keyfile:pubkey.
```

This is virtually the same command you used earlier to build the dll file. The difference is that instead of making the file private you are making it public and giving it a strong name. When you change your program, you will need to tell it where the pubkey.snk file is. Copy it to a directory that is easy to get to. I moved my pubkey.snk file and key.snk file to D:\.

There is one last thing to do before you install this file in the GAC. Because this file is not fully signed you need to prevent gacutil from checking its version before it installs it in the GAC. Otherwise the gacutil program fails. Type the following command:

```
sn - Vr ch10snvb.resources.dll
```

Make sure that the command line switch is Vr. The "V" must be capitalized. Now you can install this file in the GAC. Type the following command:

```
gacutil -i ch10snvb.resources.dll
```

Your resource file now has a strong name and is now installed in the GAC. Point your Windows Explorer to the GAC in C:\WINNT\assembly. You should see your resource file in the GAC similar to mine, as shown in Figure 10-4.

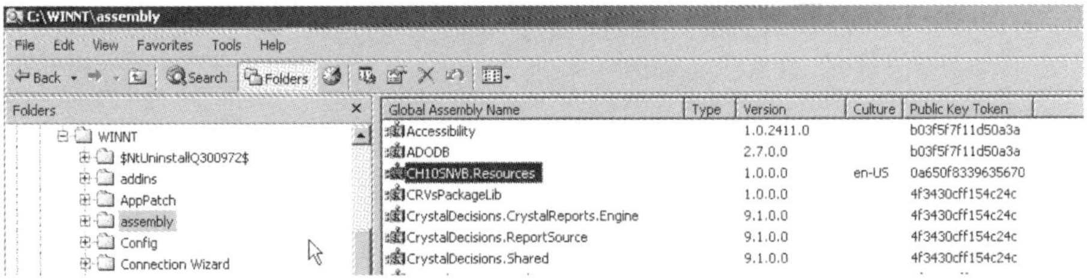

Figure 10-4. GAC showing that the new resource file has been installed

Notice that the resource file has a culture associated with it and that the version is 1.0.0.0. This conforms to the AL command you typed to generate this DLL.

Using the GAC Resource File

Now it is time to see if your program still works. Press F5 to run your program. It should fail when getting the resources. Can you guess why? Your resource file is still where you left it in the en-US directory. The answer is that your resource file is now strong named and your small program does not have the right to access it. Security at work!

How do you fix this? You need to make a small adjustment to your program to temporarily sign it with the same public key. You delay sign this program using attributes.

Open your AssemblyInfo.vb file in the Solution Explorer window. You will see a set of attributes that are kept in the assembly's manifest. You will add to this set of attributes to delay sign your program with the same key as the resource file. Enter the following lines of code at the end of the file:

```
<Assembly: AssemblyKeyFileAttribute("d:\pubkey.snk")>
<Assembly: AssemblyDelaySignAttribute(True)>
```

The first line passes the name of the file containing the public key to this attribute's constructor. The second line indicates that delayed signing is being used.

Compile the program. Now run the program and it should run without errors.

How do you know that the resources are being obtained from the GAC? Try renaming your resource file DLL in the en-US directory. Run your program again. You should have no errors.

It may seem like a lot of work to do all this. It is easy enough for you to make a batch file that performs these steps for generating the key file to sign the resource file and install it in the GAC. This batch file method is a method I would highly recommend.

Using the Full Strong Name

So much for delayed signing. What happens when it is time to deploy your application and your keeper-of-the-keys has given you the full key pair file? You need to sign your assemblies with the full strong name. The procedure is simple enough.

Go to your DOS box in the en-US directory. Type the following command:

```
sn -R ch10snvb.resources.dll key.snk
```

What this does is re-sign your assembly with the full public/private key. Now use the gacutil program to reinstall the resource file into the GAC. Type the following command.

```
gacutil -i ch10snvb.resources.dll
```

OK, now your resource assembly is properly signed. You need to do the same for your program. Comment out the second line that identifies your program as delayed. You will not need it.

Change the line:

```
<Assembly: AssemblyKeyFileAttribute("d:\pubkey.snk")>
```

to:

```
<Assembly: AssemblyKeyFileAttribute("d:\key.snk")>
```

All you have done is replace the name of the key file with which this assembly is signed. Recompile your project and comment out this line. Press F5 to run your program. It should run as expected.

I would like to mention one last thing about the GAC and managing it. You are probably wondering if you can see the GAC in Windows Explorer, can you drag a strong-named dll and drop it in? Well, in fact you can. It is not strictly necessary to use the gacutil.exe program to do this. You can also click on a dll in this view and delete it from the GAC.

I suppose I could have left the discussion of the GAC at that point, but I am a rather curious type and wanted to discover more. Here are some of the questions I had when I was playing around with the GAC.

- Why is the view different in Explorer than any other directory? The reason is that Windows uses a special Windows Explorer shell extension DLL named shfusion.dll to view the contents of this directory.

- Is this a true directory? No. What you see as files in this folder are actually trees of subdirectories. Open a DOS box in the c:\WINNT\assembly folder and type in "tree." You will be amazed at what you see.

If you want to know more about the GAC, I encourage you to investigate further.

Versioning in .NET

Versioning in .NET only works when you use strong names. The version is actually a part of the strong name. This allows you to fully identify your program as being unique from all others in the known universe.

There are many ways to version files for security, and there are quite a few tools in .NET that help you. Versioning and security in .NET could take a whole book in itself. For now, I concentrate on versioning resource files and allowing .NET programs to use them correctly.

You have made many satellite resource files throughout this book. Each one was generated with the al.exe tool. You have probably noticed that I always include a version flag in the arguments. It is always Version 1.0.0.0.

NOTE *Microsoft has strict ways to version files. If you want to version a file and refer to a version file, you must use the complete Microsoft version. This consists of a major version, minor version, build number, and revision. This is why a version is in the form of 1.0.0.0.*

When you signed the satellite DLL with the key file, the version was incorporated in the signature hash code. The version of DLL that you put in the GAC was version 1.0.0.0. Now it is time to change versions a little.

Using Multiple Satellite Versions

Part of getting rid of DLL hell is being able to put the two versions of the same file in the GAC or memory and specify which one you want to use. There is no more of this copying over old versions with new ones and breaking programs. I have stated that you can install in the GAC-version satellite resource files, and this is what you will do.

I suggest using a batch file for this process so you can play with the versions and the GAC without too much effort on your part.

First, make two new text files and call them v1.txt and v2.txt respectively. Type the following lines into v1.txt:

```
HELLO = Hello V1
PUBLIC = Public V1
```

Put the following lines into v2.txt:

```
HELLO = Hello V2
PUBLIC = Public V2
```

Make a batch file called buildv1.bat and another batch file called buildv2.bat. Enter the code in Listing 10-2 in the buildv1.bat file. I put my corvars.bat file in the root directory for easy access. You may want to do the same, as you will be using the command line quite a bit.

Listing 10-2. Batch file that compiles a version 1 of the resource file

```
call c:\corvars.bat
resgen v1.txt ch10snvb.en-US.resources
al /out:CH10SNVB.Resources.Dll /v:1.0.0.0 /c:en-US
/embed:CH10SNVB.en-US.resources,CH10SNVB.en-US.resources
/keyfile:key.snk
gacutil -i ch10snvb.resources.dll

pause
```

The al.exe line is very long. Make sure it is complete. What I am doing here is taking the v1.txt file, generating a ch10snvb.resources file, compiling the .resources file into a satellite DLL, and installing it in the GAC. You will do the same thing for the buildv2.bat file only you will use the v2.txt file as a base. Enter the code from Listing 10-3 into your buildv2.bat file.

Listing 10-3. Batch file that compiles a version 2 of the resource file

```
call c:\corvars.bat
resgen v2.txt ch10snvb.en-US.resources
al /out:CH10SNVB.Resources.Dll /v:2.0.0.0 /c:en-US
/embed:CH10SNVB.en-US.resources,CH10SNVB.en-US.resources /keyfile:key.snk
gacutil -i ch10snvb.resources.dll

pause
```

Notice that in addition to using v2.txt in Listing 10-3, I also changed the version of the satellite DLL to V:2.0.0.0.

Now that you have these two batch files, run build1.bat followed by build2.bat. Look at the GAC. Remember it is in C:\WINNT\assembly. You should see the same file differentiated only by version. What I see is shown in Figure 10-5.

Global Assembly Name	Type	Version	Culture	Public Key Token
Accessibility		1.0.2411.0		b03f5f7f11d50a3a
ADODB		2.7.0.0		b03f5f7f11d50a3a
CH10SNVB.Resources		2.0.0.0	en-US	0a650f8339635670
CH10SNVB.Resources		1.0.0.0	en-US	0a650f8339635670
CRVsPackageLib		1.0.0.0		4f3430cff154c24c
CrystalDecisions.CrystalReports.Engine		9.1.0.0		4f3430cff154c24c
CrystalDecisions.ReportSource		9.1.0.0		4f3430cff154c24c
CrystalDecisions.Shared		9.1.0.0		4f3430cff154c24c

Figure 10-5. The GAC shows the same resource file, but different versions

Pretty neat huh? Two of the same files with the same public key token and culture. They seem to be differentiated only by version. Let's use them!

Go back into your project and edit the AssemblyInfo.vb file. Press F5 to run the program. What do you see? You should see your form with the version 2 resources. This is telling you that with multiple versions of the same satellite resource file in the GAC, .NET chooses the latest version for you unless you say otherwise. So, you ask, how do you say otherwise? You use attributes in the main program that are accessing the DLL. For this you need to use the SatelliteContractVersionAttribute class. You need to instantiate this class constructor with the resource DLL version number. This class is not used in the traditional sense but is used as an attribute. Type the following line of code at the bottom of your AssemblyInfo.vb file:

```
<Assembly: Resources.SatelliteContractVersion("1.0.0.0")>
```

This now tells the resource manager to search for, and use, the resource file that is marked as version 1. Press F5 and run the program. What do you see? You should see the text from the version 1 resource file.

NOTE *There are many attributes that end in the word attribute. .NET accepts and recognizes the name of the attribute without the ending "attribute" suffix. That is why I was able to use SatelliteContractVersion instead of SatelliteContractVersionAttribute.*

This is important because it allows you to force the use of a particular version of a file. In this case, a resource file.

There will come a time when you have released a product with a certain version. You find a bug in your program and make a patch. The bug has no impact on the resource file. To release the patch you need to bump the version of the executable. By using the SatelliteContractVersionAttribute attribute you can tell your new version to use the old version of resource files. You will not have to distribute a new resource file with your patch.

Suppose you wanted to do the reverse? It is also possible to change the resource file and redistribute it with a new version even if the program that uses it wants the previous version. This is accomplished with a publisher policy file. It allows you to tell all calling programs that this new resource file is good for various program versions.

Setting the Policy

There are three basic configuration files associated with any .NET program. These configuration files allow the developer to externalize some of the properties associated with an assembly's manifest. It also allows you to override quite a few of the assembly's attributes with ones you specify in the configuration file. Each of these three files follows the same XML format.

The Application Configuration File

The first file is the application configuration file. This file resides in the same directory as the assembly it applies to. It is generally used for remoting in .NET. There are a number of XML tags that refer to dependent assemblies and which versions of those assemblies can be redirected. The application configuration file is the first file that the CLR checks for information that would override version information contained in the assembly's manifest.

The name of this file is the name of the assembly with a .config extension. In our case the name of the assembly is ch10snvb.exe. The application configuration file for this would be called ch10snvb.exe.config.

The Publisher Policy Configuration File

The next file is the publisher policy configuration file. This file is the second place that the CLR looks for manifest override information. The policy file normally overrides the application configuration file. The exception to this is when the application configuration file contains a tag that enforces safe mode. Safe mode is invoked by using the <publisherPolicy apply="yes|no"/> element. If this tag is set to "yes," then the information in the policy configuration file is removed from the binding process.

The publisher configuration file is the file you normally send to the client when sending a new version of a resource file to work with an older version of the application. This file is meant to redirect an assembly reference to a new version.

Recall that you put an attribute in the assembly called SatelliteContractVersion. This attribute told the resource file to get its resources from a particular version of the resource file. Although this version information was hard-coded into the client application, the policy configuration file can override this attribute and redirect the resource manager to get its resources from another version.

If the application configuration file is in the same directory as the application, where is the policy configuration file kept? It is kept in the GAC with the shared assembly it refers to. This means that the policy configuration file is a DLL with a strong name.

A policy file has an interesting naming convention. Its name is policy.major.minor.assemblyname.dll. If you had an assembly called MyProg.dll that was version 2.3, the policy configuration file would be called "policy.2.3.myprog.dll." Redirecting a resource file involves the same kind of policy file. The resource file you use in this chapter is ch10snvb.resources.dll. The policy file for version 1 of this resource file is policy.1.0.ch10snvb.resources.dll. The policy file for version 2 of this resource file is policy.2.0.ch10snvb.resources.dll.

Since the policy configuration file is an XML file how do you get it into a DLL and into the GAC? You use the al.exe tool to create the DLL and the gacutil.exe tool to install it in the GAC. The following piece of code is the al.exe command necessary to make a DLL out of a MyProg.cfg file to be used for the program MyProg.dll. Make sure that the following two lines of code are typed as one line only.

```
Al /Link:MyProg.cfg /out:policy.2.0.MyProg.dll
/keyfile: MyProg.snk /version:2.0.0.0
```

Notice that I am using the strong name key file that was used for the assembly. This is necessary to reconcile the policy file with the assembly. The code that follows is the gacutil.exe line necessary to install this policy DLL file into the GAC.

```
gacutil -i policy.2.0.Myprog.dll
```

Once the policy file is installed in the GAC along with the assembly it references, the binding redirection is automatically performed by the CLR.

The Machine Configuration File

This file is pretty much the same as the other two configuration files in that it uses the same XML commands to redirect versions. It also has quite a few other tags to control other aspects of the .NET runtime.

This file should not be used to hold redirection information. It is the last file the CLR looks at before loading assemblies. The settings in this file cannot be overridden.

It is interesting to look at this file and see what is in it. It can be quite instructive. Mine is in C:\IWNNT\Microsoft.net\framework\v1.0.2914\config. It is called machine.config. I advise you not to change anything in here.

There is a tool you can use to manage the machine.config file. It is an mmc snap-in called mscorcfg.msc. You can run it from the command line by typing:

```
mmc c:\winnt\microsoft.net\framework\v1.0.2914\mscorcfg.msc
```

The utility lets you manage all the assemblies in the GAC. Figure 10-6 shows the administration tool.

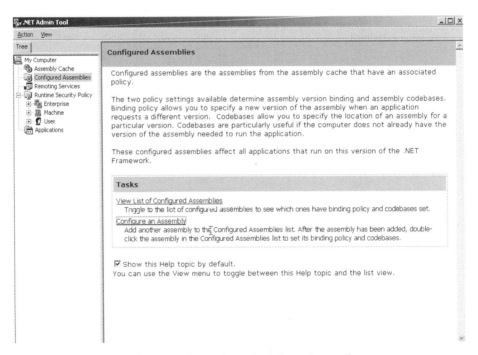

Figure 10-6. .NET machine configuration administration tool

Listing 10-4 shows a sample policy configuration file that redirects an assembly version from version 1.0.0.0 to 2.0.0.0.

Listing 10-4. Redirection policy file

```
<configuration>
    <runtime>
        <assemblyBinding xmlns="urn:schemas-microsoft-com:asm.v1">
         <dependentAssembly>
           <assemblyIdentity name="aaa.Resources"
                              publickeytoken="a35708b34e9f1417"
                              culture="en-us" />

         <bindingRedirect oldVersion="1.0.0.0"
                           newVersion="2.0.0.0"/>
       </dependentAssembly>
     </assemblyBinding>
   </runtime>
</configuration>
```

As you can see it is a fairly simple and readable file.

Summary

Throughout the examples in previous chapters, no consideration was given to versioning and the security that goes with it. Although it is possible, and most probable, you can release your code with no version-checking enabled. But you don't want to do that. If you do, you will be right back in version hell. Perhaps not with other programs, but with your updates.

This chapter has shown you the methods necessary to properly version your programs and the resource files that it depends on. I have also shown you a few tools. Some of which are familiar. They are:

- AL.EXE: This is the assembly linker. You have used it to create resource DLLs and to sign them with the proper version and strong name.

- SN.EXE: This is the strong name tool. It creates a public/private key pair that is unique. This key pair allows you to uniquely sign your program.

- GACUTIL.EXE: This is the GAC installer. It checks your program's strong name to make sure it is OK and then installs it into the GAC.

You also spent some time discovering the GAC. You now have an idea of what it really is and how to manipulate it. The GAC is a very important part of .NET.

Last, I went over the three configuration files that are important to all assemblies. Each of these configuration files allows the developer to update an assembly with attribute information. The files can also be used to redirect bindings and provide an alternate probing path to find your assembly.

Next is the last chapter of the book. In it, I go over program design in general, with an eye toward localization.

CHAPTER 11

Localization Wrap-up

THIS IS THE FINAL CHAPTER in this book. This chapter wraps up what you have learned and points out a few things about localization that do not really fit anywhere else.

Help Files

Visual Basic 5 and 6 used a Help file system called WinHelp. This was Microsoft's Help system before they standardized on HTML-based Help. Using WinHelp in earlier versions of VB was fairly easy. Microsoft had built-in support for calling WinHelp files automatically if a user pressed F1.

WinHelp, however, had some problems and was supplanted by HTML Help systems. HTML Help uses a browser window to display Help topics. You have used HTML Help when using .NET. You can see by using the .NET Help system that there are all kinds of hyperlinks and hierarchies that can be built using HTML Help.

Help Formats Explained

The kind of Help files that you create are based on what you think the users' requirements will be. WinHelp is a Microsoft-based Help system that was designed as either stand-alone Help or online Help for Windows applications. It is based on RTF (rich text format) files.

HTML Help was designed to be based on Hypertext Markup Language (HTML) files. You can run Microsoft HTML Help on any Windows 9x and up machine. Windows 95 and NT4.0 required Internet Explorer 4.x or above browser to view the Help files. Windows 98, 2000 and above uses either a browser or a built-in viewer. Table 11-1 describes some feature comparisons between HTML Help and WinHelp.

Table 11-1. WinHelp vs. HTML Help

FEATURE	HTML HELP	WINHELP
ActiveX Controls	Yes	No
Bookmarks	Yes	No
Background colors	Yes	Yes
Popup Window	Yes	Yes
Context sensitive help	Yes	Yes
Custom Windows	Yes	Yes
Dynamic HTML	Yes	No
Expandable TOC	Yes	Yes
Forms	Yes	No
Frames	Yes	No
Include Image	Yes	Yes
Include Links	Yes	Yes
Include borders	Yes	No
Tri-Pane Window	Yes	No

While the choice of which Help system to use may be a difficult one, the choice of whether to translate it is not. If you want a true world-ready program, you need to have a localized Help system that goes with it.

The Help files should be completed and translated at the same time as the translations for your program. Quite often you will have the same phrases in your Help files as you have in your program. It is important for continuity that these words, phrases, and sentences be translated identically.

The Help system can be just as important as the program itself. Often the Help files can be sent to a customer as a demo of your program.

Getting It Translated

I have mentioned throughout the book that it is wise to keep text resources in a text resource file. This file contains just key/value pairs. This type of file also can contain comments. Listing 11-1 shows a sample text-based resource file that .NET understands.

Listing 11-1. A text-based .NET resource file

```
;Resource file for MyProgram.exe
LOGIN    =    Enter Login Name
LOGOUT  = Logout from program
```

```
OPEN    = Open file
CLOSE   = Close File
'See glossary for button
BUTTON  = Press Button
;Following line must be 20 character maximum
BADPRB  = prb Is wrong type
CANCEL  = Cancel operation
```

It is most likely that your company does not have an in-house translator. More than likely, it will send this file to an outside translation service. Whether or not you send the file out or translate it in-house, you still need to make the translator's job as easy as possible.

The sample resource file in Listing 11-1 has some aspects to it that make the translator's job easier.

- Comments: Do not be stingy with comments in resource files. They help you as well as the translator.

- Line length: Let the translator know when space is at a premium.

- References to a glossary: The translator may not know your industry-specific terms. What you mean as a keypad button may be translated as a shirt button.

Make sure the glossary is kept up-to-date. It needs to be used by all people on your project. This includes developers, technical writers, marketing people, and so forth. It should become a standard to make a smooth transition between different parts of your product.

When you send the resource file out to be translated, send out the glossary. If you use a translation service that you have used before do not assume the glossary it has is up-to-date. Send a new one.

Checking Out the Translation

As you investigate translation services, you will find that the good ones do not have many translators on their actual staff. Most send out your translation work to contractors. Why do this? Well think of all the languages that your product could be translated to. Multiply that by the number of cultures that speak that language. Each culture has its own linguistic idiosyncrasies that need to be taken into consideration. Remember the CultureInfo class and the number of cultures you can localize your program to?

Not only do they have to worry about cultures within languages but the good translation services also try to find a translator who is familiar with your industry. So you have the following equation: (languages x cultures x industries) = translators needed. This is a lot of people. Hence, most translations are farmed out.

What the translation service provides is a good project manager who makes sure you get a good translation. You do not have to worry about all the details.

By the way, often this translator equation needs to be doubled. Why? Well just as you have implemented code reads among your developers, translation services often want a translation checker to go over the work that was done.

Thoroughness is important when localizing a program. Remember your company's reputation often relies on it. Speaking of thoroughness, what should you do with the translations once you get them back? Do you package them up and sell your program right away? I wouldn't. In my early days, I was burned a few times by doing just that. Despite how thorough some of these translation services are, some things may fall through the cracks.

If you are translating a program for a particular country, chances are that you have a distributor in that country who works for you. When you send out the resource file to be translated, sign up the distributor to go over the translations when you get them back. This final check can avoid some subtle translation problems that the translation service may have missed.

If you do not have a company contact in the target country, it behooves you to find one.

Translation Programs

The last few years have seen a growth in translation programs. These programs can be grouped into a few categories.

- Localization enablers

- Text extraction software

- Translation software

Localization Enablers

Localization enablers provide software to help lay out your keyboard with existing templates or custom ones. These keyboard layouts allow you to have an American keyboard but type foreign characters directly into your program. Often they include multiple font sets. You can switch between fonts depending on the language you choose.

If you have an in-house translator, this kind of product can be very useful indeed.

Under the heading of localization enablers comes another kind of software, which is multilanguage OCR software. There are programs that take a document and read it through a scanner. The software recognizes the words and can input them directly into a Word document. Where would this be useful? I can see using this to scan and read in a paper manual for redistribution on disk. This type of software could save you quite a bit of time and expense.

Translation Software

There is a category of software that tries to be the translation service. This software can take an executable file and extract all its resources. It can then do the translations and put these translations back into your executable. Instant language.

Some of these software packages are rather complex in that they can also let you edit the size of controls that text will fit into. They can also read and write XML files and databases. For example if you had an Access database it would be possible to extract and translate the text in the database.

So, are these worthwhile tools? The answer depends on your level of comfort. If you are OK with the translations performed using cookie cutter text then this might work for you. These tools are also mainly used for translations of programs that were never really designed with localization in mind. For a quick and dirty solution this may be OK.

I prefer to have a person translate my strings. I feel that only a person can handle the nuances involved in translating properly from one language to another.

Text Extractors

Text extractors are interesting indeed. A text extractor takes your source code, be it C++, VB, or Delphi, and finds all the hard-coded strings within. Here is how a text extractor would work for VB 6 code.

- The tool loads all the project's source code.

- It searches for all hard-coded strings. Such strings are usually delimited with quotes.

- It extracts all strings to a VB 6 .res file. This .res file is the compiled resource file.

- It replaces all the text strings with a LoadResString() function call that references the new strings.

This seems like a pretty cool tool. There are, however, some drawbacks and some things to watch out for.

- The LoadResString() function usually references a string via a number such as LoadResStrings(1234). This can cause severe maintenance headaches.

- Some strings may be translated that should not be. Most of these tools have a method to prevent a particular string from being extracted.

- Constant strings cannot be referenced by a LoadResString() function.

- The resulting resource file cannot be used by multiple projects.

If a resource extractor forces you to spend time adding directives to prevent string extraction then this time could be better used to extract the strings yourself properly. If you extract strings yourself you control how they are referenced and you can use the same resource file for multiple projects.

Some of these tools do a pretty good job of externalizing the strings in your project. However it usually takes quite a bit of work on your part to make sure that it is all done right. To me, their use is nebulous.

Testing Your Localized Code

There are many books on software testing methodologies. I do not attempt to elucidate the different aspects of software testing in general but instead try to give a few pointers on the localization part.

Before you send out a resource file to be tested, make sure your program works as advertised. There are many aspects of software development and testing that can be done in parallel. Testing localization is not one of those. It should be done at the end of the normal testing cycle. Why not test in parallel? How muddy do you want your testing waters? Too many variables in the testing protocol could easily confuse the issue. For instance, how would you know if a bug you found is due to the insertion of a new string or due to a real bug in the code. If the only difference between a program working or not is the addition of a particular string, then the bug would be much easier to find.

Often during the testing cycle dialog boxes are added or removed and text is changed. It would be very expensive to retranslate resource files that never saw the light of day to begin with.

The Platform Counts

If you have developed your code on an English Windows platform, it would be very difficult to test a Japanese translation on it. Buying the correct version of Windows is essential.

Windows 2000 and above can be purchased as a multilanguage version. This allows you to not only change the language that documents are displayed in but also change the language that the operating system dialogs are displayed in. This is a great help in testing your software. But is it enough? Not if you want to make sure your program really works in the country it is destined for.

Let's start with the operating system itself. It is most probable that your program will be installed on a computer that has a version of Windows that was designed for that locale. You must test on that version of Windows yourself. If you have, say a dozen translations to test this could get expensive. How would you keep the testing costs down?

Microsoft sells a product called the MSDN. The Universal version of this software gets you a package from Microsoft that contains virtually every byte of code they put out. This includes every version of Windows that is made. The MSDN also includes monthly update disks that include all service patches (always a joy) and any new software they come out with including beta software. The cost for the Universal license is not cheap, but it is well worth it. The MSDN Universal allows you to test on the target Windows version any time you want. I consider the MSDN a necessary tool for any development team.

Is All Hardware the Same?

The other part to testing is the hardware. Testing on the Cyrillic version of Windows is fine but how would a user type text? You need to buy and test with keyboards that are used in the country you are targeting. Pressing hot keys or key combinations is not a substitute for pressing the actual key that gives you a particular character.

It is also not a good idea to have some driver pop-up a screen anytime you want to input a character that does not appear in your program. Your end user will not have this program, why should you? There may be some interaction you are not aware of.

Finally, in the hardware vein I come to the machine itself. I know I said I would not expound on testing philosophy in general but I make an exception in this case. It is very important to test your software not just on different operating system versions and keyboards, but also on different machines.

During the design of your product, your team came up with a specification for the target computer. This spec described the processor speed, memory capacity, hard drive capacity, and so on. The hardware spec is always the minimum necessary for your program to run. When you test your program, you should test it on hardware that starts at the minimum level to the latest in computing power. Also make sure you do not get all your test computers from the same manufacturer. For general testing you will likely require four or five different computers.

So, that being said, let me add another wrinkle to this hardware philosophy. If you can, test your localized software on a computer that was bought from the destination country.

I have had software run just fine on my platform-testing suite only to have it fail inexplicably when loaded on the target computer. After getting the target computer sent back to me, I found that there are subtle differences in the hardware setups and components used from the computers I bought in the United States. The software I designed at the time was hardware-intensive and hardware-sensitive. I have since managed to get a "jelly bean" computer for the target country for testing purposes before sending out the software. I have found hardware compatibility problems and have solved them before the customer calls come in.

Don't Forget the Install

The install is a part of the software development cycle that often gets little attention. A professional software package needs a professional installation program. There is no excuse to go to all the trouble of localizing your software only to have an English-only install program.

Installation programming is an art in itself. The goal is to make an install program that requires almost no user intervention. This can sometimes be very difficult. For those cases where you want to get user input and give status messages you will need to do it in a way that the user understands. There are several packages available that allow multilingual installs. InstallShield is one program, and the Wise Installer is another. These are the two most popular installation programs out there. Both have versions that work with both Eastern and Western languages. I highly recommend paying as much attention to detail in the install program as you would in your final product.

Final Comments

This book has been about using .NET to localize your software. I have taken you through some general localization concepts and showed you how to apply them. I have also shown you how .NET was constructed from the ground up to make it easy to localize any program. Since the localizing capability is built into the CLR you have seen that localizing software written in one programming language is the same for any programming language that .NET supports.

Here are some major things you have learned about localizing in .NET.

- How to make VB 6 provide the same fallback functionality as .NET

- The CultureInfo class and how it is used

- The SystemGlobalization namespace

- The SystemResources namespace

- Command line tools necessary to help in localization

- The three different kinds of resource files

- How resource files are constructed and used in .NET

- How to localize Windows Forms

- A resource file editor example

- An ASP.NET example

There are quite a few languages in .NET. Only three are in the initial release but if you hunt on the web you will find languages such as COBOL, FORTRAN, PERL, PYTHON, and so on. Having this many programming languages for the same CLR is akin to translating your program into many different spoken languages. Your program is still the same; it is just how others communicate with it that is different.

Most programmers are multilingual in the programming language sense but some are not. Also, like spoken languages, some programming languages become the preferred language for some developers.

Microsoft realized this when they invented the .NET framework. No longer are developers forced to use a language they do not know or are uncomfortable with. You can use any one of a variety of programming languages as the interface to .NET. As your program is translated for easy use in other countries Microsoft has done the same with .NET.

Because .NET works in a variety of programming languages, it will become widely used by programmers from many backgrounds. You should strive to do the same by localizing your software for different cultures.

Visual Studio .NET makes localizing your software much easier than ever before.

I hope you have found the book useful and enjoyed reading it as much as I enjoyed writing it.

Resources for Internationalization and Localization Projects

THE FIRST FEW CHAPTERS of this book gave you a good overview of localization in general. Although the overview is informative, it is not exhaustive. This appendix gives you ideas of where to go for more information on localization. I've included web sites where you can pursue specific localization subjects in depth.

General Globalization Web Sites

You can find a good overview of the international support provided by Windows 2000/XP at the following web site:

```
http://www.msdn.microsoft.com/library/backgrnd/html/intl_sup_nt5.htm
```

The following site has information of a general nature on global software development.

```
http://www.microsoft.com/globaldev
```

Multilingual Computing and Technology magazine is dedicated to reporting on all aspects of the internationalization of software.

```
http://www.multilingual.com
```

To get guidance on internationalizing web sites, explore:

```
http://www.webofculture.com
```

Machine Translation Services

The following sites mentioned are interesting in that they let you type in a word or a paragraph and get it translated immediately. Since the translation is done by machine you can get a good idea as to how well this type of translation works.

```
http://babelfish.altavista.com/
http://www.freetranslation.com/
```

Places to Get Fonts

Fonts. At the end of the day, fonts are what the user ultimately sees. While the multilingual version of Windows includes quite a few fonts, you *will* need more. Also you may decide that some of the fonts from these web sites are better than the native fonts you are working with.

```
http://www.linguistsoftware.com/
http://www.unionway.com
```

Standards

Throughout this book, I have referred to various standards for culture naming and so forth. Here are web sites where you can see some of these standards.

The ISO is the keeper and updating agency for all internationalization standards. You can go to its web site and buy any of the official standards you want. The key word here is buy. The site is:

```
http://www.iso.ch
```

There are, however, numerous sites that show various internationalization standards for free. The ISO 3166 standard detailing the countries and two letter codes can be found here:

```
http://www.din.de/gremien/nas/nabd/iso3166ma/codlstp1/en_listp1.html
```

The ultimate standard is Unicode. This is what makes code pages obsolete and allows any language invented to be assigned a code point in the Unicode map. The Unicode home page is here:

```
http://www.unicode.org
```

Editors

There are quite a few editors on the market that help you type in foreign languages into your documents. Many of these are Unicode editors.

AbiWord is a freeware Open Source word processor that is available for 32-bit Windows platforms, for several versions of Unix, and for an experimental version of BeOS. In addition to its own file format, it can read UTF-8, text, Rich Text Format, XHTML, and Microsoft Word files. The site for this editor is:

```
http://www.abisource.com/products.phtml
```

What about the handhelds? Do PDAs get left behind? This editor is designed for you Windows CE folks. No one is forgotten here.

```
http://lp-group.com/store/uniwriter.html
```

Of course we cannot forget Microsoft. Microsoft's FrontPage 2000 HTML editor can be used to produce multilingual web pages with the aid of Unicode fonts and visual keyboards. Some of these visual keyboards are pretty cool. Microsoft's Visual Keyboard enhances the ability of Windows to switch keyboard layouts by adding the option to have the new keyboard appear in a floating window.

The last one in this bunch is UniEdit from HumanComputing Corp. It was recently part of Duke University. UniEdit is not free, but it is very full featured. I have used this editor extensively and find it invaluable.

```
http://www.humancomp.org/
```

While this list of web sites is in no way comprehensive, you will find a wealth of information within them. Most of them also have links to other web sites that may be useful.

Index

M

N

Apress Titles

ISBN	PRICE	AUTHOR	TITLE
1-893115-73-9	$34.95	Abbott	Voice Enabling Web Applications: VoiceXML and Beyond
1-893115-01-1	$39.95	Appleman	Appleman's Win32 API Puzzle Book and Tutorial for Visual Basic Programmers
1-893115-23-2	$29.95	Appleman	How Computer Programming Works
1-893115-97-6	$39.95	Appleman	Moving to VB. NET: Strategies, Concepts, and Code
1-893115-09-7	$29.95	Baum	Dave Baum's Definitive Guide to LEGO MINDSTORMS
1-893115-84-4	$29.95	Baum, Gasperi, Hempel, and Villa	Extreme MINDSTORMS: An Advanced Guide to LEGO MINDSTORMS
1-893115-82-8	$59.95	Ben-Gan/Moreau	Advanced Transact-SQL for SQL Server 2000
1-893115-48-8	$29.95	Bischof	The .NET Languages: A Quick Translation Guide
1-893115-67-4	$49.95	Borge	Managing Enterprise Systems with the Windows Script Host
1-893115-28-3	$44.95	Challa/Laksberg	Essential Guide to Managed Extensions for C++
1-893115-44-5	$29.95	Cook	Robot Building for Beginners
1-893115-99-2	$39.95	Cornell/Morrison	Programming VB .NET: A Guide for Experienced Programmers
1-893115-72-0	$39.95	Curtin	Developing Trust: Online Privacy and Security
1-59059-008-2	$29.95	Duncan	The Career Programmer: Guerilla Tactics for an Imperfect World
1-893115-71-2	$39.95	Ferguson	Mobile .NET
1-893115-90-9	$44.95	Finsel	The Handbook for Reluctant Database Administrators
1-893115-85-2	$34.95	Gilmore	A Programmer's Introduction to PHP 4.0
1-893115-36-4	$34.95	Goodwill	Apache Jakarta-Tomcat
1-893115-17-8	$59.95	Gross	A Programmer's Introduction to Windows DNA
1-893115-62-3	$39.95	Gunnerson	A Programmer's Introduction to C#, Second Edition
1-893115-30-5	$49.95	Harkins/Reid	SQL: Access to SQL Server
1-893115-10-0	$34.95	Holub	Taming Java Threads
1-893115-04-6	$34.95	Hyman/Vaddadi	Mike and Phani's Essential C++ Techniques
1-893115-96-8	$59.95	Jorelid	J2EE FrontEnd Technologies: A Programmer's Guide to Servlets, JavaServer Pages, and Enterprise JavaBeans
1-893115-49-6	$39.95	Kilburn	Palm Programming in Basic
1-893115-50-X	$34.95	Knudsen	Wireless Java: Developing with Java 2, Micro Edition
1-893115-79-8	$49.95	Kofler	Definitive Guide to Excel VBA

ISBN	PRICE	AUTHOR	TITLE
1-893115-57-7	$39.95	Kofler	MySQL
1-893115-87-9	$39.95	Kurata	Doing Web Development: Client-Side Techniques
1-893115-75-5	$44.95	Kurniawan	Internet Programming with VB
1-893115-46-1	$36.95	Lathrop	Linux in Small Business: A Practical User's Guide
1-893115-19-4	$49.95	Macdonald	Serious ADO: Universal Data Access with Visual Basic
1-893115-06-2	$39.95	Marquis/Smith	A Visual Basic 6.0 Programmer's Toolkit
1-893115-22-4	$27.95	McCarter	David McCarter's VB Tips and Techniques
1-893115-76-3	$49.95	Morrison	C++ For VB Programmers
1-893115-80-1	$39.95	Newmarch	A Programmer's Guide to Jini Technology
1-893115-58-5	$49.95	Oellermann	Architecting Web Services
1-893115-81-X	$39.95	Pike	SQL Server: Common Problems, Tested Solutions
1-893115-20-8	$34.95	Rischpater	Wireless Web Development
1-893115-93-3	$34.95	Rischpater	Wireless Web Development with PHP and WAP
1-893115-89-5	$59.95	Shemitz	Kylix: The Professional Developer's Guide and Reference
1-893115-40-2	$39.95	Sill	An Introduction to qmail
1-893115-24-0	$49.95	Sinclair	From Access to SQL Server
1-893115-94-1	$29.95	Spolsky	User Interface Design for Programmers
1-893115-53-4	$39.95	Sweeney	Visual Basic for Testers
1-59059-002-3	$44.95	Symmonds	Internationalization and Localization Using Microsoft .NET
1-893115-29-1	$44.95	Thomsen	Database Programming with Visual Basic .NET
1-893115-65-8	$39.95	Tiffany	Pocket PC Database Development with eMbedded Visual Basic
1-893115-59-3	$59.95	Troelsen	C# and the .NET Platform
1-893115-26-7	$59.95	Troelsen	Visual Basic .NET and the .NET Platform
1-893115-54-2	$49.95	Trueblood/Lovett	Data Mining and Statistical Analysis Using SQL
1-893115-16-X	$49.95	Vaughn	ADO Examples and Best Practices
1-893115-68-2	$49.95	Vaughn	ADO.NET and ADO Examples and Best Practices for Visual Basic Programmers, Second Edition
1-59059-012-0	$34.95	Vaughn/Blackburn	ADO.NET Examples and Best Practices for C# Programmers
1-893115-83-6	$44.95	Wells	Code Centric: T-SQL Programming with Stored Procedures and Triggers
1-893115-95-X	$49.95	Welschenbach	Cryptography in C and C++
1-893115-05-4	$39.95	Williamson	Writing Cross-Browser Dynamic HTML
1-893115-78-X	$49.95	Zukowski	Definitive Guide to Swing for Java 2, Second Edition
1-893115-92-5	$49.95	Zukowski	Java Collections

Available at bookstores nationwide or from Springer Verlag New York, Inc. at 1-800-777-4643; fax 1-212-533-3503. Contact us for more information at sales@apress.com.

Apress Titles Publishing SOON!

ISBN	AUTHOR	TITLE
1-893115-91-7	Birmingham/Perry	Software Development on a Leash
1-893115-39-9	Chand	A Programmer's Guide to ADO.NET in C#
1-893115-42-9	Foo/Lee	XML Programming Using the Microsoft XML Parser
1-893115-55-0	Frenz	Visual Basic for Scientists
1-59059-009-0	Harris/Macdonald	Moving to ASP.NET
1-59059-016-3	Hubbard	Windows Forms in C#
1-893115-38-0	Lafler	Power AOL: A Survival Guide
1-893115-43-7	Stephenson	Standard VB: An Enterprise Developer's Reference for VB 6 and VB .NET
1-59059-007-4	Thomsen	Building Web Services with VB .NET
1-59059-010-4	Thomsen	Database Programming with C#
1-59059-011-2	Troelsen	COM and .NET Interoperability
1-893115-98-4	Zukowski	Learn Java with JBuilder 6

Available at bookstores nationwide or from Springer Verlag New York, Inc. at 1-800-777-4643; fax 1-212-533-3503. Contact us for more information at sales@apress.com.

Apress™

books for professionals by professionals™

About Apress

Apress, located in Berkeley, CA, is an innovative publishing company devoted to meeting the needs of existing and potential programming professionals. Simply put, the "A" in Apress stands for the "Author's Press™." Apress' unique author-centric approach to publishing grew from conversations between Dan Appleman and Gary Cornell, authors of best-selling, highly regarded computer books. In 1998, they set out to create a publishing company that emphasized quality above all else, a company with books that would be considered the best in their market. Dan and Gary's vision has resulted in over 30 widely acclaimed titles by some of the industry's leading software professionals.

Do You Have What It Takes to Write for Apress?

Apress is rapidly expanding its publishing program. If you can write and refuse to compromise on the quality of your work, if you believe in doing more than rehashing existing documentation, and if you're looking for opportunities and rewards that go far beyond those offered by traditional publishing houses, we want to hear from you!

Consider these innovations that we offer all of our authors:

- **Top royalties with *no* hidden switch statements**
  Authors typically only receive half of their normal royalty rate on foreign sales. In contrast, Apress' royalty rate remains the same for both foreign and domestic sales.

- **A mechanism for authors to obtain equity in Apress**
  Unlike the software industry, where stock options are essential to motivate and retain software professionals, the publishing industry has adhered to an outdated compensation model based on royalties alone. In the spirit of most software companies, Apress reserves a significant portion of its equity for authors.

- **Serious treatment of the technical review process**
  Each Apress book has a technical reviewing team whose remuneration depends in part on the success of the book since they too receive royalties.

Moreover, through a partnership with Springer-Verlag, one of the world's major publishing houses, Apress has significant venture capital behind it. Thus, we have the resources to produce the highest quality books *and* market them aggressively.

If you fit the model of the Apress author who can write a book that gives the "professional what he or she needs to know™," then please contact one of our Editorial Directors, Gary Cornell (gary_cornell@apress.com), Dan Appleman (dan_appleman@apress.com), Karen Watterson (karen_watterson@apress.com) or Jason Gilmore (jason_gilmore@apress.com) for more information.